FOREWORD

By

Sheila Bellew

What an unexpected boost it was to my aged and deflated ego when John phoned me on St. Valentines Day with a request to write this foreword. Though painfully aware of my inadequacies and incompetence, I felt honoured and privileged to accept.

First of all, may I express admiration, praise and congratulations to each and every one connected with this venture, made up of so many events. They are very brave to selflessly undertake the myriad of tasks involved but mar a deir an sean fhocail,
'Nior chaill fear (no bean) an mhisnigh roimhe' and I know their efforts will be appreciated and crowned with success on May 2nd with God's help.

The book is very important as it will be 'the paper trail' when the festivities are over.
I have in my bookcase many recent publications-stories of local parishes, schools etc. all excellent. However this one will be unique in so far as it is a 'Three in one'- the story of three schools, Tample, Shanballard and Cloonkeenkerrill, all still standing but vacant, since being incorporated into the new impressive academy on the hill over looking the once famed 'Walsh's Forge'. The reader will see that the Editorial Committee have provided a veritable feast of interesting and wide ranging articles - personal memories, history, profiles and much much more. Well done to all contributors.

The poetic section is of outstanding quality. It would be well worth buying the book for the pleasure of reading the poems, even if it contained nothing else. My favourite is one entitled 'The Bachelor'. It merits a place up there with Patrick Kavanagh even at his best. Let's have more of this in the future!

Before concluding, I would like to pay tribute to the teachers and clergy who laboured in Gurteen parish during my working years. They were noble people in difficult times. 'Ar dheis De go Raibh siad go leir.'

To my past pupils, I humbly say sorry, if in any way I made your young lives unhappy. Please forgive me. Enjoy every moment at the Reunion and may God bless all your families and undertaking now and in future years.

I salute my very true friends of more than a half a century (they insist on remaining nameless). You and Cloonkeenkerrill are forever in my heart and memories.

Finally I will conclude with a quotation from the *'Desiderata'*
'Be at peace with God whatever you conceive Him to be, and keep peace with your soul. With all its shame, drudgery and broken dreams, it is still a beautiful world. Be careful. Strive to be happy.'
    God bless you all,

                                       Sheila Bellew (nee Cloonan)

A MESSAGE FROM THE MINISTER

I am very honoured to have been asked by our Schools Reunion Committee to pen this Foreword, to this very historic and informative Book, entitled "Making Shapes with Slates and Marla". At the outset and on behalf of the wider Community, can I warmly welcome all of our Readers, who have acquired this special treasure from our Community. I also warmly welcome home all of our former Parishioners, who are Past Pupils of all of our three old National Schools at Clonkeenkerrill, Shanballard and Tample. A special Cead Míle Failte to all of our Emigrants, who have come from the United Kingdom, the United States, Europe and wider afield. We are delighted to have you back for this special and historic occasion and we salute you as our People and on your contribution to the International success of over 100 million of the Irish Diaspora, spread in all corners of the Globe.

Looking back, our School days were a wonderful period in our lives. While at times we may not have liked certain occasions, we can now be certain that on reflection they were most certainly the best days of our lives. We owe a huge debt of gratitude to our former Teachers, who along with our Parents were our educators and guardians and prepared us for the long road of life ahead. I enjoyed my own School days at Tample National School, from 1957 to 1964. I would like to pay a special tribute to my first teacher Mrs Maureen Clancy, N.T. and to our late Principal that unique, distinguished and special gifted teacher, the late Ms Daisy Duffy, P.N.T. For those of us, who are fortunate to have been taught by both Mrs Clancy and Ms Duffy, we owe them a huge debt of gratitude. The lessons that I learned, the instruction that I received and the knowledge gained in my formative years in Tample National School, have been of major assistance to me, throughout my entire life.

On behalf of all of our Past Pupils, I thank them sincerely for their huge contribution and along with them, I thank all of the other former Teachers in both Clonkeenkerrill and Shanballard, for their special and outstanding contributions also. It is great to have People like Mr Michael Blehein, Mr P.J. Burke, Mrs. Pam Lyng and all of their Colleagues, who can be justly proud of their Past Pupils, and of their contribution to Primary Education in our Community.

In my last Ministry, I was responsible for Science and Technology at the Department of Education and Science. During this period of time, the Massachutes Institute of Technology proposed to locate a major Research Project in Europe. They carried out a major Study including detailed Research, on all of the Educational Systems in every Member State of the European Union. They benchmarked all Systems against the American System.

Their Report concluded that Ireland had an outstanding Third Level System, a wonderful Second Level System and that our Primary Education System, i.e. our National Schools, were unequalled in any part of Europe. Consequent on that, they decided that as a result of the grounding and the Education available at Primary level in Ireland, that the ability of young Irish Students to absorb knowledge, through the Second and Third Level systems was much greater, than our colleagues across Europe and on that basis, M.I.T. concluded that the place to put their major Research project was in Ireland. Thankfully this has happened and it will be a major boost to our research, innovation and education system, in the years ahead. International proof, if it were ever needed that our Primary School System is the best in the World.

I hope you all enjoy reading this Special Schools History. It reflects the past and present and pinpoints the way with great optimism to an exciting future, for all of our People. I hope also that you enjoy all of the events and functions, that have been organised by a very dedicated Committee for this very special year, for the Past Pupils of the combined Gurteen Schools. And as we reflect on the past, we salute the present and in particular our current Teachers in Gurteen Central National School, which was built in 1981 and on behalf of the Parents and People of Gurteen, we thank the current staff, ably led by their Principal Mr Dermot Maloney and his colleagues Mrs Ann Ward N.T. and Ms Eimear Monaghan N.T., for their continuing contribution and sustaining of the high standards of Primary Education, that has not alone served our Parish and the adjoining Parishes over the Centuries and has played a major role in the development of one of the most successful economies in the World.

Beir Bua agus Beannacht.

Noel Treacy TD
Minister for Food and Horticulture, at the Department of Agriculture, Food and Forestry.

ACKNOWLEDGEMENTS

This book has been published as a result of the efforts of a large number of people. We would like to thank the management and Staff of Galway Rural Development who have grant aided its publication.

The members of The Schools' Reunion Committee have worked long and hard to ensure that the project is a success. There was never any shortage of volunteers when help was needed.

We would like to thank our Sponsors. Their financial contributions have made our task much easier than it otherwise would have been.

The people of the parish and surrounding areas have supplied us with photos, documents and memorabilia of various kinds and these have proved most useful.

The Pupils and Staff of St. Kerrill's National School have participated in all of our projects and welcomed us whenever we visited the school.

Thanks to our contributors and guest writers who produced such a vast range of interesting material.

A word of appreciation to Marie Mannion, Education Officer with Galway Co. Council, who provided guidelines for research and pinpointed locations where sources of information were available.

Mary Qualter and the staff of the County Library in Island House have been most helpful and the same is true for Kieran Hoare, Margaret Hughes and Marie Boran in the Archives Section of NUIG Library.

Thanks too to Dr. Seán O'Cearnaigh from the Placename Section of The Department of Community Affairs, Dublin.

Galway Bay FM, Shannonside and M&NWR radio stations have helped to publicise our programmes. All of them have been most generous with airtime.

The Advertiser, Connacht Tribune, Tuam Herald and Galway Independent have also helped to bring the Reunion activities to the attention of the public. Ireland's Own and Ireland's Eye magazines have given their support and helped us to contact past pupils.

The Clergy and editors of various newsletters have informed their readers of Reunion events and we thank them for their help.

Noel Dilleen's advice and technological expertise made it possible to meet our deadlines and we thank him most sincerely.

Bridget Dilleen/Sullivan did a great deal of research and we are most grateful to her.

We owe a debt of gratitude also to Frank Kennedy and Pádraigh Judge for their untiring efforts in the area of layout and design.

Finally, thanks to all those who were willing to make their computers available, whenever required.

OUR SPONSORS

The Committee would like to thank the following people:

Tom Roche who sponsored our video.

<u>OTHER SPONSORS</u>

Bank of Ireland, Loughrea

Sheila Bellew. N.T.

Michael Blehein, N.T.

Niamh and T.J. Carr

Mary Connaire, Killimordaly

Sonny Connaire, Killimordaly

Paul Connaughton, T.D.

Brendan Hynes, U.SA.

Frank McDonagh, Mountbellew

Oliver King, Mountbellew

Herbie and Noreen Parker, Ballymacward

Paddy Scarry, U.S.A.

Fr. Sean Slattery P.P.

Maureen Thornhill, N.T. Shannonbridge

Noel Treacy. T.D.

Ulster Bank, Athenry

St. Kerrill's Festival Committee

THE LITERARY CONNECTIONS

This area has a history of literary endeavour stretching back for several decades. Dermot Burke was one of the earliest scribes and he was renowned for poetry. Ned Nevin from Killuane was a nineteenth century writer and one of his poems entitled 'Coolock Bog' is recorded in The Folklore Commission Survey of 1937-8. Ned was an ornithologist and sportsman who engaged in many activities that were frowned upon by the authorities. In the eyes of ordinary people, most of what he did was for the good of the community. He wrote three other poems at least and you can read one of them, Loughnahinch, in this book.

Martin Finnerty from Tample was another important figure in the literary field. He was a regular contributor to the Galway Observer. He compiled a collection of poems, stories and articles and published them under the title of 'An Punann Ársa. Martin was a rebel and farmer and he was always ready to challenge the British authorities. He served in Galway Co. Council. Martin's writings are often referred to by historians and archaeologists, many of whom regard them as a solid foundation on which to base their research.

John Scarry of Cappalusk carried on the local literary tradition up to the time of his death. John was a self-educated man and was employed as a journalist by The Irish Press. He wrote many interesting articles but unfortunately, they do not seem to be available at the moment.

It is believed that the ancestors of Richard Scarry also came from Gurteen. Richard of course was a writer of childrens' books and his fame extended worldwide.

Pádraic Fallon, although a native of Athenry, has strong connections with this parish. The Finnerty, Burke and Cormican families are related to him and he has written poems about different places in the parish. Two of them are included in this collection. He wrote a number of plays and other pieces and listeners to RTE radio in previous decades would have been familiar with his works. 2005 is the centenary of his birth and we look forward to a big surge of interest in his writings next year. It is generally believed that he is the most underrated poet of recent times.

One of the most prolific writers from this area was Seán Mac Giollarnáth (Seán Ford) from Killuane. Sean wrote many interesting pieces on history and folklore. Secondary School Students studied Cúdar, one of his books, as part of their course in the 1960s. Seán was a close friend of Pádraigh Pearse and he was appointed editor of 'An Claideamh Solais' for a time. This revolutionary newspaper founded by Pearse, was eventually suppressed by the English Government. As well as being a writer, Seán was an expert in legal matters and he supplied invaluable advice to local people who were arraigned by the authorities and charged with sedition prior to independence. He worked in Galway city and was made a Judge by the Irish Government.

We are happy to report that the literary tradition is still strong in Gurteen. Local writers, Tommie Mitchell, Noel Dillon, Tom Roche, Bridget Sullivan, Nancy Coen and Margot McMahon are busy producing material that is highly regarded by the reading public.
The Golden Pen Literary Awards, which is based in Gurteen, provides an outlet for new and established writers. Some of the early winners such as Eileen Casey, Gerard Hanbury and Geraldine Mills have gone on to write books that have established solid reputations for them in the literary world.
It is our fervent hope that the writing tradition which flourished here in olden times will expand and develop over the coming years.

EDITORIAL

When we began this book, we felt it would be more enjoyable if we included a wide range of material. Each contributor was allowed to write on a subject of his or her choice. The end result is a mixed bag of stories, poetry and articles. We have published a large collection of pictures and photographs and we hope you will find these interesting. We apologise for the fact that some of the photos are not up to standard. This is due to the fact that they were in poor condition when we received them or because we didn't have the originals. In the main we have concentrated on past events but some of our contributors concern themselves with current and future affairs and we think this is something to be welcomed.

Our locality has a wealth of secrets to share with those who are willing to probe and we have found many fascinating stories relating to history and folklore while researching this book. As we tell our friends, we have learned more about life in Ireland over the past few months than we had known in all our previous years.

Many individuals have helped with research and without their assistance, it wouldn't have been possible to create a book of this kind. The people of Gurteen, Ballymacward and surrounding areas have been most forthcoming with material and advice and we in the Reunion Committee are most grateful to them.

In our Acknowledgements, we have expressed our thanks to all concerned. However, if we have omitted anyone, we can assure you that the omission wasn't deliberate.

Finally, we hope you enjoy the series of events that the Reunion Committee have put together to mark this special occasion. We would like to meet and converse with as many of you as possible over the coming days.

THE REUNION COMMITTEE

ST. KERRILL'S SCHOOL ORGANISING COMMITTEE

CONTENTS

CHAPTER 1:   HISTORY AND EDUCATION   1

- Gleanings
- A Short History of Education
- The Civil Parish of Cloonkeenkerrill
- The O'Hara Family and Lenaboy Castle
- My Musings on the Schools' Reunion

CHAPTER 2:   THE PURSUIT OF KNOWLEDGE   27

- Changing Schools
- The Wonders of Life - an extract from a work in progress
- Antics in and out of Class

CHAPTER 3:   MARKING TIME   45

- The Beginning and End of the Year
- In Search of Special Days in Spring
- Classic Country Customs
- The Dark Days of the Year
- Marking Martin's Memory

CHAPTER 4:   WEDDING BELLS   57

- Wedding Bells ring out for..
- An Indian Wedding

CHAPTER 5:   LOCAL LORE AND LEGENDS   63

- Cluain Chaoin Choirill agus Cill Dubhan
- What's in a name?
- A Look at the Archives
- Gurteen Proverbs

CHAPTER 6:   SCHOOLS PRESENT AND PAST   79

- Settling in at St.Kerrills
- A Century of Change
- Coping With Classes at Cloonkeen
- From Kinreask to Cloonkeen
- Our Teachers

| CHAPTER 7: | SAINTS AMONG SINNERS | 103 |

The true identity of Saint Kerrill
Echoes of my Schooldays
At Home and Away
Mission To Liberia
My Stay in Gurteen
Punished for Praying

| CHAPTER 8: | LIGHT ENTERTAINMENT | 113 |

A burning desire to Escape
Our Youth Club
Jaw Breakers
Having a Ball at Cloonkeen

| CHAPTER 9: | THE SCHOOL SCENE IN SHANBALLARD | 125 |

Sweet Sounds of Shanballard
The Master - A man ahead of his Time
The Murphys
Good Old Sods

| CHAPTER 10: | HOW THE SENIORS SEE IT | 139 |

The Rough and the Smooth
Looking back over Nine Decades
A Fine Old Soldier
From Cappalusk to Colorado
Sonny Connaire and the Long Road

| CHAPTER 11: | MATTERS MEDICAL AND ASTRONOMICAL | 149 |

Engineering the Future
A holiday in the Sun

| CHAPTER 12: | MORE VIEWS ON LIFE AND EDUCATION | 157 |

A day in the Life of my Education
My Dad - Peter Kerrill Gavin
My American Experience

CHAPTER 13:	LEARNING LOTS IN TAMPLE	163

        Memories of Tample
        The Duffy Dynasty
        Four Generations at Tample School
        Riding High on Shank's Mare
        Tample School and After
        Snippets from my Schooldays

CHAPTER 14:	FARMING, FODDERING AND FORGE WORK	175

        From Belleville to Ballymac
        A Farm with a Post Office Stuck onto the House
        Ag Cur an Siol
        The Forge on Cappagh Hill

CHAPTER 15:	WEATHER, LAND AND SEASCAPES	187

        Do you talk about the Weather often?
        Kylemore and its Abbey
        Absence of Ocean

CHAPTER 16:	OUR SPORTING WORLD	193

        History of St. Kerrill's G.A.A.Club
        A brief History of Pearses Camogie Club
        Gurteen Soccer - The Story so far..
        Ballymacward Soccer 1975-1989
        Hurling in Tample
        Colemanstown United FC 1982-2004
        Pearses Hurling

CHAPTER 17:	LINES AND LYRICS	215

        Thatcher
        The Diviner
        The Bachelor
        Loughnahinch
        Try, Try Again
        A Child's Worry
        An Gleann Inar Tógadh Mé
        An Fear Gorm
        Homework oh Homework
        Why Go To Church?
        Pity the Poor Starling
        The Long Way Home

My New Spelling Checker
Still Life
The Old Rugged Cross
Eamon An Chnuic
Ned of the Hill
The Forge
Shanballard
Gurteen School Rhymes
Sionnach
A Memory
Life's Mirror
Mallacht Naoimh
Raftery
The Saint's Curse
Quest For Knowledge

APPENDIX 239

LIST OF TEACHERS
LIST OF PRIESTS
UNION OF LOUGHREA
VALUATION OF TENEMENTS (AS PER LAYOUT)
WORDS WHICH WERE ONCE PART OF EVERYDAY SPEECH
VALUATION OF RAINFALL AND MET MATERIAL
BALLYMACWARD (CLONKEEN) MAP
FARM MACHINERY
PRIMARY CERTIFICATE
BIBLIOGRAPHY
REFERENCES
BIOGRAPHIES
EXTRACTS FROM THE ARCHAELOGICAL INVENTORY
OF CO. GALWAY
REGISTRATION OF DOGS

JOHN DUFFY AND HIS WIFE JULIA DILLEEN/DUFFY N.T. WHO TAUGHT IN SHANBALLARD NS AROUND 1911 (ACCORDING TO 1911 CENSUS)

TOMMY MENTANE, MARY GRIFFIN, MARKEY CARR, BRIDIE CARR, THOMAS CAR,R SNR, PADDY CARR, MARIA CARR, WILLIAM DILLEEN, MOLLIE DILLEEN, JOHN DILLEEN, USA.

SEAMUS DILLEEN ON PONY AND MARY DILLEEN.

JULIA DILLEEN/MURPHY, MOLLIE DILLEEN, JOHN DILLEEN USA. CATHERINE, BRIDGET, MARY AND ANN DILLEEN.

CHAPTER ONE

HISTORY AND EDUCATION

Notes Gleaned from the National Archives

By

Brid Sullivan

The population of Co Galway in 1841 was 337374 and the number of schools in the county was 360. There were 16711 Protestants in education and 18066 Catholics were attending school in the County of Galway. In the National Schools index I found that Cloonkeenkerrill made an initial application for a national school on 17/10/1843 and a further application was received on 27/5/1871. On further checking in the Commissioners of Public Instruction of Ireland 1831, in the civil parish of Cloonkeen, the following three listings were noted,

1) Gorteen, day school, had Laurence Griffin as Master and 45 males and 28 females, with an average of 35 pupils attending daily. They were instructed in reading, writing, arithmetic, grammar and bookkeeping.

2) In Glenamucka there was a hedge school where Thomas Davock was the schoolmaster. This school had 52 males and 18 females with the average attendance of 50 daily. This school is in Ballymacward parish.

3) Finally in Cloonkeen civil parish, the other hedge school, was at Forest View and John Hannan was the master. This was a smaller school with 30 males and 15 females. I can't identify where this hedge school was.

In 1831 in Ballymacward there were 4891 Roman Catholics and 85 Protestants. According to the Diocese of Clonfert records, 550 Catholics were attending Mass in Gorteen chapel and 2400 in Ballymacward.

The initial application for a school in Gorteen was made on 18/10.1842 and a further application was lodged on 23/4/1855. Unfortunately the original copy of the data for Clonkeenkerril and Gorteen was in very poor condition and was not available to transcribe. Some registers for Gorteen School were legible and I noted that on a register report, dated 14/4/1864 that Mary Duffy was present at the time of the inspection but had left by 16/9/1872. The next teacher listed after Mary Duffy was Bridget Woods on 16/10/1872. This report stated there was an adequate supply of Books in the school. There were no complaints listed on the correspondence side or Board Orders, so everything must have being to the inspector's satisfaction. Also in the applications Books I noted that on 13/6/1871 Mr John McNally who was schoolmaster in Cloonkeenkerrill, was recommending that his wife Bridget McNally be the assistant teacher. He recorded that she had two years previous experience in Clonbur School and six years in Burriscarra female national school. In 1871 there were 80 males in the school and 50 females and Rev John Deely was the manager. The salary was £32 per annum. I suspect this was for both teachers, although it did not state this.

A SHORT HISTORY OF IRISH EDUCATION

Ireland had an excellent reputation in education dating back to the monastic schools. While most of Europe was in turmoil, Irish monks were busy copying ancient manuscripts or imparting knowledge to their disciples. Prior to that, the Druids, who dominated most areas of Celtic life, immersed themselves in education. The Druids were free to construct their own curriculum and enjoyed the support of kings and royal patrons. They instructed their students in Mathematics, History and Literature. Apparently most of the teaching was done orally. In other words students were taught to recite large tracts of literature and although the Druids themselves could write, written work wasn't considered necessary in the schools conducted by them.

The Bards were prominent in later times. The Bardic Schools carried on the tradition of education up to the time of the collapse of the Old Gaelic system at the beginning of the Seventeenth Century. The subjects were taught through Irish. The curriculum involved the study of language, literature and the history of Ireland. Latin was studied and most of the tutors would have been familiar with the writings of the ancient Greeks and Romans. Indeed one modern author claims that if it were not for the monastic and Bardic schools that the bulk of classical writings would have disappeared completely. He even goes so far as to claim that it was the Irish who must get credit for saving civilisation. We are told that the Brehon Laws were 'intensively and scientifically studied' at this time. Courses were long and it took six to seven years to complete them. In fact sometimes the period of study lasted up to twenty years!

The Bardic schools were regarded as a threat to English rule by the authorities. This is easy to understand because the Bards helped to keep the spirits of the people alive. They emphasised the oral and cultural traditions of the country and wrote poems and songs in praise of the old Gaelic way of life. As early as 1583, the Earl of Desmond was obliged to give an undertaking that no bards would be encouraged in the territories that he controlled. The Anglo Irish gentry were threatened with fines by the Government if they supported or encouraged the existence of such schools. After the Flight of The Earls in 1607, the elimination of the Bardic schools was much easier for the English authorities. However despite the efforts of the Government, their influence continued on for some time. At this stage the selection of subjects being taught in them had declined dramatically. Now they focused mainly on poetry and these Schools of Poetry continued until the Nineteenth Century.

From the time of Henry VIII, the English had set up schools that were intended for the Anglo Norman gentry. In 1539 the monasteries had been suppressed and the plunder that took place in the aftermath of the suppression resulted in many valuable manuscripts being lost. By the 18th Century education was confined to the elite and the Irish language and literature was confined to the peasants. The people of Ireland responded by going abroad to study. They set up institutions for this purpose in various parts of Europe. Twenty Irish Colleges were founded on the continent between 1582 and 1681. (The colleges were located at Salamanca, Lisbon, Prague, Antwerp, Toulouse, Douai, Paris, plus at least four in Rome). This shows that higher education in Ireland was becoming more difficult unless one was a member of the Norman gentry and it also shows that those who had the wherewithal to study were determined to overcome the obstacles placed in their path by the English authorities.

The Irish Continental Colleges prepared their charges for the priesthood, the army, medicine and the law. Those who entered them would have been relatively affluent. It is thought that the majority of students in the Irish Colleges received their basic education at home despite the hostility of the Government to Irish Culture. Catholic Schools experienced a revival during the reign of James II but this was short lived. When William and Mary ascended the throne things changed for the worse and the introduction of the Penal Laws meant that formal education was no longer an option for the ordinary Irish citizen.

Grants were given to Protestant Education Societies and many private individuals set up schools in the 19th Century. Often they were referred to as 'Bible Societies' because 'The Good Book' provided the text in all of their schools. The London Hibernian Society and the Baptists were involved in these moves. The Kildare Place Society or to give it its official title, 'The Society for Promoting The Education of The Poor in Ireland', was set up in 1811. It was one of the most prominent of the Pro-Government bodies at the time. The instruction was through English and the outlook in the institutions was anti- Irish and anti-Catholic. In 1824 there were 1727 schools in receipt of state grants but the vast majority of Irish people had little to do with them. Instead they relied on the unofficial curriculum that was provided by the Hedge Schoolmasters.

THE HEDGE SCHOOLS

The Hedge Schools had sprung up in response to the need of ordinary people to acquire a modicum of education. By the mid 1850's it is estimated that there were approximately 10,000 Hedge Schools in Ireland. The Hedge Schools were opposed and denounced by the ruling class. They were regarded as a source of subversion and it was intended to suppress them and the Catholic Church in Ireland, by applying the Penal Laws rigorously.

Historians suggest that this type of repression would have worked if the laws had been administered in a more rigid and uniform manner. As regards religion, people adhered to their old faith and the Catholic Church survived the onslaught, even though many of its priests forfeited their lives in defence of its dogmas.

THE HEDGE SCHOOLMASTERS

Instead of quenching the thirst for knowledge among the peasantry, the Penal Laws seemed to act as a spur to ordinary people. They were prepared to make substantial sacrifices to educate themselves and their families. The teachers who presided at the Hedge Schools were brave individuals who had acquired a good knowledge of the Classics and who were ready to risk their lives to pass on their knowledge to others. Many of them would have been descendants of the Bards or

Fili who had played such a prominent part in the life of the community before the old Gaelic order had disintegrated. Love of learning seems to have been one of their primary motivating factors. Padraic Colum captures the essence of these nomads in his beautiful poem entitled: 'A Poor Scholar Of The Forties'. They may have received small payments from their supporters but it would have been payment in kind rather than money that was mostly given to them. They moved from place to place for safety, as well as for academic reasons. They were highly respected and the public could be relied on to treat them hospitably in so far as it was in their power. Subjects taught were: Arithmetic, Literacy, History and Geography. Technical subjects were sometimes available also, e.g., Bookkeeping, Surveying and Navigation. Latin often featured and occasionally Greek was taught. It has been said that the Hedge Schools were so effective that the lower stratum was more literate and better educated in the 19th Century than many of the Upper Class.

INSTRUCTING THE PUPILS

There is no adequate account of the teaching methods employed by the Hedge Schoolmasters. Writing and copying headlines set out by the teacher was common. Oral recitation of the material to be learned was popular also. (Some historians claim that it was only the inferior Hedge Schools that relied on reciting or 'Rehearsing' as it was generally called, to educate their students) Textbooks were scarce and generally belonged to the teacher. Pupils were taught individually and were monitored at intervals to assess their progress. The quality of teaching varied from place to place, depending on the qualifications of the tutors and of course the ability of the students. Many of the teachers were learned individuals who did their best to take cognisance of the latest teaching techniques and incorporate them into their classes. Some were Poets and Classical Scholars; others were Bookkeepers, Writers and experts in History, Geography or Mathematics. Peter O'Connell from Carne in Clare, was one of the most famous of them. A copy of a dictionary that he wrote is to be found in Trinity College. Humphrey O'Sullivan from Callan, Co. Kilkenny was another noted scholar. Some of his work is to be found in Maynooth College Library. Paul Deighan, a schoolmaster from Ballina, published a book on Arithmetic in 1804. It is accepted that the Hedge Schools provided a marvellous service and kept the love of learning alive at a very difficult period in Irish History.

When the English Government introduced primary state education in 1831, Hedge Schools began to decline. Not that things were to change overnight. Poets like Raftery opposed them on political and religious grounds. Many felt that the new system of education would create a race of 'English' Irishmen. Irish and religion were to be kept out of the curriculum initially and those who spoke Irish at home were to be reported to the schoolmaster. It fell to him to punish the pupils, taking into account the number of times they had broken the rules by speaking in their native language. Some still clung to the Hedge Schools in defiance of the new regime, but by the time the Government had passed The Irish Intermediate Act of 1878, very few Hedge Schools were able to function.

GETTING RID OF THE IRISH LANGUAGE

The English Government policy of downgrading the Irish language was successful. Coercion helped. Physical punishment applied regularly would appear to have discouraged many from speaking Irish. However, most historians believe that political and economic factors were mostly responsible for its decline. For example, although the United Irishmen of 1798 sought to 'break the connection' with England and to establish a society in which 'Catholic, Protestant and Dissenter' would have had equal rights, nevertheless, most of their public statements and propaganda were disseminated through the medium of English. Daniel O'Connell is blamed too. Even though he was a fluent Irish speaker, O'Connell used the English language exclusively in the course of his campaign for Catholic Emancipation and in his attempts to Repeal The Act of Union. It was logical therefore for his supporters to learn English in order to be able to follow his campaigns and to read his utterances for themselves. Then came the Famine. The west and south of Ireland, where the majority of Irish speakers lived, were badly affected by the Famine. The inhabitants of these parts of the country depended on agriculture for a living and when the potato crop was destroyed, westerners starved and died in their thousands. The Famine had a demoralising effect on those that survived. Many believed that the country was cursed and fled to America and overseas to escape from the ravages of hunger and destitution. Unlike the Italians and others who settled in America, Irish immigrants seemed to lose interest in their native tongue. Before leaving the country many of them tried to acquire an adequate knowledge of English which they felt would be a great asset to them in their adopted countries.

The combination of coercion, politics and economics led to a rapid decline in the Irish language and Irish morale generally. In 1916 Pádraigh Pearse and his contemporaries favoured the Irish language but a great deal of harm had been done prior to then. Their supporters claimed to be very much in favour of creating an 'Irish Ireland' but only a minority of them were able to speak the language, having passed through the 'National' System of education themselves. The Gaelic League and others did their best but by and large Irish was a foreign language to the people of that time. Pearse founded Scoil Éanna to put his theories into practice but it had little impact on the overall educational scene. Pearse was extremely critical of the educational system that the English Government had established here, referring to it as 'The Murder Machine.' However, when the Free State Government took over in 1922, it paid scant attention to such criticisms and 'The Murder Machine' soon became fully integrated into the Irish educational system. Irish was allowed into the curriculum before the English left the country but it was never taken seriously by the public subsequently. In fact in the mid Twentieth Century there was strong antipathy to it on the part of many parents, who thought that too much time, money and effort were being devoted to Irish and that it was responsible for retarding the intellectual progress of their sons and daughters. It is not intended to discuss the merits or demerits of those viewpoints here, except to say there is no convincing evidence to show that bi-lingualism or multi-lingualism are responsible for slowing down the learning power of pupils at any stage. In the national schools traditional material of the kind employed in the Monastic and Bardic schools was ignored and it wasn't until 1937 that the Folklore Commission made some worthwhile efforts to try to recapture some of the stories and ancient lore of Ireland. The Brehon laws were also ignored by the new

Irish Government. Instead, they settled for the English Accusatorial Legal code, lock stock and barrel so to speak. Up to recently, nearly all our laws originated in acts passed by the British Parliament prior to independence.

CURRENT TRENDS

Recently attempts have been made to overhaul primary and secondary education in Ireland. It's too early yet to pass comment on the changes or to assess their impact on students generally. One of the advantages of the new programmes is that they seem to allow teachers greater flexibility in the implementation of the curriculum.

Another area that must be considered is the impact of modern technology on students and their families. One of the greatest challenges facing modern educators perhaps is the problem of how to harness scientific know-how in such a way as students and society in general will obtain worthwhile benefit from it. Hopefully, we'll advance from the rigid restrictions of former times of the type described by Dickens in one of his novels. For example, in Hard Times he portrays pupils as rows of 'empty vessels to be crammed full of imperial facts' under the direction of aptly named characters such as Gradgrind and Mr. M'Choakumchild.

LOCAL EDUCATION

There were a number of Hedge Schoolmasters operating locally. One of them apparently lived in the Colemanstown area and travelled by ass and cart to conduct school in Newcastle. Prior to Catholic Emancipation in 1829, teachers learned their trade from the older Hedge Schoolteachers. Newly established teachers were usually on the look out of suitable centres of population in which to ply their trade. After Emancipation the teachers often leased buildings for this purpose. It was common practice for them to hang up a plate informing prospective pupils of their availabilty. According to The Parliamentary Gazetter a number of teachers competed for business in Gurteen around 1834. 'Pay Daily' schools, located in Gurteen, Gleannamucka and Forest View, serviced the region with 127 boys and 43 girls on their books. These schools probably enjoyed the support of the clergy, although as mentioned already, there was strong opposition from some of the people to the new 'national' schools.

In his biography of Fr. Griffin, Padraic O'Laoi states:

'Laurence Griffin was the first teacher in the annals of Gurteen. He came from the North Clare area of Corofin. Payment varied from 1 penny/week/pupil to 25 pence/pupil/quarter year, ensuring a teacher's income of between £10 and £25 per annum. His first schoolhouse was the old thatched church in Gurteen. When he married he built a new school to service the area - his eldest son, John, succeeded him but retired in 1875 when Gurteen school closed and pupils transferred to Tample.'

As a result of Catholic Emancipation, the Catholics in Ireland became more vociferous in demanding a better system of elementary denominational education. The British Government set up a Board of Commissioners for National Education in response to this demand. The Board offered support to anyone of standing, normally a clergyman or landlord, to apply for school recognition under their regulations. The local sponsors were expected to supply the site and to make a contribution towards maintenance of the school and teachers' salaries. They also had the power to appoint or dismiss teachers. The Commissioners paid the bulk of the building costs and the teachers' salaries.

John Flynn in his book: Ballymacward - The Story of An East Galway Parish says:
'A school under the National System operated at Clonkeenkerrill in 1842 with one male teacher whose annual salary was shown as £8 in 1844. In that year there were 60 male and 30 female pupils on the roll; the average attendance was shown as 30 in 1853. In 1862 four and a half hours weekly were devoted to religious instruction over six days (Could this have been an upgraded school that was originally located in Gleannamucka - the Pay School mentioned above?)

By 1853 Gurteen School had also been brought under the National System with 68 male and 41 female pupils on the roll and an average attendance of 48. That same year the local contribution amounted to £15-10s. By 1862, when the number on the roll was 71, three and a half hours weekly were devoted to religious instruction.

By 1900 national schools had more than half a million pupils on their books and literacy in English had improved dramatically. By this time the majority of pupils spoke very little Irish.

The above data was obtained from the censuses of 1871 and 1881. It relates to both sexes and to all age groups.

If children under 7 and adults over 70 are excluded from the figures on literacy, it will be seen how well the school system promoted the use of the English language.

Generally females slightly out-perform males in all age groups.

In 1887 a new school was built in Tample. This replaced an existing building that had been used as a school previously on Ned Burke's land.

In 1896 St. Monica's School was built in Shanballard.

In 1902, St. Kerrill's School was opened in Cloonkeenkerrill. This replaced the two storey one that began in 1845.

Cloonkeenkerrill closed in 1975 and Tample and Shanballard continued as learning centres until 1981. In that year a new central school was opened to accommodate former students of all three Gurteen schools. This is a modern institution containing learning aids and technology and it stands on the crest of Cappagh Hill beside the ruins of Walsh's Forge.

Further information on the local educational scene can be gleaned by reading the articles that are written by our other contributors.

The Civil Parish of Clonkeen Kerrill
With Odds & Ends About
The Civil People of Gurteen RC Parish
(James N. Dillon alias Noel Dilleen)

Hooban's Gortronnagh c.1935

Introduction. My mother, Nancy, lived most of her adult life at Lisduff, about five miles south of Faha, Gurteen. She had this enigmatic habit of always referring to Faha, as 'Home'. So, as the old 'High Nellie' (kitted out with carbide lamp and pump) was readied for the road and one child in 'Sunday Best' hoisted onto the carrier, the other child was left at 'home', in Moc's care, pondering just where exactly home was!

She alternated her route 'Home' - at one time through Gortronnagh to call on gentle stooped Mary Hooban and her retiring brothers. By the late 'Forties' all were doomed to eternal spinsterhood, the handiwork of an authoritarian mother - 'twas hinted she had adapted too well to prudish widow weeds! With Nancy's bike safely stashed, the women talked in muted tones while slowly walking to the river ford before parting. The pace quickened a little as Nancy and offspring legging it cross-country past an odd bushy mound to Faha, her father, her sister ---- and lots of cousins.

The other route involved a longer bike journey, first calling on Aunt Bess Cormican in Shanballard, then past Kitt's tree shaded house where once Miss Lynch resided, by Geraghty's Garden where no Geraghty resides, through "Gortmore Gate" on the Shanballard/Faha boundary and a furze-lined well-trodden shortcut across a large sleeper spanned drain.

Hynes Family and Others, Faha 1935

Dare I impose on your time for one last childhood visit to Shanballymore; past Gilligans and Maria of the cool, thirst-quenching red rhubarb juice, to affable Aggie, Anne and Pakie Hynes. Oh wistful nostalgia, stay awhile with your infantile but relaxing memories of verdant, bottomless Shanballymore Lake; its dark water teeming with 'roacheens' that, like myself, never quite reached full size!

Three of Nancy's Gurteen Photos are published here and the following article is dedicated to every family whose surname has disappeared from proud homely Gurteen but especially to my Hooban forebears.

Early Medieval Times.

Even prior to the 12th century Anglo-Norman conquest of Ireland, the monastic style Celtic Church was feeling the wind of change and reluctantly undergoing massive reorganisation. In an effort to achieve universal conformity, Vatican edicts pushed a new diocesan church structure. Ireland was carved into dioceses that, in turn, were subdivided into units known as ecclesiastical parishes. Each parish had a parish church and was endowed with church land. Income from the endowment combined with tithes (one tenth of the produce of all the land in the parish) provided the clergyman's living. Some ambitious clergymen abused the system and had the livings of several parishes (pluralism). These entrepreneurial clergymen employed a curate, for a pittance, to service the extra parishes. The population of a parish may have been less than one tenth of the present number. **Ecclesiastical Parishes** were also adopted by the civil authorities and in this context were known as **Civil Parishes.** One such parish in the diocese of Clonfert and barony of Tyaquin was known as **Clonkeen Kerrill.**

About 1435, David and John Mulkerrill approached Thomas O'Kelly, Bishop of Clonfert and requested that Clonkeen Parish Church be converted into a convent for Franciscan friars of the Third Penitential Order. Pope Eugene IV gave a pontifical nod and confirmed the new status in 1441. Obviously the parish church already in Clonkeen was totally inadequate and specialised builders were brought in to construct an imposing edifice making Clonkeen Parish the envy of Clonfert! Papal documents of the day indicate that the Third Order acted as auxiliaries to the secular clergy thus making life easier for all; of course, it could equally mean that reinforcements were needed to sanctify the unruly natives? Historians believe the Third Order Franciscan were also involved in education (whether elitist or not is unknown) during the 16th century.

King Henry VIII (d.1547) 'lawfully' reassigned all RC Church's assets, such as parish churches, graveyards and glebe land and tithes, to his newly established Church of Ireland. Due to the scarcity of suitably qualified Protestant ministers, some existing Catholic clergy and hierarchy ostensibly conformed to the new church situation whilst covertly Catholic. Thus they retained the use of their livings whilst struggling to minister to the needs of their confused parishioners. Serious pressure was exerted on Clonfert's RC clergy and laity to conform to the liturgy of the Church of Ireland during the reign of James I (d.1625). Members of a Royal Visitation to the diocese of Clonfert in 1615 found Bishop Roland Lynch married but the bishop's wife, children and servants were all Catholic!

On examination of Clonfert clergy, anyone found to be a 'mass priest' was deprived of his living. Former church property and revenue in 'Cluainkeinkerrill' had been alienated into the hands of an O'Naghten sept and a curate named William McDonald (presumably CofI) was apparently entrusted with the spiritual welfare of the parish. In the whole diocese there wasn't one teacher! Counter Reformation forces, often working in disguise and spearheaded by the Jesuits, made sure that the general body of Irish Christians remained Catholic despite the setbacks of Cromwellian and Williamite persecution. Old parish churches, due to lack of a Protestant congregation, fell into disrepair and their stark ruins now sit forlornly on many old graveyards. Gough's hand engraved map of 1679 (below) shows clearly the extent of Clonkeen Kerrill with its main townlands. Gough marks the position of another church near Clough, and Larkin's Map (1818) calls it Templegerrod! Impoverished and disenfranchised Catholics experienced little relaxation of Penal Laws until Maynooth Seminary (founded 1795) gradually provided a home-educated native clergy.

The RC hierarchy and clergy, buoyed up and invigorated with the establishment of Maynooth, grasped this respite and threw themselves into a massive rebuilding and restructuring campaign --- no doubt designed to reclaim their rightful place as the one true church servicing the needs of the 'Majority Irish Nation.' Clonfert RC diocese reorganised its parish structure in the late 1700's in anticipation of additional relief under the Act of Union! Two or more old medieval parishes were lumped together making a new larger parish.

Clonkeen Kerrill was united with its sister parish, Ballymacward and a humble thatched chapel built, 1796, at a more central location in Gurteen Village which, by then, was the business, drinking and later law enforcement hub of the parish. A few western Ballymacward townlands, such as Gorteen and Glennamucka were attached to Gurteen Chapel and in time the boundary became blurred as the old medieval parishes merged and fused together.

Profligate King George IV, eldest of the many sons of mad King George III, disliked Roman Catholicism almost as much as he disliked his estranged and eccentric wife, Queen Caroline. When news of Napoleon Bonaparte's death reached London in 1821, a breathless messenger rushed to court and said to the King: "Sire, Your most bitter enemy is dead." King George coolly replied: "Is she by God."

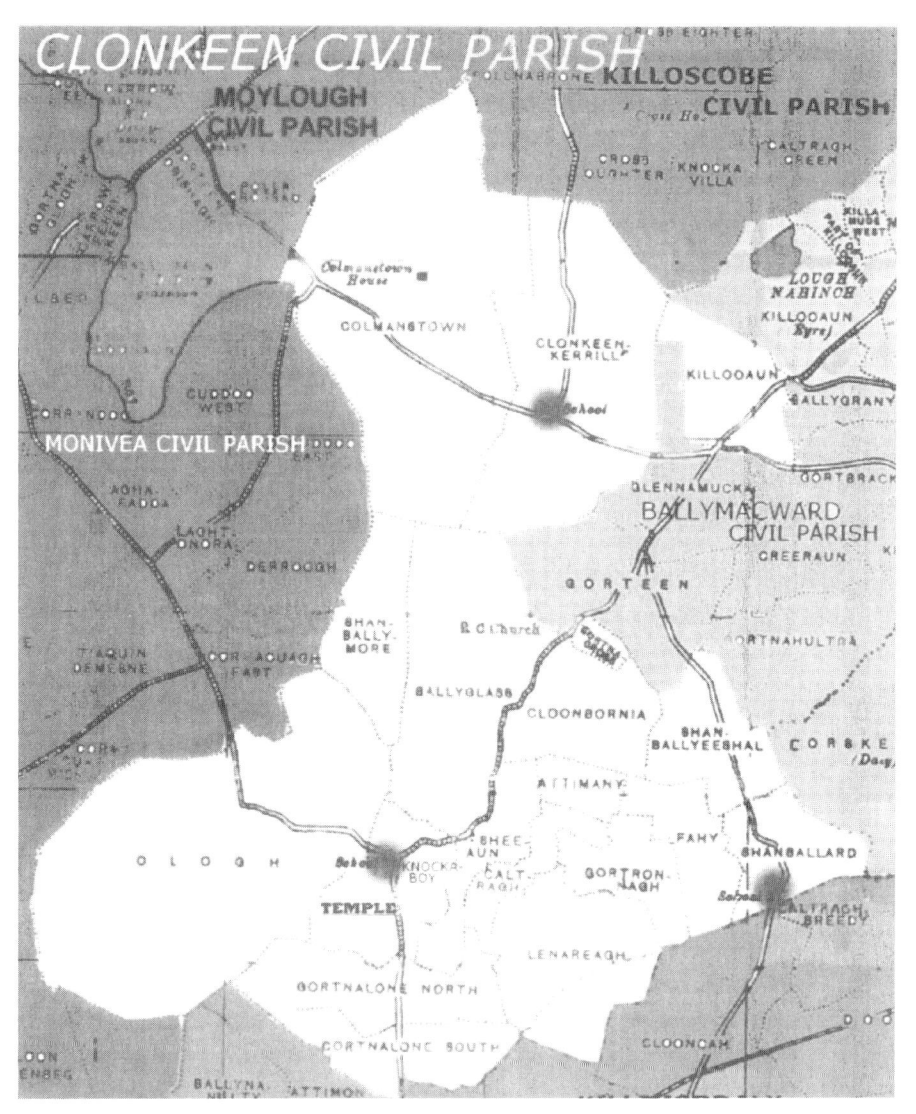

Despite George's vehement opposition to full RC civil rights, his Prime Minister, the Duke of Wellington finally pushed Daniel O'Connell's Catholic Emancipation through parliament in 1829.

The earliest RC parish registers (baptisms, marriages and deaths) in Ireland generally date from historic 1829. But the earliest registers for Ballymacward / Gurteen only date from 1856. So, as no separate parish registers can be found for Clonkeen Kerrill they were either lost or never existed before 1856!

Following the great Ordnance Survey of Co. Galway in 1838, the townland boundaries of Clonkeen Kerrill were clearly defined. Fields, buildings and other unusual features were, at last, accurately mapped. A simplified abstract of this is included (above left) and readers can use it in conjunction with the townland data tables further along!

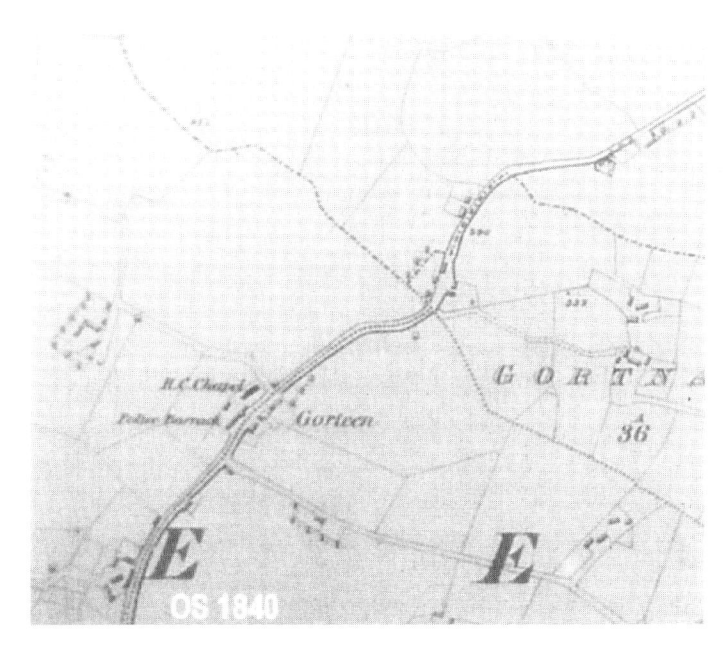

'Good Men' of Gurteen on Christmas Day 1837

Gurteen men have always held a high opinion of their physical prowess and indeed the boast "I'm the best man in the Parish of Gurteen" was frequently heard in the small hours as Francis Fynn, Publican, reluctantly closed his business premises. One Gurteen man (for the moment known as James H.) moved up a gear when he claimed, "Meself and John M. are the two best man in the whole country." His bravado was destined to cost him his life and have tragic consequences for two of his neighbours. On the evening of the 25th

December 1837, several people were drinking in Fynn's Public House in the village of Gurteen. James H, a bachelor, in the company of his brother Pat, sister in law, Mary and niece, Mary Junior were washing down the taste of greasy goose. The happy group had spent a sum of three shillings and sixpence on drink, equal to about thirty or more pints of porter or a labourer wages for seven days hard graft. Gradually a subtle change -- perhaps induced from over imbibing -- crept into the tone of the conversation between James H. and Michael K., a member of neighbouring group of revellers. James' continuous bragging that himself and John M. were the two' best men in the country' annoyed the touchy Michael who counter claimed: "I can 'bate' any man in the world". A member of James' faction retorted, "You can with your tongue."
Before long an angry dispute arose which the landlord feared would end badly. With extreme difficulty Francis Fynn succeeded in excluding the antagonists from the premises. Outside an encouraging group, sensing a little entertainment to round off the day's festivities, gathered around as the erstwhile friends circled and belittled each other. Mary H. Sen ran to the nearby chapel, scooped up some holy water (records fail to say if it was Kerrill's) and showered James in spiritual protection. Maybe the exaggerated shaping up and lack of real action enticed an over eager onlooker to throw a stone that hit James H. Mathias K (a servant of Publican Fynn and also Michael K's nephew) unexpectedly became embroiled in the action and hit James H across the skull with a chunk of wood. James H fell unconscious to the ground. He lived till next day and died without the comfort of doctor or priest.

A Dr. Wm. Heissey, (Hussey!) saw the deceased on the 27th Dec. 1837 and gave medical evidence at the inquest:

> There was no external marks of violence; he took the cap of the skull and found it fractured on one side over the ear; it was a very long one and in his opinion caused by a very heavy blunt instrument; there was excessive bleeding which caused a compression of the brain; there was a great quantity of congealed blood on the brain; the wound was sufficient to cause death by compression of the brain. The Jury returned a verdict against three persons and the Coroner has issued his warrant for their arrest.

Only two, Michael K and Mathias K, were lodged in Galway Gaol until the Spring Assizes of 1838 when the case came before Mr. Justice Crampton in the Crown Court, Co. Galway Assizes. The Jury returned a verdict of 'Not Guilty of Murder' but 'Guilty of Manslaughter'. The learned Judge sentenced Mathias K to seven years Transportation and Michael K got eighteen months hard labour. Unfortunately the story ends here and we have no way of knowing if young Mathias served his sentence in some distant Australian penal colony before eventually returning to the familiar surroundings of his native Gurteen - or did he prefer to remain in exile and make a fresh start for himself?

An Affair of Honour.

Even some of Gurteen's gentry had a fondness for single combat. Two former friends had a serious difference of opinion, which they were unable to resolve amicably. No reason for the falling out was given; one can only surmise that a lady was mixed up in the situation ---- what else could inspire such an impetuous course of action! The two, Henry Concannon of Waterloo near Tuam and **Edward Rochfort** of **Shambelard,** Esqrs., did agree to settle their differences with pistols.

Accordingly a hostile meeting took place on the 25 August 1838 at Corofin, in County Galway. Mr. Concannon was attended by Wm. F. Bodkin Esq., of Kilclooney and Mr. Rochfort by E. Costello Esq., of Galway. After exchanging four shots each, either with such poor marksmanship or such good fortune that neither was injured, the gentlemen present interfered to prevent further hostilities. The former friends fully agreed and the parties were compelled to leave the field. Edward Rochford, Gentleman, died a natural death after a short illness on February 23, 1873, at his residence, Woodbine Cottage, Shambelard.

The Families of Gurteen
Early Censuses and Census Substitutes

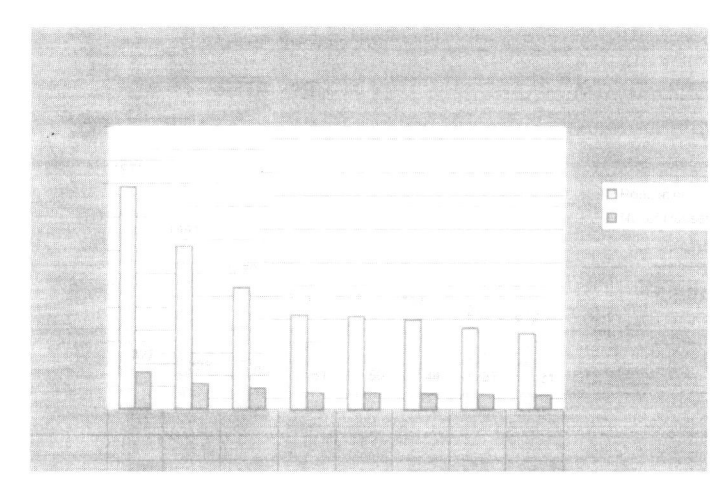

Early Censuses of Population for Ireland was carried every ten years starting in 1821. It was just another intelligence operation carried out by the 'Peelers'. Enumeration forms for our first four censuses were stored in the dungeons of the Four Courts until 1922. But this irreplaceable archive was deliberately fired during our Civil War. The British destroyed the censuses (1861 to 1891) so that the only censuses with original enumeration forms date from 1901 and 1911. Books of boring statistical data for Co. Galway still exist for each of the censuses from 1841 to 1891. This data appears to be of little value but if arranged by civil parish and graphed (above) it provides a picture, no matter how skimpy, of the catastrophic annihilation of families and homes occurring between 1841 and 1911.

With no church records until 1856, no civil records for Births, Deaths and Marriages until 1864 and no full census until 1901 - who then are the people of Clonkeen Kerrill or modern Gurteen? The answer will always be incomplete at best but three great sources, if properly exploited, could help make substantial progress! The first and most difficult source is, to this day, sitting untapped in Clonkeen Kerrill Cemetery. A wealth of genealogical data spanning the period 1780 (or earlier) to 1900 would be released if the position of all old headstones was carefully mapped and their inscriptions deciphered and recorded!

To this day many a townland has a field or garden bearing the surname of a 'Displaced Family' - - - still a living tribute to a family long gone, their erstwhile presence now just a vague recollection of today's busy population and the stones of their beloved homestead buried under newer structures!

From 1871 to 1911 the downward trend of townland population showed signs of "bottoming out" almost certainly due to birth-rate catching up with the combined effects of death and emigration! The censuses of 1901 and 1911 survived the disturbed period of Irish Independence and ensuing Civil War. Statistics for individual townlands have been included in a data table entitled **"Townland Statistics Clonkeen Civil Parish"** on the following page

Tithe List of Land Occupiers for Clonkeen Civil Parish

A meticulously compiled list of land occupiers for every Gurteen townland was compiled in 1826 - twenty A3 pages of gripping data and wouldn't you know it - all for the purposes of Church of Ireland taxation (Tithes). This tax burden was lifted from the shoulders of tenants twelve years later and landlords made liable. But what a hollow tenant victory as the landlord class simply compensated by raising rents! But good news at last; the obsolete list was saved and it is the only pre famine list of occupiers for Clonkeen Civil Parish. It gives the size of each holding, its valuation and the Tithe payable to the C of I by the occupier.

Richard Griffith's Valuation of Tenements

Griffith and his team's mammoth task, valuing all buildings and land in Ireland, was carried out for the county of Galway after the famine. Poor Law Rates, a local taxation used to fund Workhouses for the poor, was the initial driving force of the survey but Poor Law Valuation

Land Occupiers of Pre Famine (c.1826)

Occupier	Area Titheable in Acres	Valuation in £	Yearly Tithe in £
John Quin	1.6	1.37	0.04
Michl. Walsh	51.25	39.75	1.33
James Cunniffe	10.9	9.55	0.31
Jas & Thos.------	49.8	35.12	1.17
Michl. Cunnane	13.5	8.03	0.26
Patk. Cunnane	6.7	4	0.12
Jas. Royan	6.7	4	0.12
Peter Gilmer	31.9	19.25	0.65
Willm. Walsh	12.8	8.14	0.27
Peter Tierney	12.8	8.14	0.27
Chapel Yard	0.24	0.15	0.01
Edmd. Gallagher	3	2.55	0.06
Martin Manion	12.8	8.12	0.27
Thos. Walsh	12.8	8.12	0.27
Dan Costello	10.1	5.62	0.2
Thos. McNamara	9.6	6.75	0.22
John Kerrane	16.8	9.27	0.31
Thos. Kerrane	16.8	9.27	0.31
Mark Kerrane	16.8	9.27	0.31
John Fynn	60.1	31.42	1.05
Matw. Giblon	43.77	18.41	0.61
John&Patk. Silk	14.5	6.01	0.2
Michl. Hooban	14.5	6.01	0.2
Thos Kerrane/Peter Connors	14.5	6.01	0.2
Thos. Kerrane(again)	12.26	6.01	0.2
Jas McDonagh	11.24	5.56	0.18
Patk. Cavanagh	12	6.02	0.2
Wm. Walsh	23.74	11.65	0.39
John Walsh	11.75	5.8	0.19
Jas. Kerrane	11.75	5.8	0.19
John Tierney	12.2	5.82	0.2
Patk Tierney	12.2	5.82	0.2
Jas Royan	12.2	5.82	0.2
Patk. Cunnane	7.8	5.66	0.18

Post Famine (c.1853) Ballyglass

Occupier	Area in Stat. Acres	PLV Land in £	PLV Buildings in £	Total PLV in £
John Finn	83	30.25	5.5	35.75
Matthias Giblin	72	13.5	0.75	14.25
Patrick Silk		2.35	0.35	2.7
Thomas Kirrane		2.25	0	2.25
John Silk	76	5.15	0.6	5.75
Peter Connor		2	0.5	2.5
John Hooban		0.5	0.2	0.7
Patrick Kirrane		4.9	0.85	5.75
Thomas Kirrane	53	6.75	1	7.75
Patrick McDonagh		6	0.5	6.5
Thos Kirrane jun.				
Thomas Kirrane	52.5	18.25	0.5	18.75
John Kirrane				
John Kirrane	38.6	12	0.5	12.5
James Ryan	51.5	6	0.75	6.75
Thomas Kirrane		27	1.5	10.65
Thos Kirrane jun.			1.5	10.65
Mark Kirrane			1.25	10.4
Mark Kirrane	Bog 36	0.9		
Michael Kilkenny	7.75	1.25	0.25	1.5
James Duffy	177.25	72.3	4.2	76.5
Mark Kirrane	10.25	4.75	0.75	5.5
Michael White	10.1	4.75		4.75
Mark Monahan	55.2	11.5	0.75	12.25
RC Chapel	0.25		8	8
Police Barracks			7.5	7.5

Several Post Famine occupier's names are repeated because they collectively leased vacant holdings and divided it between themselves (groupings shown in shades of grey). Eight vacant prefamine houses were downgraded to cottier (labourer's) houses but the list gives no indication if they were occupied or not. Lord Dunsandle (Landlord) lumped several vacant holdings into a large grass farm which was leased on an annual basis.

Compiled by James N. Dillon

Townlands Statistics Clonkeen Kerrill Civil Parish

Townland	1841	1851	1861	1871	1881	1891	1901	1911	1841	1851	1861	1871	1881	1891	1901	1911	Area in stat. acres	Griffith PLV in £	LANDLORD c.1850
Attimany	21	9	9	7	11	10	13	7	4	2	2	2	3	2	2	2	86	9	Lord Dunsandle
Ballyglass	285	204	133	111	115	116	111	101	49	36	21	19	20	18	17	16	723	261	Lord Dunsandle
Caltragh	7	5	5	7	10	7	5	6	1	1	1	1	1	1	1	1	140	91	Lord Dunsandle
Clogh	280	219	176	167	159	146	131	145	45	32	26	27	26	25	25	25	1639	403	Lord Dunsandle
Clonkeenkerrill	175	158	103	76	51	60	55	51	27	25	17	12	10	12	11	11	905	260	Myles W. O'Reilly
Cloonbornia	121	78	37	26	20	21	33	22	25	19	10	6	4	5	5	5	315	100	Richard Graves
Colmanstown	244	181	121	103	114	110	96	86	38	25	22	23	26	20	21	20	1457	423	Myles W. O'Reilly
Fahy	46	30	28	18	19	18	13	15	8	5	5	4	3	3	4	3	209	34	Lord Dunsandle
Gortnacross	36	19	20	11	7	16	16	10	5	4	3	2	2	2	2	2	37	15	Richard Graves
Gortnalone N.	34	89	70	34	29	34	42	37	5	13	12	6	4	7	8	8	337	117	John E. Trench
Gortnalone S.	49	4	4	19	26	6	3	4	7	1	1	4	5	2	1	1	277	71	John A. Daly
Gortronnagh	45	25	29	18	20	15	14	13	8	4	5	4	4	4	3	3	184	29	Lord Dunsandle
Killooaun	70	87	68	7	40	41	26	18	11	16	15	1	7	6	6	6	302	65	John F. Browne
Knockaboy	67	19	17	15	15	16	12	10	13	4	3	3	2	2	2	2	77	45	John E. Trench
Lenareagh	133	95	73	63	52	55	40	32	20	14	14	10	7	8	6	6	480	83	Lord Dunsandle
Shanballard	93	61	42	32	34	35	30	26	17	10	8	7	8	9	6	6	254	78	Lord Dunsandle
Shanballyeeshal	130	78	54	52	45	34	31	37	25	13	10	9	8	7	7	6	261	57	John E. Trench
Shanbally More	27	15	24	11	14	14	11	10	3	2	3	3	2	2	2	2	263	31	Lord Dunsandle
Sheeaun	94	42	38	33	24	18	26	19	13	7	6	5	4	4	5	4	178	87	Richard Graves
Temple	14	28	29	31	30	27	21	18	2	5	4	4	5	6	4	3	204	97	Richard Graves
Totals	1971	1441	1076	835	827	799	729	672	327	228	189	151	150	145	138	132	8212	2354	

Townlands from the West End of Ballymacward Civil Parish

Townland	1841	1851	1861	1871	1881	1891	1901	1911	1841	1851	1861	1871	1881	1891	1901	1911	Area/acres	PLV in £	LANDLORD
Ballygrany	179	89	72	57	51	37	29	27	27	22	16	15	12	10	9	8	151	50	Lord Dunsandle
CorskeaghDaly	21	20	13	10	13	15	16	18	3	3	3	2	2	2	2	2	737	226	Lord Dunsandle
Creeraun	14	21	18	12	12	8	8	5	2	3	3	6	4	2	2	2	245	129	Margaret O'Kelly
Glennamucka	40	86	39	42	43	31	42	34	7	13	7	7	5	4	6	6	347	151	Lord Dunsandle
Gortbrack	95	86	52	36	41	32	26	23	13	14	11	9	10	9	7	5	99	40	Robert H. M. Eyre
Gorteen	151	93	82	70	68	33	44	38	26	17	14	11	11	9	9	8	429	157	Lord Dunsandle
Gortnahultra	26	11	0	7	7	5	10	12	3	1	0	1	1	1	1	1	370	140	Lord Dunsandle
Killooaun Eyre	74	26	32	16	29	32	37	28	11	5	8	4	5	5	5	5	403	92	John F. Browne
Census Year	1841	1851	1861	1871	1881	1891	1901	1911	1841	1851	1861	1871	1881	1891	1901	1911	Area/acres	PLV in £	LANDLORD

Compiled by James N. Dillon

was also used by landowners and agents in assessing expected rental income. Dwelling houses, farm sheds and land were all liable for PLR. Because of the enormity of comparing Tithe with Griffith for a full parish, only the townland of Ballyglass is selected.

Land War - Propaganda or Reality

Up to 1905 many townlands in Clonkeen Civil Parish were part of the giant Dunsandle Estate. After a protracted and sometimes ruthless struggle, William Daly of Dunsandle, acting on behalf of himself and his younger brother, agreed to sell his tenanted lands to the occupiers. Gurteen Branch of the United Irish League (UIL) pushed to have a united tenant front at the negotiating table and managed to secure this by setting up a Dunsandle Estate Tenants Committee. The final stage of haggling over prices fell on the shoulders of Chairman, Patrick Carr of Carraroe, (opposite Bookeen Barracks) and Secretary, Martin Finnerty of Knockaboy, Gurteen. Below are three gems abstracted from newspapers sympathetic to the tenant cause.

Treacy's Unexpected Turkey Dinner

Michael Treacy lives on four acres of land in the townland of Clough, the cultivation of which would baffle the resources of agricultural science. He sows potatoes on mountain land about seven miles away and has the satisfaction of observing a large Dunsandle grazing farm extending right up to his door. His industrious wife rears a clutch of turkeys to supplement his meagre income. Occasionally, after the nature of their kind, the roving turkeys trespass on the grazing farm.
On one such occasion the lord of the soil, William Daly, Esq. of Dunsandle, was looking over his domain in the company of his humble herdsman, when some of the nomadic turkeys came between the wind and Mr Daly's nobility! The herd, at a nod from his master, raised his gun and dispatched one of the offending birds. Mr. Daly continued his inspection with unruffled composure.
This incident, insignificant in its own way, is still a good barometer of landlord/tenant relations. Treacy works as hard as he is able but were it not for the assistance he gets from his two sons in America, he would not have turkey for dinner -------- unless his landlord honour him with more frequent visits!

Permission to rent a Turf Bank

In the village of Cappalusk there were six tenants who, about 1868, state they were deprived of 65 acres of good land in order to facilitate the formation of a Dunsandle grazing farm. They eke out a miserable subsistence on smallholdings of three to eight acres of the worst description. Their children emigrate to England each year as Harvesters and with the money thus earned they manage to keep the pot boiling - though an analysis of the contents would not always be satisfactory from a nutritional point of view.

Each year Fardy Kenny, John Keane and Peter Scally have to make a pilgrimage (on foot) to Dunsandle to ask permission to cut turf. Sometimes the landlord is away (or maybe not receiving visitors of this class) and they trudge the nine weary miles home again and wait for a luckier day. Fardy Kenny recalls, from some years back, having traipsed three times in one year to Dunsandle before that minor monarch, the bog bailiff, appeared in Cappalusk with the necessary permission for the tenants to cut their winter turf.

Kenny, who happens to be a member of the United Irish League, was refused permission to cut turf locally a few years back and of necessity was compelled to travel three miles to a bog in a neighbouring estate. The appearance of the houses in Cappalusk is neat and clean and the people impress one as being industrious and honest.

Mary Swanzy, a well-known artist, painted William Daly's portrait. It was sold at auction about twenty years ago. The following image was taken from the sale catalogue and the poem's author used the pseudonym Tipperary.

William Daly of Dunsandle
By Mary Swanzy

Dunsandle's Vow

From Gurteen Town to Tallyho,
From Larah Hill to Raford gaily.
From Cappalusk to Carraroe
No rents are paid to Willie Daly.
Too long were paid Dunsandle rents,
Fished out by bailiff's, mouthed mealy.
Willie tyrants laws, at all events,
Ground peasants under Willie Daly.

Too long 'gainst bailiff, clerk and lord,
The tenant strove to guard his eyrie,
Knockatopher's sons were forced abroad,
Kiltulla cleared by tyrant Daly.
"But never more a pound we'll pay,
We swear by blessed book and candle".
Weep, Kinneen Jack; no Office Day!
And that's the vow of bold Dunsandle.

The O'Hara Family & Lenaboy Castle

By

William Henry

The name O' Hara descends from the important and distinguished Irish family of Eaghra, pronounced Ara. He was chief of Leyny in County Sligo, and one of his descendants became a King of Munster. In Gaelic the name is O'hEaghra, which is anglicised to O'Hara. About 1350, this clan split and formed two divisions, the chiefs of which were called O'Hara Boy and O'Hara Reagh respectively. In the Composition Book of Connacht, 1585, the seat of O'Hara Boy is at Collooney, and the O'Hara Reagh is at Ballyharry, which should read Ballyhara. Another branch of this family migrated to County Antrim. The famous manuscript known as The Book of O'Hara, which is still in existence, contains concise records of the O'Hara chiefs. In his Tour to the Hebrides with Dr. Johnson, 1773, Boswell, tells us of the respect which the native Irish held for O'Hara's during the eighteenth century. By the following century they owned extensive land in County Sligo. The O'Hara's of Cooper's Hill and Annaghmore possessed more than 21,000 acres and are still of importance in this county. Among the many distinguished O'Hara's were: Kane O'Hara (1712-1782) author of the popular burlesque Midas. James O'Hara (1752-1819) the American revolutionary was the son of John O'Hara, an Irishman. Kean O'Hara along with Lord Edward Fitzgerald, took part in the 1798 Rebellion, he escaped from Ireland after the rebellion failed. Three bishops of Achonry were O'Hara's. One of the founders of Pittsburgh USA was an O'Hara. In 1706, one branch of the Sligo O'Hara family was given the title, Baron Tyrawley. In Ireland today, the O'Hara's are chiefly found in Counties Sligo and Antrim.

The O'Hara family of Lenaboy, Galway and Raheen, Gort, County Galway, are descended from John O'Hara. He was the first known member of this family to settle in County Galway, probably arriving in the county sometime in the late 17th or early 18th century. John married Joanna Cook and they had three sons, James being the eldest was born in 1717, John and Geoffrie. John also served as a Town Major in Galway, and died in 1729, his wife, Joanna, survived him by ten years. The eldest son, James, became master of Lenaboy and their second son, Robert, who became master of Raheen Robert served as a Lieutenant Colonel in the 88th regiment of Connaught Rangers. During his military career he fought in ten battles and sieges of the Peninsular War, against the French armies of Napoleon Bonaparte. The following is a list of his battle honours: Vimiera, Talavera, Sabugal, Fuentes D'Onor, Miranda de Corvo, Corunna, Coa, Busaco, Redinha, Badajos. There is a very fine Gothic Revival style plaque erected to him in St. Nicholas' Collegiate Church in Galway City. Robert married Frances Taylor, granddaughter of Walter Taylor, of Castletaylor, who had acquired the property during Cromwellian times. Robert and Francis had eleven children, six sons and five daughters. One of the daughters, Elizabeth, married a member of the Gregory family of Coole, Gort. Robert's third daughter, Anne, married James Hardiman Burke of St. Clerans, in 1817. On the occasion of their wedding, Anne's dowry was £4,000. Sir Richard Martin of Dangan was a close friend of the family and as a wedding present he presented them with two tables made from Connemara marble. Richard Martin was better known as 'Humanity Martin', a name given to him by King George IV, because he was the first person to initiate laws for the protection of animals. However, he was also known as 'Trigger Martin', because of his reputation with a duelling pistol. James and Anne moved into their new home at St. Clerans. It had been completed by James in 1811 and during its construction most of the old Burke castle was demolished and some of the stones from it were reincorporated in the building of the new stables and the out-houses. James and Anne Burke had seven children: John, Robert O'Hara, James, Fanny, Elizabeth, Hester and Anne Celestine Burke. The second son, Robert O'Hara Burke became the noted Australian explorer. By all accounts Anne O'Hara Burke was a very beautiful woman, full of tenderness and sympathy. The good nature of Anne O'Hara Burke is borne out in the family documents. They record that once during a fever epidemic in the old Claddagh village, Anne went among the unfortunate people and nursed the sick. The Claddagh was an ancient Irish village at the mouth of the River Corrib. Because of her kindness to these people, she was always made welcome in the village. She travelled throughout the county in a phaeton drawn by a pair of grey-coloured Connemara ponies and was well known by the local people. The fact that she could travel about the countryside in safety demonstrates the high regard that people felt for her. Anne O'Hara Burke died in 1844 and was the last Mrs. Burke of St. Clerans.

John and Joanna O'Hara's eldest son James who was the first of this family to live at Lenaboy married Elizabeth Shaw in 1744. She was the daughter of Robert Shaw, a former MP for Galway. It seems that the marriage produced fourteen children of which only four survived him. James became Mayor of Galway in 1747, but served only one term. While James was mayor, the Disney's another prominent family assembled a rival council and nominated their own allies for the main Galway corporate offices. Although the Privy Council supported the Disney's, James O'Hara refused to accept the decision and it seems that he had to be forcibly removed from office by the military. This decision caused James O'Hara to set up his own rival corporation, which possibly lasted about a year. His eldest son who was also named James was born in 1748 and in turn he became master of Lenaboy. He served as Recorder of Galway for sixty years and died in 1838. His son, also another James, who was born in 1796, went on represent Galway as MP and also lived at Lenaboy Castle. In fact Lenaboy passed down through five generations of the O'Hara family, all of them named James. Finally in 1913, Colonel James O'Hara leased the castle to Mr. David Syme, manager of the Guinness Company in Galway.

In 1920, Lenaboy Castle became the headquarters of the British Auxiliaries in Galway. The castle has a dark side to its history, during this period a young priest, Fr. Michael Griffin was murdered at Lenaboy. Fr. Griffin was born on September 18th 1892 at Gurteen, County Galway. He was ordained in 1917 and by June 1918 was assigned to the parish of Rahoon in Galway. By 1920, the War of Independence was well under way. In Galway City on the night of September 8th 1920, Sean Mulvoy a member of the Irish Republican Army was shot dead while trying to disarm Constable Crumm of the Royal Irish Constabulary. The other volunteers involved in the incident were Sean Turke and Frank O'Dowd. It is not known for sure which bullet killed Mulvoy, but Crumm was also shot dead. The infamous Black and Tans immediately set out for revenge. In the early hours of the morning they took Seamus Quirke, a first lieutenant with the local brigade of the I.R.A., from his lodgings near Galway docks. They dragged him to the corner of the docks where they shot him seven times. They left him for dead, but he managed to crawl back to the lodgings where he later died. Fr. Michael Griffin was sent for to administer the last rites. On Friday September 10th, High Mass was celebrated in the Pro-Cathedral for both I.R.A. men. After the Mass, Bishop O'Dea led 10,000 people, and over forty priests in the funeral procession to St. James' Cemetery, Mervue, where Sean Mulvoy was buried. The funeral of Seamus Quirke continued on to his native Cork. In recent years two roads in Galway were named in memory of these men.

On the night of November 14th 1920, Fr. Griffin was lured from his presbytery in Sea Road, presumably by members of the Black and Tans. He was taken to Lenaboy Castle and questioned, possibly regarding republican activities. Shortly afterwards, Fr. Griffin was shot through the head in the grounds of Lenaboy. His body was then buried in an unmarked shallow grave at Cloughscoiltia near the village of Barna, County Galway. The following day, Canon Davis the Administrator of Rahoon Parish, called to the police station at Eglington Street and reported the disappearance of the young priest. The authorities immediately appealed for help and a search began. On November 20th, his body was discovered by a local farmer, and brought to Galway City. On the day of his burial, mourners gathered from early morning at the church of St. Joseph in Galway City, for the funeral Mass. Almost one hundred and fifty priests, the Archbishop of Tuam and the bishops of Galway and Clonfert attended the funeral. After the Mass, his remains were taken to the Cathedral grounds at Loughrea for burial. A road was also named after Fr. Griffin and plaque marks the house from which he was taken. For years, mystery surrounded his murder. However, the late Fr. Padraic O'Laoi, author of Fr. Griffin, has completed extensive research on the subject. He concluded that Fr. Griffin was murdered in reprisal for the kidnapping and execution of an informer, by the Irish Republican Army. In July 1998, the skeletal remains a man were discovered in the Barna area and it is widely believed that they were the remains of the informer.

Acknowledgments & References
Mrs. Jacqueline O Brien for proofreading this work and making valuable suggestions. Ms. Marie Mannion, Mrs. Mary de Vere Chamberlain Taylor, The staff of the James Hardiman Library, National University of Ireland, Galway.

Fr. Griffin, by Padraic O'Laoi, (Connacht Tribune Ltd., Galway, 1994)
Galway History & Society, Interdisciplinary Essays on the History of an Irish County, 'The Politics of Protestant Ascendancy: County Galway 1650-1832', by James Kelly. Editor: Gerard Morgan, Associate Editor Raymond Gillespy, Series Editor William Nolan, Geography Publications, Dublin 1996
Genealogical and Heraldic History of the Landed Gentry of Ireland, By B. Burke, (1912), (Revised by A.C. Fox-Davies) Harrison & Sons, London
Humanity Dick Martin, the King of Connemara 1754-1834, by Shevawn Lynam, (The Lilliput Press, London, 1989)
Irish Families, their names, arms and origins, by Edward MacLysagh
Records of the Galway Family History Society
St. Patrick's Parish Magazine 1980-81, 'Sean Turke', by Canon P. Laoi P.P.
The Burkes of Iserclerán, by Captain Tom Powell, 1932-33
The History of the Town and County of the town of Galway. by James Hardiman, 1820. Facsimile Edition, Connacht Tribune Ltd., Galway, 1985.
The O'Hara Family Connection with St. Clerans. by William Henry, (Merv Griffin, 1999)

MY MUSINGS ON THE SCHOOLS' RE-UNION

By

Jimmy Cogavin

Thanks to everybody connected with the idea and the organisation of this event. Every one I have spoken to seems to be absolutely thrilled and considers it a wonderful idea. Unfortunately, I opened my mouth too wide and promised Joe, I would jot down a few notes on my memories. Now the time has come to put pen to paper. I am one of the few who attended two of the three schools.

My first faltering steps away from home were off to Tample in June 1941 as a weakling of just 4 years 1 month of age. I was entrusted into the care of Peggy Griffin and Maureen Carr. I have since been told that one morning my shoelace became undone and try as they would, I refused to allow them near it. We continued on until we reached Wade's forge. There, my grand uncles Tom and Martin (both blacksmiths) were asked to do the necessary. I wonder did this demonstrate traits such as strong family values or just downright chauvinism?

The school was in the control of two great teachers Miss Daisy Duffy and my Aunt-in-law Mrs. Bride Cogavin. I have little recollection of the syllabus or my progress in the school except for one detail. The third page of the first book became dog-eared, thickened, smudged and torn with the persistent opening, closing and thumbing of it. Whether there was a conspiracy or not between school and home, I was not allowed to move on to the next page until I knew the one I was on. Throughout the rest of my life I never again had such difficulty. That particular lesson is etched in my brain and at this stage is unlikely to leave. My mother, who is 95, also went to the same school, and she still remembers the lesson and refers to it as "the four little words". They were IT, IS, AN and AS.

My father who was born in 1896 went to Tample also. He was taught at the end of his school days in 1909 by the same Bride Monaghan (later to become his sister-in-law). She came to Tample as an assistant teacher at fifteen years of age from Co. Cavan, and later married my uncle, Michael. In those days, Botany or at least an elementary course in plant growth, was taught in the school together with a good grounding in the three Rs., as well as, Catechism.

When Mrs Hurley, (nee Duffy, a sister of Miss Duffy), died in Cloonkeen about 1945 Bride was appointed to the school as teacher. At this stage, there were six of us in the family at home, Maura, Phil., Joe, Noreen, Mairead and myself. John and Ann had yet to arrive. We were an important commodity in the sense that numbers were urgently needed for Cloonkeen School. Together with the Connors in Shanbhaile, another big family, we changed horses and moved to Cloonkeen. We collectively improved the "average" considerably and Miss Sheila Cloonan came in, as assistant teacher. They became a powerful team. She taught me Algebra and Geometry, as extras to facilitate my start in secondary school. Not alone did she achieve her objective, but, she lit a spark of love in me, for the wonderful world of mathematics and science. As it happened, I had learned enough to carry me through secondary school and into university. Thank you Sheila.

On my way home from school one day in 1948 or 1949, Tommy Roche invited me in to their house to show me, possibly his earliest engineering feat. With great pride he threw a switch in the kitchen and a bulb hanging from the ceiling, lit up. This was the first hydro-electricity scheme in Gurteen. He had made a wheel race, put it in the river, which flowed down by the gable end of the house, harnessed power from it and turned it into electricity. It was still a few years more before the Rural Electrification Scheme brought power to our community. Well done, Tommy, I imagine you were thirteen or fourteen, then.

Since undertaking to put those thoughts together, I have read a fair bit on the subject of primary school education, with a view to tracing the origins of our schools. If others have done like-wise I apologise for invading their pitch. Most of the material was recovered from libraries and from the National Archives in Dublin. It needs more local input. Help would be greatly appreciated.

A TURNING POINT IN IRISH HISTORY

The biggest battle ever fought in Ireland was the Battle of Aughrim. It took place less than twenty miles from Gurteen in 1691. More people died there (est. 20,000 between the two sides), than have been killed in most of the battles and troubles since then. That includes the 1916 Rising, the Civil War and the recent Northern troubles. King James 11 and his French allies were defeated by his son-in-law, the Dutch king, William of Orange and their array of forces from all over Europe, including a contingent from the Vatican. William, a Protestant, ascended the English throne and with his wife, Mary, ensured that the Irish gave no more trouble. A century of oppression followed.

The Penal Laws, enacted by William and later by his sister Anne, meant that Catholics had no entitlement to own property, to vote, to attend Roman Catholic services, to be educated, to take positions in state concerns, or to join the armed forces at home or abroad. The same applied in England incidentally. At least a hundred years of oppression and impoverishment ensued.

The American War of Independence in 1776 gave the English a salutary message and after many defeats, they were forced to surrender and go home. The Americans still commemorate this great victory over the English on July 4th. The French revolution increased worries about how 'the motley' could behave. The English Government started to make concessions. They set up Maynooth College in 1795 to try to have some control over the clergy. They wanted to prevent the slide to revolutionary thinking of the kind that had engulfed France and which was proving very dangerous, for kings and rulers generally. The Dutch were also restive. The Act of Union was introduced in 1801. It was really only a talking shop for the landed and wealthy that played at the business of governing Ireland.

On the education front, things were beginning to change dramatically and the covert Hedge

Schools were developing into privately owned schools where teachers charged for their services. Daniel O'Connell's Catholic Emancipation Act 1829 was a significant step forward. The National Board of Education was founded in 1832. This brought standardisation to schooling in Ireland. It helped to pay for teachers, introduce a syllabus, provide a standard book list, and aided the equipping of buildings provided by local effort.

THE LOCAL SITUATION

At this stage, we come to our own schools, the first being Cloonkeen. In 1843 the Education Commissioners, received an application, from a Major O'Reilly requesting a grant for a teacher's salary in Cloonkeenkerrill. This was a very extensive document with 86 questions in all to be answered, including the dimensions of the proposed building. It appears that he was the landlord that owned the building. He was from Co. Louth near Balbriggan. The building had a height description of 13 feet. I think this is now Finnerty's barn/cart-house. In 1871, 1883 and 1885 further applications were made, in his (Reilly's) name, for grants in respect of teachers' and assistant teachers' salaries. Most interesting is his announcement that he proposes, to build a new school, to equip it with farm implements and tools of a size suitable for young boys. They were to learn the use of such implements as scythes, spades hacks etc. Most adults in the area did not have these items at the time.

The Roll Number is 3842. Another Roll No. 15429 is used in later dates. I am not sure what this means. The Major got the parish priest in Ballymacward to act as Communicator (Manager) and he himself is referred to as the patron from then on. The school was free to the community and no rent was charged. The attendance on a day of inspection in the 1880's was 74 (47 males and 27 females).

Next, came Shanballard, Roll No. 14663. In 1895 a lease on a piece of land was taken out in the name of trustees. Most Rev. Dr. Healy, archbishop of Tuam, Rev. Larkin, Adm. Ballymacward, and Owen Lynch Gurteen. A school was built immediately and in 1904 a residence was built on adjoining property. A loan of £250 was made available. This house was a bit of a disaster and had to be rebuilt in 1910. A big row erupted between the clergy in Ballymacward, Aughrim, Eyrecourt and New Inn. It was said that dances were being held in some of the schools in Dec. 1917 for the benefit of Sinn Fein. Shanballard was named as one of the schools but this was firmly denied. The landslide victory by Sinn Fein in the elections of the following year was the beginning of the end for British rule.

As an aside, I understand that my father, Tom, was secretary at the polling booth in Cloonkeen for that election. He held the position of secretary, or presiding officer, at all elections in either Cloonkeen or the Courthouse in Gurteen, until the 1983 referendum. I wonder is this a record?

At the time of writing I have not found anything on the origin of Tample School. By the time we meet in May, I expect the situation to have improved and that more information will have come to hand. Help from local sources will be very welcome.

No commentary or history of education in Gurteen would be complete without looking at the contribution of one family, the Griffins. Pam and Claire have spent all of their professional lives, living in the parish and teaching locally. Their aunts, Miss Duffy and Mrs. Hurley, did likewise, and so did their maternal grand parents Mr. and Mrs. Duffy. I can only imagine that their paternal great grand father Laurence Griffin would have taken great pride in the knowledge that his great grand daughter, Pam, taught in the present school until her retirement.

He would also have been overjoyed with the location of the present school in Gurteen, 150 years after Cloonkeen, 100 years after Shanballard and Tample. The Griffith Valuation Reports for East Galway, compiled in the 1840's, and published in 1852, indicate that he was the owner of a school in the village, back then. I believe he was born about 1810. It may indeed have been his father who set it up and continued the tradition of education, at that point.

WHAT IS HISTORY?

This tradition began in Ireland with the Celtic bards and poets, right through to the hedge schoolmasters and then to the professional teachers of later days. The old Williamite laws forbade the education of Catholics. As a result of the Relief Act in 1782 things improved. The change in law however did not allow Catholics to teach without taking the Oath of Allegiance. The Act was further amended in 1792 when the need for the oath was removed. This opened things up for private teachers.

I hold a sceptical view of most of the history that I read and tend to support the view that it is "an agreed statement of what happened at the time". It will give me great pleasure if this article can spur discussion and maybe, sometime in the future, if agreement is reached, perhaps we can call it history.

I have made no reference to, or distinction between the living and the dead. When dealing in memories they are all alive.

THE NEW SCHOOL IN GURTEEN

THE OLD SCHOOL IN CLOONKEENKERRILL

CHAPTER TWO

THE PURSUIT OF KNOWLEDGE

CHANGING SCHOOLS

By

Mai Dwyer-Laheen

I had the privilege of attending Cloonkeen and Shanballard schools. When I was in Second Class Cloonkeen school was in such a dilapidated condition, that the teacher advised us to go on strike until something was done about it, so we all stayed away from school and we even got headlines in the Connaught Tribune PUPILS ON STRIKE! We felt very important. After a few carefree weeks the Priest in Gurteen put pressure on the parents to send the children to another school. So my two brothers and I set off through the bog to Shanballard school with a certain amount of apprehension. I'll always remember the warm welcome we got from the teachers and the pupils. I enjoyed every minute there. Mrs. Kitt was a kind and dedicated teacher. She prepared me for my Confirmation. I was just nine years old. My abiding memory of that time is walking through the bog on a Summer's morning and listening to the curlew and the cuckoo call, and watching the lark soar into the sky.

When Cloonkeen school was refurbished I didn't want to return but again pressure was put on the parents to send us back to Cloonkeen. I was overwhelmed with sadness saying good-bye to my newfound friends in Shanballard.

Returning to the refurbished school was exciting. Mrs. Hurley encouraged us to learn and speak Irish, and those of us who could converse in Irish were given badges with the inscription "Labraim Gaedilg". We were supposed to wear this badge and speak in Irish to anyone we met but of course we never did. In fact on our way home from school if we met a Connemara man who used to work for Mary Forde we would get up on the ditch and shout "Ghaeilge bradach briste agus Béarla ghlas bhinn". The usual response was a string of curses in Irish and then he'd chase us with the spade. The folly of youth! We could have learnt some useful Irish conversation from a native speaker if only we had sense.

Cloonkeen school in common with all other National schools had that system of cramming. We had to learn tables, Irish and English poetry all off by heart. It was fine for the bright child, but for those who were slow those who failed to crack the code of reading and writing even though they had many other talents, it was a cruel and harsh regime that blighted the childhood of many. No talk of dyslexia then. No remedial or resource teachers.

Those children were put at the back of the classroom, sometimes their faces to the wall, and called dunces. They left school feeling they were failures, when in fact it was the system and the country who failed them. It was that generation who left Ireland in their droves to take up menial jobs in the big cities of England, and now again they find themselves on the margins of society. Some are destitute. Surely the Government who spend millions catering for refugees from far flung places who never heard of Ireland until a few years ago, should turn their attention to this lost generation of Irish people who were treated so cruelly in their childhood.

The Church too is very vocal in welcoming the strangers, but has shown scant regard for those people down the years. They should be invited back and be allowed to live out their lives in dignity in the country where they belong.

I take this opportunity of wishing the Committee every success and I look forward to meeting some old friends on May 2nd.

THE WONDERS OF LIFE

An extract from a work in progress

By

TOM ROCHE.

Our house was a picturesque thatched cottage situated at the end of a narrow boreen which crossed the river. It had one chimney in the middle of the roof, three small windows deep-set into the walls and a door with a half door outside it in the middle of the front wall. The doors and windows were painted red and the walls whitewashed with lime produced locally at the limekiln a mile or so away. The white walls, red window-frames and doors and golden straw thatch set at the end of a small green field was a striking image. Wild roses, pink and white, grew against the walls to the south and west. The northern and eastern aspects had a high hedge of hawthorn and willow bushes some twenty feet or so out from the house. These were trimmed back neatly once a year This scene with the river to the front, would capture the attention of any landscape artist - a beautiful picture.

The boreen was about a quarter of a mile long from what was known as the "head" onto the main Gurteen to Mountbellew road. The first hundred yards or so had high whitethorn hedges intermingled with blackthorn sloe bushes, blackberry briars and a myriad of wild flowers. A little further on came a wide stretch known as the "Junction". At one time there were other houses to the left and right at this point. I remember one family by the name of Cookes living to the right. They were moved to Keave, Woodlawn where they got a new house and farm around 1935. The "Junction" was a great meeting place. The remainder of the boreen was open. The river was just a small stream - a tributary of the Corrib.

My first memory was of when I lost my cradle to my sister Ann, who was a new arrival in the family. My father made the cradle from timber, which he recycled from an old bacon box that he got from the local shop. It looked crude but it was very comfortable. I had grown to like it for the two and a half years that I had exclusive rights to it. Now all of this was changed. A brand new contraption known as the 'cot' was moved into the kitchen-cum-living room of our house. It was placed by the wall in the corner nearest the fire. My father also made this bed-like piece of furniture. It had four legs, six inches or so from the floor with three rails around the outside above the internal base on which the homemade straw mattress rested. It was very comfortable but I did not like it. I cried and cried for my cradle but to no avail. My mother tried to console me by taking me onto her lap, cuddling me and feeding me. After washing and changing I felt very sleepy but when I woke up in strange surroundings I again expressed my dissatisfaction by crying.

The fireplace was open and always interesting. The flickering and dancing of the flames and the various colours they elicited from the wood-logs and sods of peat turf changed by the second. The crane supported some hooks on which pots of potatoes and ovens for baking bread could be suspended over the fire. This was the only means of cooking, baking, drying and heating. With the skill of my mother's hands, the most wonderfully tasty oven cakes and griddlecakes were made. The rashers cut from the flitch of bacon hanging from the rafters above the fire, the currant buns and the caraway seed cakes all produced their own sweet smell in the kitchen and never failed to stimulate the appetite. Oatmeal porridge, bacon and cabbage and the flowery Kerr's Pinks were all cooked on the open fire. The pig's pot, a large bellied metal vessel with a pothooks fitted to the two 'lugs', was always ready to be put into action over the fire. Oaten meal, cabbage, turnips and potatoes were cooked and mashed together with the wooden pounder. This was the feed for the pigs in the small sty at the rear of the house.

Otherwise the furniture of the kitchen was simple. A grandfather chair with its sugán back and seat were at the near side of the fire beside the cot. My father's chair of the same kind was always at the far side close to the hob and the ash hole cover. Further out in the centre of the floor was a large table. This table was a workbench as well as a dining table. A long bench-like seat with four legs of split ash and a wooden plank top was called the stool. There were four or five light kitchen chairs in a row by the wall near the back door. The bin at the top wall was a large box with a sloping lid. The flour, wholemeal, and oaten meal were stored in three different compartments in this bin close to the dresser. Against the wall between the front door and my father's chair was the settle-bed. This was an ingenious contraption with hooks and hinges. It was deployed when an occasional visitor came to stay for the night. In the closed up mode it looked like a seat. It often looked like a shelf with shoes, books and clothes neatly stacked on it. High up over the fire was the mantlepiece. This was a board ten feet long and one foot wide supported on three wooden pegs fitted to the beam attached to the chimneystack. The stack itself was made from yellow fire clay daub and twisted ropes of straw. Where it appeared through the roof on the outside, daub was used to form a funnel-like exit for the smoke. This chimney funnel was white washed every time the outer walls of the house were whitened. Lime was used for this purpose.

My father and mother slept in the upper room and my Grandfather had the lower room. My cot and Ann's cradle were brought into our parent's bedroom at night.

The days and nights passed and the months went by and I was getting strong of muscle and almost able to climb from the cot onto the flagstone floor. I was longing to get out of the cot so that I could explore the new territory outside the half door. One day, perhaps a year later, I made my way across the floor through the open door to the lawn and flowerbed. I pulled up some tulips, scattered the soil and chuckled with joy. My mother had been attending to my sister Ann and had not missed me from the room. When she discovered me, she exclaimed that 'We are in for it now- keeping an eye on this young lad when he gets his feet under him.'

The first major memory is of the day my grandfather took me with him to Burke's post office and pub in Colemanstown, three miles away. He was 76 years of age and in receipt of a small pension which he collected weekly. This was in 1934. We went by donkey and cart. I remember my mother issuing instructions as we left. I sat on the floor of the cart and Grandad sat on the seat board which was athwart the cart. It was held in place by the side laces. We arrived at the

pub in jig time and he tied the donkey to a small gate and lifted me carefully onto the road. He took me by the hand and brought me into the bar.
He was greeted by a chorus of, 'Hello Matt. Is this your grandson?'
Matt said, 'This is young Tommie.'

A man with a white beard gave me a penny. Another man with a hat give me a big currant biscuit. Mr. Burke came on the scene, shook my hand and said,'Welcome'. He gave me a small glass of fizzy lemonade. I have never forgotten the taste of biscuit and lemonade. My Grandad got a pint of 'Guinness', collected his pension and paid for the pint. He bought a bag of 'bull's eyes' and put them into his pocket. We returned home to my mother who was waiting anxiously at the door. When he had unharnessed the donkey, Grandad gave the sweets to my mother. We repeated this trip many times.

Grandad was taken ill in the Sring of 1935. Doctor Crowe from Mountbellew examined him. He advised my parents to call the priest. Father Pelly came and spent an hour in the bedroom with him. When he came out he said, 'Matt is not too good but the doctor is coming in the morning to see him again. Let all his friends and relations know.'

He died the following day. A wake was held in the house that night. Clay pipes, tobacco, and a half-barrel of porter came from Burkes. We were all shocked. My mother sent myself and my sisters to stay with Emily Stephens, a neighbour, on the night of the wake. My uncle, Martin Kilkenny, arrived with a horse and sidecar next day. The coffin was carried from the house and placed on the 'well' of the sidecar. The funeral procession started on foot to the new church in Gurteen, a mile or so away.

At first I didn't fully understand what was going on but after Grandad's body had been removed from the house, I was overcome by a feeling of deep gloom, followed by extreme sorrow. I began to cry and continued to do so non-stop until my parents returned from the church. Emily Stephens looked after us while the body was being brought to the church. She told my mother about the ordeal that she had gone through as she tried to stop my crying. My parents were cross with me. My mother looked up and addressing Emily said, 'They were always very attached to each other. Tommie was the apple of Granddad's eye. The Lord have mercy on his soul. We will all miss him'. Then she started to cry. My sister and I joined in. I saw tears coming from my father's eyes. Uncle Tommie, my father's brother and his sister Mary began to cry also. Emily Stephens looked sad too but advised us to 'pull ourselves together.'
She said. 'Remember there is the burial tomorrow.'
The big black, metal kettle was filled with crystal clear water from a white enamel bucket. We got the water from Cooke's Well which was situated about a hundred yards away, beside a boreen. The tea was made in a delph teapot with a picture of a cow on both sides of it. The willow-patterned delph from the dresser was set out on the table. Currant loaf and beautiful homemade, white bread garnished with lots of butter, was served to all who called. The food was most enjoyable. The settle bed was prepared. My father and uncle slept in it as they had done many times before. Aunty Mary slept with my mother, while Annie and I were put to sleep in a cot. Emily went home by the path through the meadow field to her own house. Her next-door neighbours, Kate and Tom accompanied her. It was believed that no sane person would venture out on his or her own on the night after a bereavement. They had a tin lantern with a candle light inside. My father had bought this from the tinkers about two years previously. He paid a shiny new shilling for it. As he was paying the bearded tinsmith for it, the latter said,

'There is a special blessing going with that lamp.'
'What is it?' asked my father.
'Fairies and ghosts will always keep clear of it', he replied.
My father told this story to Kate, Emily and Tom, as they set out for home that night.
The removal from the church to Cloonkeenkerrill Graveyard took place the following morning. When Mass was over, the priest recited the prayers and the coffin was carried shoulder high and placed on the 'well' of Uncle Martin's sidecar once more. The grey Connemara pony had no difficulty pulling the sidecar and coffin on the way to the graveyard. My father sat on the left-hand side and Uncle Tommie on the right hand side of the sidecar. On arrival, the mare was tied and the coffin was placed on St. Kerrill's Bed, as is customary before interment. When the funeral was over about twenty people came to the house for a meal. The women cooked rashers and eggs. There were four sittings altogether. The men enjoyed a mug or two of porter from what remained of the half barrel. Tongues had loosened considerably by this and many stories about Matt were related. Local news and the latest gossip featured also. Then the callers left one by one and an atmosphere of gloom and grief permeated through the house again.

THE FLOWER GIRL CALLS

After a few weeks had gone by, things began to return to normal. My mother was looking over the half door when she saw somebody coming down the path field. She put her hands to her head and exclaimed. 'The Lord between us and all harm.'
She called my father, Jimmy, from the backyard and told him that Biddy, the flower maker, was coming down the hilly field.
'Arrah what harm is she?' said Jimmy.
'Take down that flitch of bacon and hide it until she has gone. She is always looking for more than I can afford to give her', replied my mother.

With that Biddy arrived at the half door.
'The Lord have mercy on the dead- Poor Matt. I'm going to say three Hail Marys for him'.
She knelt down on the large stone outside the door and recited the prayers. My parents joined in. She was invited into the kitchen.
' Musha God spare you the health and may God bless you. 'Tis hard times trying to bring up childer. Could you give me a graineen of flour?'
My father gave her a scoop of flour from the bin. "Thanks Jimmy, may God increase your store. God and His Holy Mother bless you Mam", she said, turning to my mother. "I have nine children all under twelve years of age. A grain of tay and sugar would help and God Bless you." She produced a Fry's Cocoa tin from inside her shawl- "You can put the tay into that Mam and I have a bag for the sugar."
"Alright", replied my mother, "But that is all you will get today. Sit down and I will make you a cup of tea."
" May the blessings of the Sacred Heart of Jesus fall on you Mam. The tay will help me along. It's hard on the roads this time of the year with the days so short. I do not like the dark Mam as I got a scare last week. I was coming home from the Gurteen direction by Scarry's well and there in front of my eyes was a small woman sitting under a bush. She was holding a rush candle in her hand. I am blessed to God but I am telling the truth, the hair stood up on my head. I was hardly able to walk past her with fright. When I got close to her she turned herself into a black dog. Praise be to the Lord above I do not want to be out late anymore."
My mother told her that she had heard of people that saw a light at that well last year. Jimmy said

that it was probably Will-o-the-Wisp because he hangs around there but he is harmless. "Now the tea is ready so sit at the table and eat a bit of bread and butter." "Thanks Mam; God bless you and would you have a little slice of mate for himself."
"No, said my mother, "I will not give you anymore."
"Maybe you would have a cupla pennies as I need some stuff at the shop badly and I am short of money."
With that she produced a beautiful red rose made of paper from inside her shawl.
"I will sell you this flower for sixpence." It caught my mother's fancy because she loved flowers.
"I have only four pennies left and you can have them for the flowers."
"That is alright," she said, handing my mother the flower.
"Thanks Biddy and goodbye now. I have a lot of work to do today."
She left and I questioned my mother about the ghosts. She said,
"You are alright as only some people see ghosts and fairies." I was always afraid when passing by the same well. I never saw anything spooky. There are always logical explanations in my view for happenings like that. For example Uncle Tommy was returning from the pub one dark night. He was groping along down the last stretch of the boreen when suddenly he tripped and fell forward. He was then raised from the ground by something black and hairy. He thought it was the Devil. The strange creature carried him twenty yards or so before throwing him off. He returned to the house as pale as a sheet. He had lost his hat and pipe. My father lit the candle lantern and both went to investigate. They discovered that it was a tinker's stray donkey that had transported Tommie and deposited him on his head on the roadside. Apparently he had been lying asleep when Tommie tripped over him. No doubt he had woken up in a fright and had sprinted a short distance before dumping his 'passenger'. My father had a great laugh at Tommie's expense and the latter used to blush with embarrassment whenever the incident was mentioned.

A TRIP TO SCHOOL

Time passed quickly. The next thing I remember was being carried on my mother's back to Cloonkeen School. I was welcomed by Mrs. Walsh, who was to be my teacher. She taught Infants, First and Second Class. Mrs. Hurley, the principal taught Fourth, Fifth and Sixth Class in what was known as 'The Big Room'. Mrs. Hurley said she was looking forward to having me in Third Class. My mother said, 'Slán', and went home. She collected me again at two o'clock.

I was put sitting beside a fair-haired girl with blue eyes, who wore a flowery dress. This was to be my girl while I was in baby infants. I hugged her every morning. Sometimes we giggled and were slapped for disturbing the class. We were taught how to sing every morning:

> Proudly the note the trumpet is sounding
> Loudly the war cry…etc.

We all stamped up and down as if marching. This got the blood flowing in our veins. There was not much else to warm us until the fire kindled. Then the Catechism. Who made the World? God made the World. Who is God? God is the Creator of Heaven and Earth. We were told that there were three divine persons in the one God; Father, Son and Holy Ghost. We marvelled at this and asked the teacher how could there be three people in the one person. Her reply was, 'All things are possible to God' and she gave the example of the Shamrock- three leaves on one stem. A.B.C, and sums, books had to be bought. Copies, scribblers, pencils, English and Irish books, pens with nibs and blotting paper. All of this cost about three shillings. This was a large sum of money in those days. Uncle Tommy gave me one shilling and I got two shillings from my mother. I was very proud to be able to hand this money to Mrs. Walsh by the end of my first month in school.

Things got more serious later on as we prepared for First Holy Communion. The priest, Fr. O' Reilly, came to the school once a week. Garda Snee from Menlough came once a month. The Inspector came twice a year. We were all very frightened and felt very intimidated by those people in fancy suits and uniforms. Often driven to despair and stiffened by fear, we found it difficult to learn under those circumstances. If we did not make a good effort the teacher would beat the living daylights out of us with a long Sally rod. Things got even worse when we moved into the big room. I do not lay blame on anybody. This was the order of the day. I cannot say now whether we would be better or worse if things were different. We were still happy and proud.

GROWING UP

In the following years my body grew stronger and I was able to bear the cold rains and frost and snow in the winter months. The journey to school became much more pleasurable, especially during Spring and Summer. Autumn of course had its own magic.

In Spring the swamp pool in Mannions field became a hive of activity. Bullfrogs croaked loudly as they guarded their territory. The hen frogs paddled lazily around the pool and awaited the approval of the big males. The frogspawn soon spread all over the water in the pool as each day went by. It soon became speckled with small dots of life. I watched in fascination as tiny hands and feet formed. The breaking into tadpoles from the eggs soon transformed the waters in the pool to a black moving mass. The tadpoles grew their enormous black heads and tail fins which very soon shed. The froglets moved one by one into the wet meadows driven by instinct to better pastures.

In Spring I was always in a hurry home from school. My father and mother would be preparing to sow the potatoes in the bog field behind the house. Now aged six, I was able to help at that important job. My father would line out an area of about half an acre for ten or twelve ridges of potatoes, turning the fóidín with a special spade called a laighe, one sod to the left and one to the right, leaving a narrow green strip in between. This was known as the fódóg. Now twelve ridges are outlined. My job was to spread the dung on the ridge. Rotted farmyard dung was used for fertilizer. My mother would load this onto the donkey cart and place it in small heaps between the fóidíní. I spread it out evenly like a blanket. The slits, cut some weeks before, were placed in rows of three across the ridge. The green fódog would then be cut in short strips and with the green side down it would be placed on the top of the ridge. Then the black loamy soil would be dug from the dikes and placed on top of the slits on the ridge by my father. When twelve ridges, sixty yards long, were complete, it looked very much a work of art, created by an architect with divine inspiration - six ridges of epicures for early use and six ridges of Kerr's Pinks for later on in autumn.

Last year's potato plot would be sown again by hand. Four rows of white cabbage, six rows of common flat Dutch cabbage for animal feed, a few rows of Swede turnips for the house and eight or nine rows of purple top Aberdeens for the pigs and cows. Onions, carrots and parsnips took up the remainder. All of this fertilized by organic decomposed dung, watered by April showers and heated by the sun in May, June and July. A wonderful crop of vegetables and potatoes would be produced. This meant self-sufficiency.

The hens laid eggs - the surplus sold to pay for sugar, tea and flour. Bacon was obtained from the pigs and milk and butter from the cows. We were a very happy family and proud of our ability to be self sufficient and able to eke out a living from eight acres of reclaimed, black, moor bogland. We had very little money, but we did not need much. We had our pride, dignity, health and happiness. We had love in abundance for life, God and our fellow man.

A SUMMER SCENE

The summer mornings seemed to me like a huge curtain, ready to reveal the mystery of life at a moment's notice, just as the haze and fog would disappear in the mid morning to reveal the countryside swathed in glorious sunshine. O what a magical and wondrous time and place in which to live. The birds were busy building their nests. Honeybees sped past and grasshoppers called out to their mates. Hares and rabbits bolted through the fields at the sight of dogs or birds of prey. Grey crows and hawks watched and swooped down to catch a field mouse whenever they saw one, or perhaps a rat or baby rabbit. At dusk on a summer's evening, we often sat on the turf bank in silence, watching hares and rabbits, while up above the lark sang a melodious serenade as it hovered in the same sweeping orbit. The corncrake could be heard croaking in the meadow where cowslips and bluebells bloomed in profusion. The drumming snipe was there too, descending rapidly through the air, showing off his superior speed and ability to manoeuvre gracefully. There is nowhere else on earth to match the beauty of the meadow field beside our house and I felt that it was a corner of heaven. 'A hole in Heaven's Gable', as Kavanagh wrote in his poem, 'A Christmas Childhood'.

I watched the setting sun and the evening dew falling on the numerous cobwebs suspended in the long grass. They looked like jewels on a crown as the dew droplets reflected the setting sun. I made my way home, tired but intoxicated with excitement. That night in my dreams, I relived some of the marvellous experiences that had delighted me earlier that day.

Up early in the morning for school again. First Holy Communion the following Easter was the next important event in my life. There was a great deal of preparation to be done and I was determined to put my heart and soul into the task. However, this was some distance into the future and I still had the summer holidays in front of me and of course I was all-agog waiting for their arrival. I knew I would be working in the meadows and in Cualac Bog and this was a real treat to be savoured in my young mind.

Even though I had been anticipating it eagerly, the advent of summer almost took me by surprise. One evening I heard hammering and scraping noises coming from the turf shed and it suddenly struck me that July was only six days away. I would be getting holidays from school and I would free to work in the open air once more. I was so excited by the idea that I began to jump up and down with joy.

When dinner was over my mother told me that I could go into the turf shed which was now transformed into a kind of workshop in which spades, shovels and implements were being put into

shape for the forthcoming campaigns. My mother warned me to be careful.
'Your Father is working down there', she said, 'He's using sharp tools, you better behave yourself or you will be sent into the house again.'

I bolted through the door at high speed but as I approached the shed I slowed down. The door was half-open. My father greeted me with a smile.
He said, 'Come on in but you are not allowed to touch any of those tools. I will show you something.'
With that he reached up to the rafters. He took down a small wooden hay rake that he had made for me. I was overwhelmed. It confirmed in my mind, at least, that I was an important member of the family team. I could now show the world that I was a fully-fledged worker; being the proud owner of my own special hayrake!

THE SCHOOL HOLIDAYS

The first week of July, 1936 is indelibly imprinted on my mind. Beautiful weather. Long days and the swish, swish, swish of the scythe blade. Long rows of hay called swaths were made by my father as he cut the four-acre field close to the house on the western side. The smell of the new-mown hay intermingled with the reek of the smoke from the peat fire in the house. A heavenly fragrance.

My job all that day and for three days to follow, was to assist my father by having the sharpening stone to his hand when required, his jacket when he needed to smoke his pipe, the sweetcan of spring water which was half submerged in the drain at the end of the field to keep it cool. He took a drink, smoked his pipe, and had a short rest every two hours or so. The target, to lay low one acre a day was already in sight for day one. One more hour to go and we would be on the way home to the bacon and cabbage. We were quite hungry as we had only one small collation at twelve o clock. I took the sharpening stone and my dad took the scythe and hung it high up on the branch of the ash tree at the back of the yard. I took the sharpening stone into the house. I washed my hands and feeling very tired, I sat for the dinner beside my father. This was the first occasion that I felt proud of my sense of purpose. I had proven my ability,

During the following two weeks, the sun was shining from eight o'clock in the morning to eight o'clock in the evening. The four-acre field by then had been transformed into forty tram-cocks of silvery, dry hay, enough to feed the cows, calves and donkey for the winter. I had played my part in the business by using my small rake.

With the hay saved, everybody in our house was exceptionally happy. My mother seemed more attentive and excited than normal. When she was tucking me away in my cot one night she said, 'I will tell you a secret. Please do not tell anybody about it.'
I sat up expectantly and said: " What is it Mom?"
"We are to get a new baby soon," she said.
" Oh!" said I, " Will it be a boy?"
"I am not sure" she said, "but we will welcome whatever God sends us"
"But did you order a boy? I need somebody to play football and hurling and to come fishing with me. Oh! Please, Mom, get a boy."
"We will see what will happen", she said as she settled me down for the night.

The following morning I was up early. I could sense that some special excitement was in the air. "Your father has gone to Pat Walshe's forge to have the donkey shod. He also needs two gudgeon pins for that barrow in the back of the turf shed. We are preparing to go to the bog to cut the turf next week," she told me.

I was ecstatic with excitement at the thought of this adventure. I could remember the babble and laughs about last year's drama. Some funny stories, which I did not understand had regaled the adults. I anxiously awaited my father's return from the forge. I ran out to him and the first thing I told him was the secret of our getting a new baby.
 "Oh!" he said. "I am very gladdened and excited by this good news".
I replied, "But please do not tell Mom that I told you, because it is a secret."
I knew that my Dad was in good humour, so I popped the question,
 "Can I come to the bog at the turfcutting this year?"
 "You may", my Dad replied, 'Provided that you behave and do what you are told".
"I will, I will, I sure will", I replied. "Thank you Dad".

HIRING HELP

The following Sunday my father went to Mass on his bicycle. My mother, my sister Ann and I walked slowly to the church, a short mile or so away. When we returned home, the potatoes were washed and boiled for dinner. We had egg omelettes with the succulent, flowery potatoes, garnished with fresh butter and a glass of new milk. My mother put a portion aside for my father. It was 2.30 p.m. and there was no sign of him coming down the boreen. I asked my mother why and she replied that he had gone to Athenry to hire a man to help us cut the turf. She said,
'Big strong men from Connemara come there every Sunday looking for a week's work. All of them are gentlemen with great skills using spades, shovels or sleans. They are all native Irish speakers with just enough English to get them by. If he is lucky enough to find one to help us for the coming week, we will consider ourselves lucky.'

 I saw him turning into the boreen at last. I ran out to meet him. He gave me a small bar of Cadbury's chocolate. He had two more in his pocket - one for Mother and one for my sister Ann.
"Did you hire a helper?" I asked. My father replied, 'Yes. I was lucky to get Jimmy Joyce.' My mother was delighted as they both knew Jimmy. He had often worked in this locality previously

Jimmy Joyce arrived much later that evening. My mother had prepared the settle bed. A bacon sandwich was left on the table with a mug of fresh milk. We all had retired to bed except my father. He waited up to greet Jimmy. I was still awake and I heard talk in strange broken English going on between the two of them. "Ach dheabhail" said Jimmy, "'tis warm on the road. My bicycle got soft on the wheel. Tá sí out by the river bridge. Ach, we will repair the tube tamorrow night.'

I peeked through the keyhole on the door. Jimmy had his cap turned backwards. His shirt was open half way down his chest exposing a thick thatch of black curly hair. He wore blue braces on which a grey báinín flannel trousers was suspended. He was enjoying his sandwich. I could not see any more through the keyhole. I was frightened and found it difficult to go to sleep. My father came into our bedroom and reassured me that Jimmy was a real gentleman and would not do me any harm.

In the morning early, my father called out, "Get up and get ready." Jimmy Joyce had tackled the donkey and yoked him to the cart. My mother made the breakfast, while my father helped Jimmy load the turf barrow onto the centre of the cart, with the two handles facing backwards. The shovel, spade, fork and slean were all wrapped up together in a jute fertilizer bag to keep them clean, sharp and safe under the barrow on the floor of the cart.

Breakfast over by 7.30 a.m., the two men set off for the bog. Jimmy sat on one side with his legs dangling down. My father sat on the other side to create a balance as it were. As they moved out over the bridge, it looked like a picture of a gun carriage used in the '14-18 war. They met my uncle Tommy at the bog. He had gone ahead to collect another barrow which was lent to us by a neighbour, Ned Navin.

All three met at the turf bank which had been prepared earlier in the year. The top screw had been removed for about one foot down to reach the soft turf. Twenty-eight yards long by six feet wide, by fourteen sods deep had to be cut and wheeled out onto the bank. All three of them lit their pipes as strategy was discussed. My father on the breast slean, Uncle Tommy and Jimmy Joyce on the barrows. "She is half past eight now,' said Jimmy as they wheeled out the first barrow load of twenty sods on to the spreading bank.

My mother and I remained at home to organise the dinner picnic. I had to be ready to go to the bog at twelve-thirty. A big fire burning furiously on the open hearth was raked out wide. My mother was baking griddle and oven cakes. A large cut of bacon from the flitch was boiling in a saucepan with a lid. A dozen eggs were being boiled in the tinker's saucepan. A homemade wicker basket was dressed out with a white cloth. Two pint bottles of milk and one lb of yellow butter wrapped in tinfoil reclaimed from the inside of a teachest. Cocoa tins were filled with tea and sugar. The one-gallon sweetcan with a lid was filled with spring water, all ready to go when Uncle Tom arrived back with the donkey and cart. This was pre-arranged for eleven o'clock. The air of the kitchen was hot. It had a beautiful aroma. My heart and soul was full of excitement when I spotted the donkey's cart coming in over the bridge. The basket and a small wooden box were loaded. "I hope everything we need is in there", said my mother. She lifted Annie and myself onto the cart and followed on herself. The house was deserted for the rest of that day as the whole family had a role to play on the first day in the bog. When we arrived, my mother selected a dry hill at the front of the boghole. A fire was lit and I collected dry bog dale and some small caoireans of turf. The redhead friendly match lit some old paper in the centre of the fire. Soon the smoke was flying up towards the sky. We had fifteen minutes to spare when the sweetcan full of water was hung over the fire on an iron bar with a hook. It just started to boil when the three turfcutters slowly ambled out from the bank, their jackets on one arm and a few sods of dry turf to sit on under the other. The meal went down well and everybody seemed very happy. There was very little conversation after the first bog picnic of the week. My mother packed the utensils and the remaining food into the basket. She requested my father to come home walking by the short-cut path. He agreed to that and said that they would be home by six-thirty for the evening meal. My mother left for home on the donkey cart.

I was allowed to stay in the bog which was a place of great wonder and excitement to me. I stood there on the highest point of the high bog, looking around me in all directions. I could see Lough-na-Hinch lake to my left and further up the hill to Mount Bernard. The five trees that marked the triangulation point with views to the North, South, East and West were visible. This point is marked on the map as 425 feet above sea level. It is said that this was the first land sighted by invaders as they approached the Irish coastline.

A PLEASANT SCENE

Nearer to me I could see four thatched, whitewashed cottages along the roadside. The land sloped down in undulating fashion to meet the Cualach bog. I could see cattle browsing in the afternoon sun right in front of me. The purple heather was blooming. Bog cotton with its white heads and stem-like straws waving in the wind. Yellow whin bushes and bulrushes already casting shadows. To the south I could see the church in Gurteen set into the foreground of the Caltra hills. To my right I could see Tiaquin woods and a little more clockwise the Knockcrow hills at Abbeyknockmoy. Behind that stood the peak of Croagh Patrick in the far distance. I knew I was seeing a special vista which aeons of time had not changed. A wonderful feeling flowed in my heart as I realised this landscape to be something eternal.

My father, Tommie and Jimmy were sitting on the barrows enjoying a smoke and a short rest. I was called upon to find out whether there was a can of water available for a drink, as they were thirsty. "Yes" I said, "I saw my mother putting it in the shade".

I fetched the sweetcan of spring water which had a handful of pinhead oaten meal added to it. This mixture was known as 'whitewater' and was especially good for the thirst. My mother had left a small tin saucepan tied to the handle of the sweetcan. My father filled the tinker's saucepan and passed it to Jimmy. He gobbled it down and said to my father.
' Ach . can I have another? Tá me thirsty.'
He swallowed the refill. Uncle Tommie and my father also satisfied their thirst. The gallon container was more than half empty by now so we put it down into a small nearby drain to keep it cool.
"Thanks", said Jimmy "She is good for the thirst".

It is now 5.00 p.m., only another hour left to work before we set out on foot for home by the usual shortcut. My mother had the table set for the tea when we got home. Two boiled eggs each for the men and one for me. Oaten bread fresh from the griddle with freshly made butter loaded on to it while still hot. The food tasted delicious and we set about satisfying our appetites without delay. My mother was complimented by all the men. Making oaten bread was a very skilled job.

I got out spoons, patches and a bicycle pump. My father helped us to repair Jimmy Joyce's puncture.
"I hope she keeps hard - I will need her early Sunday morning to go to Athenry", said Jimmy.

A DAY AT THE WELL

We all retired to bed early. I could still see the sun setting on the western skyline. It sat there like a big ball of orange and red fire as it slowly sank into the western horizon. It is said that a sunset like that always heralds very fine warm weather. One way or the other, I can say it was a beautiful picture. We followed the same pattern on the following days. Now, with the turf cut we were finished with the bog for the time being. Spreading, footing and re-footing had to be done later on. The 29th of June, the feast day of St. Peter and Paul was around the corner. This was always a big day out for our family. My mother's brother, Martin Kilkenny, owned the land adjacent to a holy place called Tobar Moillhe. The 29th of June is 'Pattern Day'. The people from surrounding areas make a pilgrimage to this place on the 29th of June every year. The well is situated on marshy ground and one had to wear wellingtons to do the station rounds there whenever there was heavy rain. In fine weather it was like a corner of Heaven. You could see the wild birds flying past in formation, as they made their unhurried safaris to distant destinations. Smaller birds such as the Thrush, Blackbird or Robin - all could be heard singing their delightful songs in the hedgerows. Underfoot, the damp earth smelt like incense, suggesting an atmosphere of tranquillity and sanctity. People were constantly moving around the well as they prayed for loved ones, family and the welfare of their animals - not forgetting their neighbours. Tradition relates that a blind boy fell into the well and when he was taken out his sight was fully restored - a miracle of faith. There is not much known about Moillhe - he probably was a priest and may have celebrated Mass there during Penal Times. We do know that he was a very holy man and that he used to pray near the well on the feast day of Peter and Paul. He was often joined there by parishioners.

This Pattern has been kept up to the present day. It was also traditional that the first new crop of potatoes of the year should be dug and made into callie (colcannon) for dinner on that day. The old people used to say that potatoes planted on St. Patrick's Day would bear full fruit for SS. Peter and Paul's.

I have been joining the procession for many years with my mother. It was also a social occasion for my mother's family. Mrs. Gibbons from Aughrim, Mrs. Tuohy from Carana and Mrs. Green living in England would all get together at their brother Martin's home. They would enjoy the callie and the crack after doing their station at the blessed well. They have all gone to their eternal reward now. I pray for them still at the holy well.

A month had elapsed since the turf was cut. By this time the heat of the sun had drawn the water from the sods. They were ready for footing in small gróigíní. Four sods put standing against each other with one on top. Each sod had to lifted by hand from the damp bank. Stooping forward and bending up and down soon took its toll on the back. Standing up straight, with hands on hips, one felt like screaming for relief. Self-pity didn't help. "Keep at it, make yourself think that footing turf is good for you. The job must get done.' This was our guiding philosophy as we struggled with the sods, wresting them in a dogged manner from the heather platform to which they were attached.

We continued to work hard and soon all the turf on the bank was standing up like soldiers on parade on St. Patrick's Day, saluting our success. After that it was re-footed - six or seven small gróigíní to make a big duchán. By then it was almost ready to bring home and the show was over for another year.

CELEBRATIONS

My sister Mary was born in October of 1936 in the thatched cottage. My father borrowed the grey mare and trap from Fords - the shopkeepers at the head of the boreen. He went to Woodlawn to fetch the midwife, Nurse Daly. They arrived in good time it seems, because when Annie and I woke up in the morning we were told that we had a new baby sister and the midwife took her to our room for us to see. I was delighted, but I had little pangs of regret because it was not a boy. Of course my sister Ann was delighted. We grew up together, one boy (myself) and two sisters.

The next important date in my life was preparing for my First Holy Communion. I got over the examination by the Priest, Fr. O'Reilly with flying colours. We must have been well prepared. All the First Communion class answered their catechism questions correctly. I was asked to say the Act of Contrition. I thought that this was very easy.

It was Easter Sunday, 1937. There was excitement bordering on panic. My mother had made a new suit for me, black, with a white collar and white buttons. The top was blouse like, with a row of buttons down the front. The pants was a good fit and was buttoned on to the bottom of the blouse. The material was got from flour bags, washed, bleached and dyed black. I felt like a prince as I walked hand-in-hand with my mother to the church in Gurteen. I sat in the front seat with twelve other children who were making their First Communion that day. There was an air of sanctity around as we were marshalled up the aisle by our teachers. It was a wonderful, happy and exciting time for us all. I got sweets and lemonade at the church gate after Mass. Now, having got food for the soul, it was decided to get some food for the body. (We had been fasting from twelve midnight the night before). On the way home my mother told me that my father would have the breakfast ready. We had rashers and as many eggs as you could eat - that was the tradition at Easter then. I was looking forward to this huge banquet so much that I thought we would never get home.

In the afternoon my mother brought me to see Emily Stephens. She had white lozenges. They had a pleasant peppermint taste that delighted me. Then we went to visit the Mannion's next door. They had a brownie box camera which was got for 20 full packs of cigarette cards. Maggie Mannion showed us the camera with great pride.
She also took a photograph of me in my First Communion suit. I was not sure what all this was about. I did not understand photography but the result speaks for itself.

I have to finish now, as this school reunion book has limited space available.
The time is also limited. A deadline has to be met. (With God's help) I will be back with the full story in the near future. We have a wealth of material to share with each other.

I HOPE YOU ENJOYED CHAPTER ONE

       THANK YOU,

            TOM ROCHE.

ANTICS IN AND OUT OF CLASS

By

Julia Kilkenny

I went to Shanballard School in 1918 at the age of 6. The distance was 3 miles across the fields. The Naughtons and Kilkennys were attending at the same time. They came out onto the road near the school at Kitt's house. Shoes were not worn much that time especially between May and October. Mrs. Kitt and Mrs. Duffy were teaching there then. They both taught in the same big room - back to back with a blackboard at each end. During my first days, Mrs. Duffy's daughter and another of the big girls used to take us upstairs in the residence where they kept us amused playing 'Puicin' and games of that kind. Then there was music from a great big gramophone. We had never seen the likes and our eyes nearly popped out of our sockets as we watched and listened to that marvellous machine. We couldn't stop staring at it and we wondered if the man who sang 'The Mountains of Mourne' was actually singing inside in the box.

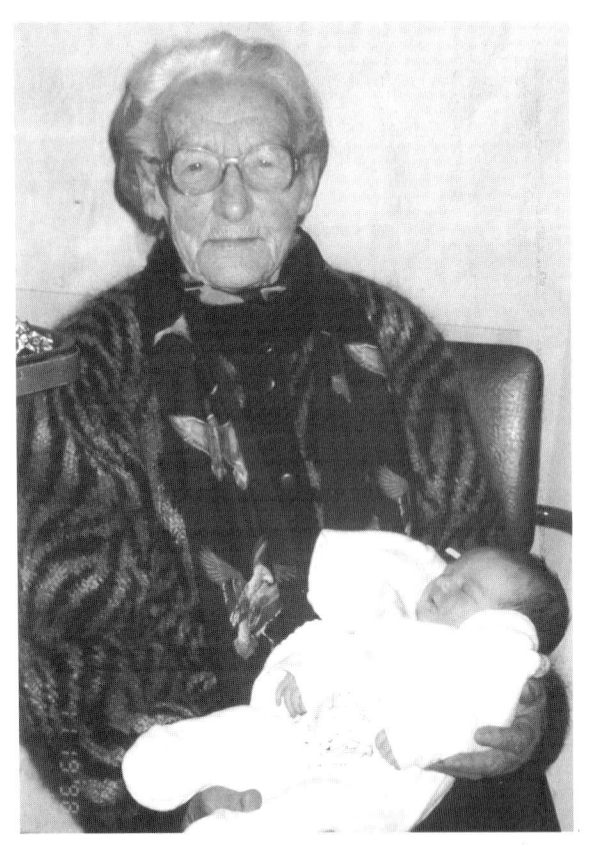

For lunch we had oaten bread and milk. Others had soda bread which was considered a great novelty at the time. One of the big boys used to take lunches from the other children. He had a long board with a nail on the end. He used to threaten those with tasty lunches saying, 'Tull, tull or else give out,' giving them a jab of the nail at the same time!

The Inspector called annually and this caused a great fuss. The teachers knew when his visits were due and we had to be on our best behaviour and wear our best clothes on these occasions. The same was true when the priest called. We wore our good shoes during the visits but when the priest or inspector had gone, we took them off and carried them home under our arms - not to be used again for weeks or months perhaps.

There was a great emphasis on the three R's. It was essential to know the chief towns in each county as well as the main rivers and mountains of Ireland. There was a large map of the world hanging on the wall. Once the teacher asked a student to point out Timbuktu on the map. The boy was in a panic. After a feverish effort, he eventually found it and in his excitement shouted out, 'Timbuckthree!'. Of course we all burst out laughing and even the teacher couldn't hide her amusement. On another occasion when Mrs. Duffy was explaining something, she noticed one of her pupils looking out the window. She said,
'Just look at Pat. He has one foot in Galway and the other in Dublin and he's not the least bit interested in what I'm saying.'
She got very annoyed once when someone knocked an ornament from the mantlepiece.
'What have you done?' she cried, 'You've broken a precious keepsake that my mother gave me.'

Even though it was an accident she punished the culprit on the spot.

One of the funniest incidents happened during the summer. There was a vacancy between the girls' and boys' toilets and the boys used long sticks to poke the girls whenever they were attending to the call of Nature. Tom Power heard somebody using the girls' toilet and he began to poke her energetically with the stick. When he heard a scream he realised his mistake and dashed back into the classroom. When Mrs. Duffy returned (It was she that had been at the toilet) she was furious and demanded to know what boy had been out last. Eventually Tom had to admit to the fact.
'What made you do such a dreadful deed?' she asked.
'Sure I thought it was Nora Lyons,' replied Tom.
By the time Mrs. Duffy was finished with him, Tom's thoughts were far removed from Nora and the girls' toilet, I'm sure.

Another time Mrs. Duffy stood in front of the class. She asked us:
'Now tell me in what way I'm like a clock?'
One pupil said, 'Because you have a face.' She complimented him and continued on and someone else said: 'You have a pair of hands,' and so on.

Then she asked:
'In what way am I not like a clock?'
One of the boys said: 'Because you don't have a pendulum.'
We thought it was very funny but Mrs. Duffy was not amused.

One of the Connaire boys had very strong teeth. He was able to hold the blackboard in his mouth and walk across the desks, with the blackboard between his teeth. I heard that he often caught smaller boys and carried them as a cat carries a mouse with his teeth, while crawling around on all fours!

At lunchtime we played 'tig' and hide and seek.

'Buckedy weydy' was a game played by some of the Attymon children. It was some kind of seesaw and I believe they used to perform it on the bridge overlooking the railway. When they were playing it, one of them used to swing directly over the rail tracks. It was a great wonder that nobody was killed or injured.

We played a game at school called Lúrabog, Larabog. The rhyme is as follows:

Lúrabog, Larabog
Be-o-nail - nail a probáin.
Súil- a- súil - a- stickín,
Uistín - Buistín,
Coppa-coppa-néistín-cois.

It was recited by a child holding a stick. All the others sat in a circle feet outstretched.
The child with the stick tapped each child's foot as she went around the circle while reciting the above. When she came to the word cois, that particular pupil got a good whack of the stick and withdrew the leg. The game went on like this until everybody's leg had got a good strong smack.

The 'Black' Mentane was great fun and used to do a lot of antics behind the teacher's back. He wasn't interested in lessons and would slip home whenever he got a chance. He had a lot of funny sayings. He had a habit of reciting the following lines whenever the fancy took him,

The bee, the bat, the butterfly,
The cuckoo and the swallow,
The corncrake stuck out its head
And bade them all 'Good Morrow.'

'The Black' took early retirement from the classroom. He was slapped one day for something he'd done and he dashed out the door and made a beeline for home. That was the last we saw of him in Shanballard. The teacher tried to coax him back but to no avail. It seems his parents supported his absence from school and the teachers were told that he wouldn't return until his 'beard covered his belly'.

Irish was new to us and to the teachers. The teachers were enthusiastic about the language and many of them went to Connemara to improve their skills. The Connaire family who lived near the school had a good knowledge of Irish. Often the teachers took us out of doors in fine weather and when the Connaires were passing by they would consult them concerning the pronunciation of various words.

The teachers could be cross at times but generally they were nice to us. As I mentioned, we were brought to the residence to listen to music or to play games. The teachers usually went to lunch at the residence which was just a few yards away from the school. Senior pupils looked after us then. Sometimes this worked out all right but at other times things didn't go so well at all. Once when one of the boys was put in charge, the rest of the pupils put out their tongues and began to taunt him. The boy lost his temper, grabbed a stick and began flaking everyone within reach. By the time the teachers returned, the pupils were as quiet as mice and were found hiding under desks, in presses and behind doors. That particular boy wasn't put in charge of us after that.

All in all we had good fun and I hope that children nowadays enjoy themselves as much as we did.

CHAPTER THREE

MARKING TIME

THE BEGINNING AND END OF THE YEAR

New Year's Eve is a special night. It's the time when large crowds assemble in towns and cities. Bells are rung, bunting proliferates, balloons are released into the air as people join hands and sing 'Auld Lang Syne' in a spirit of camaraderie and solidarity. Even the most unmusical and least boisterous individuals in the community are tempted to join in the festivities. Special concessions allow young people to stay up late to watch the events on television when it's not possible for them to be physically present.

Seoladh na sean bliana (Seeing off the old year) This is something I've heard talked about but I've never actually seen it in practice. Apparently a group of young people would come together at a church or crossroads on New Year's Eve at midnight. They would play music and dance until the early hours of the morning before returning home.
Entertainment was free and it is said that it was a delightful experience, especially on a calm, moonlit night.

In former times, exchanging gifts was almost as common on New Year's Day as it was at Christmas. It was a great visiting day. Traditionally Christmas was spent at home so on New Year's Day one met one's relatives and reestablished old bonds of friendship. Visiting meant enjoying copious quantities of food and beverages and few rustics allowed the occasion to pass without shedding the blood of an innocent fowl, which eventually found its way to the oven and from there to the plates and palates of diners. Storytellers and musicians combined to make music and revelry available to guests, and all in all it was an ideal opportunity for relaxation and celebration.

In the Fifties those who didn't have visitors or who were unable to provide homemade entertainment could rely on radio to provide an array of wholesome fare to cater for family tastes. This usually took the form of variety shows or plays by major artists.

LIFE BEFORE 'THE BOX IN THE CORNER'

In pre-radio and pre-television days, all entertainment was homespun and there was no shortage of participants for the various capers which enticed country folk from their cosy cottages in mid-winter.

In parts of Wales for instance, it was customary for children to go around the neighbourhood wishing householders 'A Happy New Year' while at the same time asking them for gifts. According to one source the young people carried an apple or orange on a skewer or stick. Flowers were decorated with gold and silver tinsel and the young people wore hats or caps decked with them. (A foreshadowing of The Hippies of the Sixties?)

In this country 'trick or treat' games were sometimes organised for January 1st. although these weren't quite on the same scale as they were at Halloween or on St. Brigid's Day.
In recent times 'Mummers' festivals, which try to represent and renew some of the best aspects of life in ancient Ireland, are all the go and many of them are held at this period. When I was growing up I felt that New Year's Day was an awesome time which required a great deal of planning and forethought because I was told that whatever one did on this day was certain to be repeated on almost every day throughout the year. A daunting thought for any youngster!

Another idea which once found favour around here was the belief that if you fed your fowl with any available fruits which are well chopped on this day, they would continue to lay for the rest of the year. Poultry farmers and free-range egg producers take note!

OTHER CUSTOMS

New Year's Day or Hogmany was particularly popular in Scotland. Here as elsewhere there were many strange ideas about the first day of the year. For example one myth in circulation was, that if a person washed a dishtowel and threw it on a hedge to dry and then rubbed the horses with it, the animals would then grow fat. Could the author of this doctrine be held responsible for the willful neglect of steeds I wonder? Or perhaps it's a vindication of the well-known saying: 'Live Horse and you'll get grass.'?

The game of Shinty was traditionally played on this day. In the past the game was boisterous and lacked formal rules, ending when the leader of one section cried, 'Enough' Nowadays 12 players per team play 45 minutes a side with a break in the middle. The ball is made of leather-covered cork and hit with a camán, much the same as in Gaelic hurling.

The 1st. of January was, and still is, a time for new resolutions. As with Lenten promises, these are generally short lived and rarely survive the remaining 29 days of the month. In some parts those who desired to have their new year wishes granted were told that this would happen if they went to the well for a bucket of water immediately after sunrise on New Year's Day.

Water collected on this day was believed to have special cleansing and healing powers. Unfortunately, statistics that support or refute this theory are hard to come by.
Others believed that whatever dreams one had on New Year's Night would come true.
Sudden or unexpected noises on New Year's Eve night were a source of worry to superstitious people, being regarded as portents of death or disaster during the coming year.

A smouldering log or one which does not fully burn out on New Year's Day, is regarded with horror by some who believe that such an occurrence brings sickness or death to the family in whose house it is lighting.

Another strange practice which was observed in days gone by was to make small cakes. These were named after family members. The housewife used her thumb to make a hole in each one. If the hole became baked up then the person to whom it was assigned would die within the year. Candles were used in a local variation of this game. On January 5th. Little Christmas Eve (Oíche Nollag na mBan) families used to light small candles and place them on a cake. One member of the family identified with each candle and it was said that whichever candle quenched first, the person associated with it would die soonest. Sometimes the candles were made of rushes and treated with goose grease. People claim that these used to be taken indoors and inserted into hardened dung before being lit.

Troscadh Oíche Nollag was when fasting took place on Christmas Eve. Visitors used to call to different houses and at eleven o'clock cooking preparations would begin. Around the same time twelve candles in honour of the twelve days of Christmas or possibly in honour of the Twelve Apostles would be lit. All those assembled would begin to feast shortly after midnight.

The meal consisted mainly of potatoes, milk or salted bacon that had been steeping for a time. In the case of those who lived close to the sea, salted fish would be chosen instead of bacon. The process of salting the fish might have taken place 2 to 3 months previously. Then the salt would be removed by steeping in water a few days prior to cooking.

Another popular custom was to take twelve onions and name them after the months of the year. A quantity of salt was put on each. If the salt has melted by the sixth of January, the corresponding month will be wet, whereas if the salt remains, the month will be dry. Perhaps this theory should be taken with the proverbial ' pinch of salt'?

A more relevant and measurable theory is the notion that a sunny or warm January promises a cold Spring and an unsettled Summer.

RELIGIOUS CELEBRATIONS

New Year's Day comes midway in the feast of Christmas and prayer and religious ceremonies are a prominent feature of the day's celebrations, especially among the elderly. Though no longer a holy day of obligation for Roman Catholics, never the less many people attend Mass on this day. Rosaries are lengthened to pray for family members overseas and for exiles generally. Cards and good wishes are sent to correspondents who somehow got overlooked in the frantic mailing spree prior to Christmas. Consolation presents can still be purchased and delivered before 'The Season of Goodwill' officially expires on the Feast of the Epiphany, thus saving the blushes and possibly keeping the friendship of the parties involved intact - for another year at least.

For young people New Year's Night was the next big night for dancing, after St. Stephen's Day, when of course every able bodied young person took to the floor. Before the advent of dance-halls it was often said that heat from country ceilis was sufficient to disperse the frost or fog from the country boreens on New Year's Night. Also prior to pollution, there was nothing more invigorating than a brisk walk or cycle home in the pure clear air after a night's dancing.

Despite the weather being cold and bleak, the first days of the year begin to get brighter and longer. According to an old Irish saying, they are longer by 'a cock's footstep' on the 6th of January, than they were before Christmas.

Shelley's, lines:
> If Winter comes:
> Can Spring be far behind?

express the feeling of hope and anticipation that many people experience as they bid farewell to the old year and welcome in the new one.

THE END

CLASSIC COUNTRY CUSTOMS

An account of former summer practices in rural Ireland

'The Merry Month of May' is synonymous with festivities - a time of celebration with the hope (however misguided) of a long, glorious summer ahead. In times past, celebrations were muted by the fact that the first of the month marked 'Gale Day' when the half yearly rent had to be paid if householders wanted to hold onto their property. It was only with the advent of The Land League that tenants acquired some measure of security as a result of the three F's- Fair Rent, Free Sale and Fixity of Tenure. Prior to that a tenant could be evicted at any time and if he or she failed to meet the rent deadline, eviction was almost certain to follow immediately. Rates were a problem then and they too were paid in two 'moieties.' The majority of farmers were obliged to sell some of their best animals in order to meet these commitments. At the end of the month or early in June, tithes had to be paid on the sale of lambs and wool.

Letting of grazing and meadow took place around this time also but of course most of the grain crops would have been planted at this stage. It was common enough for farmers to plant potatoes and turnips in May.

HIRING HELP

It was in May also that hiring fairs reached their peak. In this area, Athenry was the venue for these. Early on Sunday Summer mornings, labourers would gather in the town square to await the arrival of farmers who came in great numbers to hire help for the busy season that lay ahead. The 'Spalpeens' or travelling labourers were strong and adept at farm work. They came from Connemara mostly and spent their summers sweating in the bogs and meadows in order to earn their daily bread. It was customary for the hirers to provide food and sleeping quarters for the Connemara men. Horse and carts were availed of to transport labourers from Athenry to Gurteen and other areas. However, the spalpeens usually departed the farms on foot when it was time to leave. Conditions varied from farm to farm but generally speaking working hours were long and wages were low. On the other hand farmers and their employees were rewarded with an ample supply of wholesome food in return for their work on the land.

WELCOMING IN THE MONTH

Summer of course was a time of celebration. The dark days of winter were well and truly over and the Celts and their descendants in later centuries were determined to enjoy themselves. They did this by organising festivities of various kinds. All over the country newly leafed branches were used to create May boughs. In Cork the leaves of the sycamore were particularly popular while in parts of Leinster large branches of whitethorn were used. These were hung outside the doors of farmhouses and byres and were sometimes adorned with flowers, ribbons and candles. After dark the candles and bonfires were lit and dancing began. The May bough was believed to bring its owner good luck and if it was stolen the luck was gone.

On May Eve people picked flowers for decorating inside and out and they strewed them along paths leading to their houses. Maytime is always associated with dancing. Maypoles remained quite popular in rural Ireland as late as the 1950's. In parts of the country 'May Boys' dressed in white linen shirts and dark trousers often collected money and then cut down long poles which they would dance around until the early hours of the morning. Maypoles were also used as 'Greasy Poles' and prizes were given to those who were supple enough to climb them. Admission to Maypole dances was free. Other festivities also took place close to the maypoles. These included sack races, jumping, tug- o-war and donkey races. Two of the most unusual events that I've heard of were: a competition to find out who could hold on to a greased pig's tail and blindfolding party goers to get them to catch a man ringing a hand bell. Electing a May King and May Queen were regular features of the festivities too.

THE MAY MORNING DEW

In the past young girls would get up early on the 1st of May to bathe their faces in the morning dew. This they believed would increase their beauty and cure any blemishes that they might have. Collecting well water was another common practice and one was considered especially lucky to draw the first container of water from the well. This was supposed to guarantee good fortune for the rest of the year.

Stockowners were wary of strangers and there are numerous myths about milking on May Day. Superstitious people were convinced that their herd could be deprived of its milk yield if a stranger milked the animals on this day. Therefore they paid particular attention to protecting crops and animals. There are several legends about hares siphoning milk on May Day. When these animals were chased they found their way into farmhouses and were transformed into old ladies. Some went so far as to claim that the elderly ladies left a trail of blood as a result of being bitten by the chasing dogs while they were in the shape of hares!

THE CHRISTIANISATION OF MAY

The Church tried to alter ancient pagan rituals and have dedicated the month to Mary. Although flowers still feature prominently, they are now used to decorate altars built in honour of the Blessed Virgin. The Late Canon Sydney McEwan's recording 'Bring Flowers of The Rarest' is a beautiful tribute that celebrates the Christian ideal of summer and can be heard on many radio stations throughout the country at the beginning of May.

It is still common to find altars dedicated to Mary in many houses. Candles and yellow flowers brighten the altars and families say special prayers in honour of the Virgin for the entire month. When the weather is fine (and very often it is), Nature and the countryside can be seen at its best. On the other hand farmers like to have wind and lots of moisture at this time because it is said that,

'A wet and windy May,
Will fill the haggard with oats and hay.

Whatever one's outlook is, one thing is clear: the summer is on its way and the countryside becomes more fresh and invigorating as its surface begins to be covered with an array of crops and beautiful flowers. And of course there is the added bonus that the longest hours of daylight are close at hand in this part of the world.

THE DARK DAYS OF THE YEAR

A look at Halloween customs past and present

Halloween, which has become a Christian celebration, begins on October 31st and is followed by All Saints' Day on November 1st. All Souls' Day is on November 2nd. Originally All Hallows was celebrated on May Ist. The first record of the feast dates back to 610 AD. All Saints' Day was changed to November1st. in 834.

Halloween is a sombre time of year- a time when daylight begins to shrink rapidly in this part of the world- an occasion to listen to ghostly tales and perhaps be terrified by supernatural sagas involving ghosts and goblins. When I was growing up my sister and myself had mixed feelings about the stories. We longed to hear them but of course we were frightened by the graphic accounts of the mysterious events that were supposed to take place at Halloween. Who wouldn't be upset at thought of meeting deceased relatives on a dark country road? And who hasn't heard of the mysterious dark dog often encountered on the Clonkeenkerrill Road or at Creeraun Gate? Not to mention the sighting of a strange lady that was to be seen combing her hair beside Scarry's Well.

We wondered what was the meaning of these unusual occurrences and what dreadful consequences lay in store for us if we were unfortunate enough to encounter them? Thankfully neither of us ever did experience apparitions of this kind and we continued to visit our friends as normal. Not only that, we actually summoned up the courage to participate in the trick or treat rituals that were common at that time.

The increase of darkness at Halloween seems to have cast dark shadows in the minds of our ancestors also, if we are to judge by their customs. Long ago the feast was dedicated to Saman, the Lord of Death. It marked summer's end - the feast of the dying sun and was the last day of the Celtic year. It was widely believed that Saman summoned the souls of evil people and condemned them to inhabit the bodies of animals. In order to protect themselves, The Celts lit bonfires and housefires were extinguished. These were rekindled later as a kind of greeting for the returning souls of the dead. Food and other offerings would signal a welcome for the cycle of rebirth that began at Bealtaine - the 1st. of May.
The two important divisions of the Celtic year were of course Bealtaine and Samhain.

CELTIC FEARS

In the past the Celts were particularly cautious at Halloween. They worried about witches, evil spirits and fairies. Some of them, when going out of doors, hid their faces to prevent the fairies from recognising or snatching them. Children were kept indoors and those who did venture abroad generally did so in the company of others. The Celts had great faith in the Rowan tree. They thought that its wood was capable of protecting one from the power of the witches. Things changed with the coming of Christianity, although many religious people were still reluctant to engage in the festivities because they felt they were linked to devil worship and witchcraft. Few Christians have any misgivings about participating in these activities nowadays.

THE BEGINNINGS

Most of the Halloween customs do indeed have their origins in pre Christian times. They include 'trick or treat', apple ducking and games of divination. Nowadays one occasionally comes across these games being played. Blind folds were used for 'Snap Apple' and also when playing 'Divination.' In this game one had to choose from saucers or small containers while wearing a cover over the eyes. One container had water; another a rosary beads and usually one had a small portion of soil. These were moved about in random positions. It was believed that the person who selected water would travel overseas, whoever chose the beads, would become a priest or nun and the unlucky one that picked the container with soil would die within a short time. Thankfully, Blind man's Buff and apple ducking are generally much more popular than games of Divination.

OUTDOOR GAMES

Some people used to get tremendous satisfaction from wearing masks and dressing up in outlandish outfits to play in 'trick or treat' games. Pumpkin or turnip lanterns were used to guide them on their way. Those that complained about the pranks would be noted and would probably receive worse treatment the following year. It was advisable therefore for victims to remain silent. It must be said that only a tiny minority ever did object and most people regarded the pranksters with amusement and contributed generously to them whenever they called.

As with the Brideogs, Halloween 'Trick Or Treat' games are disappearing rapidly from the scene in rural areas. In our area for example nobody called to us last year during Halloween or on St. Bridget's Day. Previous years saw just a few 'trick or treaters' and they were children. In previous decades these feast days were availed of by adults to indulge in fun and games at the expense of fellow rustics.

A RELIGIOUS CELEBRATION

Pope Gregory dedicated the feast in honour of all the canonised saints. However the fear of evil still persisted and often St. Bridget's crosses were used to protect people and animals from harm. At one stage the Feast of All Saints was a day of abstinence. This meant that meat wasn't eaten. Instead apple cake or bairín brack were used. Young girls would be delighted to find the rings that were implanted in these- a sign that they would marry or become engaged in the not too distant future. Colcannon (made from potatoes, milk butter and onions) was also a favoured dish for the occasion.

In the Isle of Man the traditional meal consisted of potatoes, parsnips and fish mixed with butter. Oatcakes took pride of place in Scotland. More recently special Halloween cake in orange and black were eaten at fancy dress parties.

All Saints Day is a holiday of obligation for Catholics. The 2nd of November is dedicated to the Holy Souls. People visit cemeteries and pray for the dead. Christians believe that special indulgences benefiting the suffering souls in Purgatory can be gained for their departed loved ones by visiting burial places and by offering prayers for them at Halloween. Many use it as an opportunity to tidy up plots that may have been neglected during the year.

CUSTOMS ELSEWHERE

Of course Halloween celebrations were not confined to the countryside.
Children in Belfast, Dublin and Cork used to dress up in fancy clothes and go from house to house in search of apples and nuts. In Wales bonfires were lit on hillsides and youngsters often blew horns as they danced and sang around the fire.

In remote parts of Ireland, as at Christmas, candles in memory of departed relatives were placed in the windows.

HALLOWEEN IN MODERN TIMES

At present Halloween is seen as a welcome break between Harvest and Christmas.
For some it is a time of reflection during which they ponder on the mysteries of life and the inevitability of death. For others it is a time to remember relatives or family members who have died. In the Catholic Church special prayers and Masses are celebrated and envelopes are distributed to the faithful on which they can inscribe the names of their deceased relatives whose souls will be prayed for in subsequent religious services.

For the less religious, Halloween a time to refresh themselves by taking a short vacation or simply by taking things easy. In Nature it signals a period of rest and hibernation and in the farming world, animals are brought into sheds and byres to be fed and cared for over for the next 6 months. The rest of us just button up well as we try to console ourselves by thinking of the long, bright sunny days that will soon replace the cold, dark, dismal days of Halloween.

THE END

MARKING MARTIN'S MEMORY-CUSTOMS AND LEGENDS OF ST. MARTIN

The Feast of St. Martin held an important place in the calendar of this area up to recent years. It was a time set aside for the killing of fowl or animals in honour of the saint. The feast day falls on November 11th and the killing had to be done on the 10th, otherwise it was felt that the sacrifice would not be acceptable. Wealthy families used to kill sheep on this occasion but the less well off settled for fowl, and geese were the most popular offering among them.

Householders made special preparations leading up to the Feast. A week or so before the 10th a bird or animal was segregated from its fellows and treated to a special diet before it was killed. It was essential that the person recognised as being 'Head of The House' performed the killing. When this had been done the four corners of the house would be sprinkled with the blood of the dead offering in honour of St. Martin. Often the doorposts were included also. Performing these rituals, it was felt would protect the family from evil during the following year.

A difference between this and the ordinary killing of fowl or animals, was that the blood of those killed for St. Martin could not be used for cooking or pudding making. It was considered so special that a cloth dipped in it and applied to affected areas was believed to be a cure for aches and pains. Quills from the dead fowl were often made into pens. Children who used them were thought to have a better chance of improving their writing and literary skills. Sometimes sick animals were dedicated to the saint. Drops of blood from the animal in question would be shed. However, if the creature got better it ought not to be sold or killed because this would dishonour the saint.

Another custom associated with this feast was where a person suffering from skin ailments would go out on St. Martin's Night and kneel in a field where weeds were growing. The individual would close his or her eyes and pull a plant. The plant would then be rubbed to the problem areas and it is no exaggeration to say that many people had more confidence in the effectiveness of this remedy that they did in ordinary medicine.

The highlight of the festival was the main meal on the 11th of November. Special prayers of thanksgiving were offered by members of the family after the meal had been eaten. It was a common practice for each member to take three sips of water. This was understood to be in honour to The Blessed Trinity.

STORIES AND LEGENDS

This custom was observed in many parts of the country until a decade or so ago. Those who ignored it were looked upon with some misgivings by their fellow rustics. It was felt that bad luck would befall them during the year and several stories are offered in support of this theory. One such legend concerns a miserly lady who killed a cat in place of a fowl. She was punished instantly by the death of all her fowl next day.

A second story also concerns a cat. In this case the children wanted to kill a sheep. The father wasn't present at the time but his wife was determined not to be at the loss of a valuable animal. There was a big row between mother and children with the result that the children were sent to bed without any food. During the night the house went on fire. The two youngsters survived but the mother died in the fire.

There is a tale about a poor person who found a sick sheep lost in the snow. He felt sorry for it and took it home and cared for it. The sheep soon recovered and the farmer became rich as a result of his good deed. When the 10th of November came round he wanted to kill a good sheep now that he was relatively wealthy. As in the previous stories, his wife did not agree and urged him to kill an old sheep instead. They did so and both he and his wife suffered for their meanness by becoming poor again.

One of the most unusual legends concerns a woman who had nothing at all to kill for the feast. She thought it might be acceptable if she shed a few drops of blood from her baby but when she tried to do this, the blood continued to flow and the baby died. Later that night a beggar called. She gives him food and lodgings for the night. Then the stranger revives the infant. The stranger was none other than the Saint himself who had rewarded the woman for her dedication by giving life to the child.

HOW DID IT BEGIN?

The origin of the custom of sacrificing fowl and animals on the feast of St. Martin is a mystery. The day is dedicated to St.Martin of Tours and although he was a soldier, he died peacefully in 402 AD. In fact he has the distinction of being the first non-martyr canonised by the Western Church. Not much is known about him except it is said he had the power to dispel mist and fog. Some claim that his feast is being confused with that of Pope Martin 1st who reigned from 649 to 655 AD and who was imprisoned by the Emperor of Constantinople, as the city was called at the time. He died in jail on September 16th 655 as a result of ill treatment. His relics were brought to Rome on November 12th and were kept in a chapel dedicated to St. Martin of Tours. November 12th was decreed a holy day by the Church but in this country the feast was always celebrated on the 11th.

Another explanation for the bloodletting is that St. Martin conferred a monk's tonsure on St.Patrick. St.Patrick was reputed to have given presents of pigs to all nuns and monks and that these were to be killed and eaten on the anniversary of St. Martin's death.

Many other suggestions have been offered to explain this custom which was so prevalent in Ireland in previous centuries. However most people are of the opinion that it was one of a number of pagan customs adopted by the early Christian Church. Of course one must remember that sacrificial offerings were a common feature of life in biblical times also. Almost everyone is familiar with the story about Abraham who was prepared to offer his own son, Isaac, as a blood sacrifice to God The Father. Abraham's readiness to offer such an immolation was proof of the tremendous faith that he possessed and he was promised that his descendants would be the Chosen People of God as a result.

Changing times mean that these ancient customs have almost disappeared. This is something of a relief I'm sure for those who dislike the sight of blood. Housewives are no longer under pressure to make a sacrificial offering in November and it's likely that many of them or their families would be unable to name St. Martin's feast day, much less offer a blood sacrifice in his honour. This is in stark contrast to previous decades when the ritual was a regular feature of life in Gurteen and in other country places. At that time it would be considered something akin to heresy if the day were allowed to pass without the necessary sacrifice being made. At present the housewife's cleaver no longer poses a threat to fowl or farm animals, who can breathe easy in their resting places, and who can thank the decline of religious and rural values for their safety as St. Martin's Eve draws near.

CHAPTER FOUR

WEDDING BELLS

WEDDING BELLS RING OUT FOR

Michael Roche And Caroline McGuinness

Pairic Hynes and Andrea Curran

Wedding bells ring out for
Sharon Kelly and Donal O'Reilly

AN INDIAN WEDDING

By

Agnes Heaney

My father often spoke of his trip to America and of his arrival at Fresno, California, where he hoped to meet uncles who had settled there several years previously. They had a picturesque ranch house almost hidden by tall cottonwood trees. It had a covered porch on one side, an open one on the other. Inside, it was roomy and comfortable and furnished in fabulous style. Of course there were no mod cons then; just oil lamps and stoves. Drinking water came from a pump. Uncles employed Chinese people to do household chores e.g. cooking, feeding stock and wood chopping. Two big prairie dogs slept outside to warn of approaching dangers. Beyond the orchards were barns for poultry and pigs, also large corrals for the horses and burrows (mules). Chinese and Mexican workers looked after the vineyards and orange groves, and they usually worked from sun-up to sundown. Alfalfa was sown for fodder and cattle and sheep grazed on rolling pastureland.

My father spent his first day in Fresno gazing at the magnificent mountains - their snow capped peaks high up against the clouds. The orange groves bloomed in the valley; their sweet scented blossoms filled the air. The brightly coloured birds were fascinating. These included Green Parakeets with red beaks, singing Bulbuls and Humming birds. There was a wonderful variety of wild flowers including the Poppy. This is the Californian state flower and was to be seen everywhere. Every day seemed to offer something new and exciting. When exploring the orchards one had to be wary of snakes, as these were particularly dangerous when emerging from hibernation.

The uncles had a fund of thrilling stories to tell about the time they arrived in Fresno. At that time it was scarcely more than a village with a population of six hundred people. They got their hands on 2000 acres which they converted from parched prairie land into a bountiful ranch. They were unaware of the hardship they would endure as they set out with oxen and mules to clear dense forests, build log huts and fight off Indian attacks. They needed horses and ploughs to cultivate the land and they decided to trade with the Navajo Indians in order to do this. In return the Indians taught them survival skills and horse training. They also showed them how to grow corn and to rear native wild turkeys. Originally these came from Mexico but it was the Indians that tamed them. The Indians called them 'gobblers' and used their green and bronze feathers to decorate their headdresses. The uncles gained the respect of the Indians through honest dealings and gradually hostilities between them ceased. They learned some of their language, and they were among the first white men to make friendly contact with Indians.

THE INVITATION

Shortly after our family arrived in Fresno, they were all invited to an Indian wedding. Uncles considered it an honour and a sign of confidence - they simply could not refuse, because they could be dangerous enemies too and a refusal might offend them. Father was told that it would be an opportunity for him to meet and make friends with them if he intended to become a rancher in the area. Needless to say he was very nervous, but felt it was a challenge and he reluctantly accepted. He thought they were risking their lives because these people were reputed to be savages and hated the whites for taking their land. On a morning of brilliant sunshine four brave men - Uncle Patrick, father, and two neighbours - guns strapped to their hips, set out by horse -and-buggy on a three day trip to Seeping Springs, the Navajo encampment. They brought plenty of food for the journey, grain for the horses and a pile of blankets to sleep on. Two young braves (Indians) led the way and they carried water in five-gallon saddlebags: in the desert water meant life. Following ancient trails through rugged terrain uncle pointed out flocks of small, hardy sheep living on high ranges where cattle could not climb. They were herded by range-riders who had to protect them from the ravages of wild beasts- coyotes, wolves, and grizzly bears. One grizzly could kill up to 50 sheep, killing only the mother sheep and eating their milk bags.

GETTING THERE

Their first overnight was spent in a small log cabin, which was sometimes used to house forest rangers. In a sheltered nook the Indians built a fire, they fed their horses and hobbled them, ate their meat and bread, rolled up in blankets and were soon asleep on the ground under open skies.

On the 3rd day the 'guests' crossed part of 'The Painted Desert' and almost covered in red dust, arrived at the Navajo oasis- a beautiful vale beside a foaming waterfall. Indian chiefs came from their hogans to welcome them. At the white men's salute they gave the sign of friendship saying, 'Does the white fathers come to honour the Navajos?' After smoke signals had been sent out, a stream of mounted Indians poured into the glade. Moki and other tribes rode wild looking Mustangs and drove ponies and burrows, carrying blankets and supplies. These russet-skinned warriors were dressed in colourful regalia, their jet-black hair held close with bands around their foreheads. Uncle and his friends gave them gifts of groceries, vegetables and fruit, with a plug of tobacco for each great chieftain. 'The pipe of peace' was then passed around. The Navajo worship the Sun as their god and their faith was rewarded on this occasion because it was a beautiful cloudless day. As they began their chant in honour of the sun, the bride was brought in.

Her hands were tied in front of her-a sign of obedience. She appeared to be very young and had a sad expression even though one would have thought that this was a very special day in her life. On her long, black, braided hair she wore a crown of white feathers.

The bridegroom's name was Desert Hawk. Uncle thought this was an appropriate name for him because he had a nose like a hawk's beak and his hands resembled claws. He described him as a grim old warlord who owned many squaws already.

SHORT AND SWEET

The ceremony was brief. Children were scattering flowers and the women sang strange sounding songs as they brought food and drink. Ample quantities of food were served in black earthenware vessels. Fear had taken my father's appetite away but Uncle Pat and his friends made up for him. They ate everything placed before them including homemade popcorn, which was served in a deerskin bag. He was told that the Indians were the first humans to sample the delights of popcorn.

As they sat by the campfire, everyone except my father was relaxed. He didn't trust the fierce warriors who were staring at them intensely as if they intended to serve them up as one of the after courses later on that evening. To add to his discomfort an array of mosquitoes appeared to focus on him as part of their pre-prandial appetiser. It was a tension filled afternoon for him and looking back on it, he considered himself lucky to have escaped with his life. Uncle Pat didn't see it like that at all. He enjoyed meeting his Navajo friends and felt it was quite an honour to be invited to such a celebration. It was the only Indian wedding my father attended and no doubt it remained fresh in his memory long after that sun-drenched day in California.

CHAPTER FIVE

LOCAL LORE AND LEGENDS

CLUAIN CHAOIN CHOIRILL AGUS CILL DUBHAN

By

Declan Greaney

In our family until recently we always went eastwards to Mass and westwards to school. I have often wondered why that was. Can nature be so persuasive? The ground is quite high around where we live and maybe we were just naturally being lured by The Abbert to the west and The Ahascragh to the east, both winding their way in opposite directions towards the same destination. I wonder.

The village in which we grew up lies midway between Saints Peter and Paul, the Parish Church of Ballymacward, and Cluain Chaoin Choirill National School in the parish of Gurteen. The church, village and school, all three, are located on an east-west link road between Ballymacward on the R359 (Killane Cross - Castleblakeney) and the Castle of Garbally on the R339 (Caltra - Galway).

I have walked under the hot sun, run in the rain, cycled in the snow, frozen in the frost and been carried back and forth umpteen times on that stretch of road. There were berries and briars in the summer and the tar blistered bubbled on the road. From long before I knew roads needed numbers, I have a vivid pre-school image of Mr. Kilgannon passing by our house, on a frosty, wintry morning, cycling from his home in Liscune, where he was still living, to Cluain Chaoin Choirill where he was the Headmaster. The road had not yet been tarred. I admired his tenacity even then. That moment, 'frozen' in time and place 'upon that inward eye' was my first intimation of the school I was going to attend.

Today's children, bestowed as they are with so many creature comforts at home and in school, could not easily identify with how basic our classroom surroundings were in the late fifties/early sixties. Imagining I close my eyes, I can hear again: the clattering noise of slates being collected in after Mrs. Lyng has finished doing sums on them with the lower and higher Infants; nibs being scraped about in ceramic inkwells during Transcription; feet treading quietly on well-worn wooden floors; the odd bottle of hot cocoa going 'pop!' in winter because it has been left too long to warm up in front of the turf fire; pupils volunteering to go out for a 'gabháil' of turf from the shed; window frames which rattled in the wind and doors which positively invited the wind in when it blew.

In the atmosphere of silent study we were eager to do routine tasks which we might not have been so enthusiastic about doing at home, like for instance: putting down the fire of a cold morning; sprinkling the dust on the floor before sweeping it; mixing ink powder with water in a glass bottle and filling up the afore-mentioned inkwells through a special straw-like dispenser built into the cork; polishing the hearth and - the most coveted job of all - scrubbing the floor at the end of the school year with three or four of 'the chosen few' for which we earned the handsome sum of five shillings each. This was a king's ransom to twelve or thirteen year olds in those days. Pockets bulging with Mr. Burke's sweets and with heightened prospects for the summer holidays stretching out before us, we sauntered home eastwards or westwards, tired but happy.

MAEVE GREANEY
RECENT

Granted, it was basic in many respects but, in a strange way, the school brought us close together. Laffeys, Browns, Dempseys, Naughtons, Mannions, Finnertys, Brodericks, Coppingers, Roches, Rafterys, Boltons, Glynns, Greaneys, Flahertys, Lallys, Flannerys, Finns, Kilkennys, Briens... all together, at that time, under the one roof. Having to do without made us more self-sufficient. Games in the playground were simple but great fun: football, catch, four corners or pitch and toss. Mr. Kilgannon took us out hurling.

Seeds were sown. Friendships were forged, Traditions were passed on. We all had a stake in the 'Island of Saints and Scholars.' There had been a golden age in our history, after St. Patrick, when zealous missionaries carried to most of the European nations the glad tidings of the Gospel. We heard about St. Columba, Saint Bridget, Saints Brendan, St Kevin, St Kieran and St Kerrill. They were a hard act to follow.

From pre-Christian Ireland we were introduced to the myths and legends of 'The Táin' and its epic heroes: Cú Chulainn, Ferdia, Ailill, Maebh... and to the preceding tribes who invaded the country: the Tuatha Dé Danann, the Firbolgs, the Formorians... Míle Easpain was also mentioned. Over the past twenty years or so there has been an explosion of interest in the Celts and without that original grounding in Cluain Chaoin Choirill, I, personally, would have had a very narrow base from which to explore our national identity. For example, at the moment, people may or may not know, that the Galicians, in Northern Spain, are making a very plausible argument for being the seventh official Celtic nation in Europe and that it was from there that the Celts invaded Ireland, after coming from Egypt, eventually defeating the Tuatha Dé Danann and establishing themselves as the genetic stem of the Irish race. It makes you wonder about the origins of place-names like Galway and Donegal.

In my time at Cluain Chaoin Choirill, we had three main teachers: Mrs. Lyng, Mr. Kilgannon and Mr. Burke. I appreciate more and more the start they gave us in that two-roomed 'little kingdom'. They complemented each other in my view. I am grateful to Mrs. Lyng for making the home-school transition a happy one - I remember being so nervous on the first day that I made a bee-line to a desk after entering the room, sat down and filled the best part of a page with naughts - and because she taught me my first words in Irish. Mr. Kilgannon imbued in us a love of our heritage, our culture and Gaelic games. On the Monday morning after the Galway football team had brought home the Sam Maguire for the third time in a row, the pupils in the senior room burst into a spontaneous round of applause as he entered the room waving the daily paper in the air. It was great! Mr. Burke had a love of music and language. We sang 'Men of Harlech' in three-part harmony, started to learn French and German and studied a wide range of literature in Irish and English. He taught algebra and geometry after school. 'Coincidentally', I have been an MFL teacher for more than twenty years. My degree is in English, French and German.

AOIFE AND PIERCE GREANEY

Except for the occasional visit from the Garda Síochána, the impromptu call from 'An cigire', the Bishop's annual confirmation exam and the weekly catechism call from Fr. Egan, there were few other callers to the school. We did have a visit from a travelling showman once. Magic!

Just over a year ago, at my mother's graveside (Ar dhéis Dé a h-anam.) in Killeuawn, I lifted my head at one point, and looked out across Cúl-loch towards the abbey ruins in Cluain Chaoin. It was like an epiphany. It was as if I had never seen that view before. I was taken aback by the sweep and depth of the panorama. It struck me that this ground we were standing on was hallowed ground too. As children we had taken for granted these old stones which had stood for centuries in the distance down behind our house. Cluain Chaoin and Killeuawn went back a long way. I decided to have another look into Jacky Flynn's (Bail ó Dhia ar an bhfear uasal sin.) tour de force on Ballymacward.

I paraphrase. St Jarlath came from Tuam to preach the Faith to the Sodháin who are the ancestral

people of Ballymacward in the ancient territory of Hy Many. The earliest built church on the western edge of the parish would appear to be in Killmiude, close to the bog of Cúl-loch. The foundations of this church are, in all likelihood, those of the church of St. Modiúit, a very well-documented Bishop whose diocese was probably Sodhán. Killeuawn (after Cill Dubhán) church was built around the 1300s and became the site of the medieval vicarage taking in the western section of Sodhán. Across the way in Gurteen the site of St. Coireall's church became the site of a 15th century Franciscan monastery. The new Franciscan monastery was given land in Killmiude/ Killeuawn which had probably been church land in ancient times. There had also been another medieval vicarage on the eastern side of the parish, Cill Maolchosna, called after Maol Chosna, the site of which is located in the grounds of the old Ballymacward graveyard.
It had finally sunk in.

Admittedly, the road we took to school is not the one the monks must have used to cross Cül-loch - which can still be traced - but the starting and departure points are more or less the same. As children, we had been walking in the footsteps of those gone before us without realising it. Providential or what? Don't you just wonder sometimes at the extent to which we are all being looked after from above. It meant a lot to me to have spoken again to my three former teachers during the funeral proceedings. (Go maire siad céad.) So many things seemed to have come full circle in that little graveyard. It felt like a way of life was drawing to a close. These days, as I drive by the school with my own children, I remind them that Cluain Chaoin Choirill is where our family has gone to school for generations. In the Tithe Applotment Lists of 1825 an antecedent of ours by the name of Denis is entered in the Killoane area. In 1856 Michael, Denis and Patrick Greaney paid rent to Lord Dunsandle who owned Ballygrany. All our relatives on my father's side come from the Tiaquin/ Newcastle area. There was a Thomas Greany living in Cudoo West in 1827.

Ó Íosa mhilis, éist linn,
Cuir sinn i bhfochair na naomh
Anois, agus le saol na saol.

Rath Dé orainn.

WHAT'S IN A NAME? A LOOK AT LOCAL PLACENAMES

Finding out the meaning of placenames can be very interesting. Most people know that 'Gurteen', the name of our area, means 'The little ploughed (tilled) field' but how many of you know the meanings of the names of the villages in which you live? The following translations are based on the work of P.W. Joyce, Seán Úí Chearnaigh, Deirdre and Laurence Flanagan as well as the oral and written folklore that is currently available. Ballygreaney, Kinreask and Garrymore are in the Ballymacward sector of the parish but are included because most of their inhabitants sent children to school in Gurteen.

We begin with Attymany. Áit Tí Máine or The House of Maine (or Hymany?) is one meaning that is offered. Alternative ones include: (2) Áit Tí na Mánaigh = The Site of the House of the Monks (3) Áit Tí na mBan = The Place of the Women's House.
Supporters of the latter title claim that it got its name because of a house used there as a refuge for women while a fierce battle raged in olden times.

Ballyglass - Baile Glas = The Green Village or town. There is no shortage of greenery in this village.

Ballygreaney - Baile Uí Ghráinne = The Village of The Greaneys so called because of the many families of that name that lived there. This townland had a different name two hundred years ago. It was called Gort a Charnáin = The Field Of The Small Mound. Some think this may refer to a church or school that existed there. Others feel that it got its name because Indian meal was supposed to be distributed to poor people there during the Famine. Some say the name is Gort a Chearnach = The Field of Victory - which may have to do with a fight that took place there sometime in the past.

Caltragh - An Chealtrach = The Burial Ground - usually for unbaptised children.
Cillín = Small Church or Graveyard was another name for a place where such souls were interred. Fr. Lawless celebrated Mass in memory of children buried in these places, a few years ago.

Cappalusk - Ceapach Loiscthe = The Burning Plot i.e. Field where stubble is burned. However, if the name is Ceapach Lusca, this would suggest that there once was a cave or underground passage in the vicinity.

Clough - An Cloch = The Stone. It is likely that it refers to a stone castle that existed in the area.

Cloonkeenkerrill - Cluain Caoin Chearbhaill = Kerrill's Pleasant Meadow. This is the generally accepted meaning of the name. However the former author, Martin Finnerty, suggested that it might be Clann Chian Chairill which would mean The Family (or descendants) of Cian Carroll.

Clonbornia - Cluain Boirne = The Stony Meadow. (Was there ever a shortage of them?)

Colemanstown - Baile Uí Chlumháin = The Village or town of Coleman. Some authors have said that Coleman was a brother of St. Kerrill. Joe Mannion in his book on St. Kerrill says that there was a family of O'Clumháin living in the area. He describes them as a bardic family who were poets and historians to the O'Haras of Co. Sligo.

Corskeagh - Corr Sceacha = The Hill of The Bushes. It seems there was a profusion of white thorn bushes growing there at one stage. Ollie Ruane says that his father removed some of the bushes and planted an ash tree where they grew.

Creeraun - An Criathran = The Boggy Disrtict. Despite the name there is a large portion of good land in this district. There are also remnants of an important ring fort which is mentioned in Lewis's Topographical Dictionary. Tradition says that Creeraun was one of the ancestral homes of the O'Kelly clan and that the forbears of Sean T. O'Ceallaigh,
former President of Ireland once lived there.

Faha - An Fhaiche = The Lawn or Square.

Garrymore - An Garraí Mór = The Big Garden. (They are very scarce these days)

Glanamucka - Gleann na Muca - The Valley of the Pigs. This is a small patch of ground between Killuane and Cloonkeenkerrill. There was once a school in this townland.

Gortbrack - An Gort Breac = The Speckled Field. This place is said to have got its name from the array of flowers that grew there.

Gortnalone - Gort na Lon = The field of The Blackbirds. Another theory is that the correct name is Gort na Lann = The Field of the Lances or Spears - a reference to an ancient battle that took place nearby a long time ago.

Gortronnagh - Gort Dronnach = The Ridged (humped) Field

Killuane - Cill Dhuáin = The Church of Dubhan - It's called after the Saint who built a church where the cemetery now is.

Kinreask - Cinn Riascach = The Marshy Headland. Large numbers of trees grow in Kinreask nowadays and there is an abundance of flora to be found on the roadside there.

Knockaboy - An Cnoc Buí = The Yellow Hill.

Lenareagh - An Léana Ríabach = The Striped (or Grey) Lawn

Shanballard - Sean Bhaile Árd = The Old High Village. A school existed there from 1896 - 1981.

Shanbaleeshal - An Sean Bhaile Íseal = The Old Low Lying Village

Shanballymore - An Sean Bhaile Mór = The Big Old Village. The most commonly used road to this village is beside the Post Office. There are two lakes there.

Sheeaune - An Sián = The Fairy Mound. There are several legends referring to this area (see the section on Folklore).

Tample - An Teampall = The Church. The old school is the main landmark to be seen there now.

FORGOTTEN PLACENAMES THAT WERE ONCE FAMILIAR

Several placenames have disappeared from the area over the years. These were often field names or names of houses but occasionally they referred to townlands.

Bauvin Castle in Clough is one such place. Some of the legends associated with Bauvin can be read in the Folklore section.

Gort na Croise = The Field of the Crosses. This was a field owned by the Late Laurence Griffin which once contained a group of houses. It is possible that Gurteen may have derived its name from this spot.

Sgeach Mhairéad = Margaret's Bush - refers to a place in Tample where a woman of that name lived. There was a wall here called Flax House which obviously refers to linen industry which flourished here in former times.

Cros An Éilimh = The Cross of Demand. This was located in Clonkeenkerrill where it was alleged an old Fenian used to collect a ten-penny bit from passers-by on Sundays. He is not named in the Folklore Collection but the story says that one Sunday a coffin was seen to float by in the sky and that he stopped collecting that day. He was killed soon afterwards.

Cnocán na bPáiste = The Hillock of the Children and this apparently was another name for the place where children were buried in Gortnalone.

In Tample there is (1) Tobar = A Well, (2) Gleannta = Valleys or Low Meadows and (3) Baile na Búiche = The home (village} of The Hyacinths. It's possible that this may have been Baile na Búrcaigh = The Home of The Burkes, as this family has been prominent here for quite some time.

Cluain Mór = The Large Meadow is in Lenareagh.

Geata na Mine = The Meal Gate (Shanballard -Cloncagh area) -This obviously refers to the distribution of food during The Famine.

Coill na gCapall = The Horse's Wood is also in Shanballard.

An Sean Choill = The Old Wood is also in this region.

Sruthán = (1) A Stream, (2) Corr an Phreacháin = The Crow's Hill, (3) Sean Gairdín = The Old Garden, (4) Gort a Chuineagáin = Cunninghams's Field and (5) Lios = Enclosed (Fairy) Mound. All of these were in Clough.

Rath = Fairy Fort was a spot in Lenareagh where the fairies were supposed to dance each night.

Acres was the name of some fields beside Knockaboy.

Bóthar Báite = The Road of the Drowning. This was in Woodlawn and it was said that a man and his horse drowned there on their way to the Fair in Ballinasloe.

Port Árd = High Bog (Creeraun). It got its name because the ground was higher than the surrounding area.

'Grouse Lodge' is described as 'a small bog garden on the banks of Gurteen River.'

Curragh Ruadh - Corach Rua = The Red Swamp is given as 'a village on the brink of the bog in Gurteen.'

Corr na Gaoithe = Hill of The Wind in Tample was believed to have got its name on account of the fact that it was a hill surrounded by a bog on which no shelter could be found.

Glynn's Park in Faha is also among the forgotten names in the locality.

Gort an Tobair = The Well Field was in Gurteen.

Gort a Mhainnín = Mannion's Field in Tample was called after its owners.

In Sheeaune there was Poll Tuarín = The Bleaching Hole, where the river goes underground and where we are told people used to wash linen. There is a clump of trees growing beside it.

Poll an Chapaill = The Horse's Hole. This was in Colemanstown where we are informed that a man, 'and his horse and plough went down.'

There was a graveyard in Ballygreaney called 'An Teampaillín'. A church stood there at one time also.

An interesting spot in Gurteen was called 'Gort an tSagairt' = The Priest's Field. This four acre field was at Tample. According to tradition a priest asked a farmer for land to build a house on. The farmer said he would give as much land as one man could mow with a scythe in a day. The scythesman the priest employed is reputed to have cut four acres in a day. (Would this have anything to do with the expression: 'How's she cuttin' ?)

Monaveen -Móinín na bhFian = The Meadow of The Fianna was located at the Ballymacward side of the parish. This may explain why Woodlawn was called Móta Ghráinne Óige = The Moat of Young Grace. Woodlawn has the same Irish name as Moate, Co. Westmeath. According to legend such places acquired their names owing to the fact that Young Grace (The daughter of Cormac Mac Art) used them as resting-places for herself and Diarmuid when they were attempting to escape from Fionn Mac Chumhall.

These and many other names were familiar to our ancestors but have long since passed from common usage as have the legends and lore that has been associated with them for countless decades.

PEOPLE AND PLACES IN THE THIRTIES

The following villages were highlighted by The Folklore Commission Survey carried out in this district in 1937-8.

CLONKEENKERRILL - Fifty-nine people lived there. There were four septuagenarians: Martin Barry, John Ruane, Mrs. Barry and Mrs. Conallen. Flannery was the most common name.

COLEMANSTOWN - Fifteen families lived there, giving a total population of eighty-two people. Ruane was the most common name. Only one seventy- year old, John Hansbury is listed.

BALLYGREANEY - Eight families totalling thirty-five people resided there. Nevin was the most common name and there were five seventy-year olds: Ned Nevin, Mike Nevin, Mary Gavin, John and Mrs.Tuohy.

GORTBRACK - It had four families with a total of ten people. Molloy was the most common name and thatched houses were numerous there at that time. Mrs. Molloy is the only seventy-year old listed.

GURTEEN - There were eighty people consisting of ten families. Scarry was the most common name and three septuagenarians are named: Mrs. Scarry, Mrs. Kenny and Mrs. Lyons.

KINREASK - Kilkenny was the most common name here. Four seventy-year olds are named: Thomas Flannery, Mrs. Kilkenny, Mrs. Hession and Martin Hession.

GURTEEN FOLKLORE - A LOOK AT THE ARCHIVES

A substantial amount of material was collected by The Folklore Commission in this area in 1937-8. One of the first pieces from Tample concerns a treasure that was found in Hardiman's field in Clough. It was found by Patrick King from Ballyglass who was cleaning a drain. The find consisted of two bars of gold. According to legend gold was hidden by Queen Maeve close to Bauvin Castle. Apparently she was fleeing from soldiers at the time and couldn't take all her gold with her. The story goes that Patrick didn't think that it was real gold but nevertheless he took it home by the fire to dry. A traveller called a short time later and offered Patrick a saucepan for one of the bars. The offer was accepted but the storyteller doesn't tell us what became of the remaining bar.

There is also the well-known folktale of the sheepskin. A father wanted a wife for his son. He gave him a sheepskin and told him not to part with it until he met a lady that would give him the skin back as well as the price of it. Eventually the son met a girl who took the wool from the skin. She paid him for the wool and gave him back the skin. The couple were married in due course.

There is an amusing account concerning a tailor and a 'gentleman' that lived in Colemanstown. Both of them were fond of nuts. Before the gentleman died he ordered that his family should make an extra large coffin and that the space not taken up by his own body should be filled with nuts. When the tailor found out about the arrangement he went to the graveyard in Cloonkeenkerrill shortly afterwards. He dug up the coffin and sat down on it eating the nuts. Then one of the monks from the monastery came out and saw him. He rushed to tell the other monks that there was a ghost sitting on a coffin eating nuts!

There is an intriguing yarn about a woman from Tiaquin. She and her husband went to Tuam to buy a sack of flour. The man put the sack on the woman's back and they set off for home. When they got about half way, the man 'failed'. The woman then put him up on her back and carried him and the sack of flour home.

Apparently women from Clough used to walk to Athenry for flour. They carried their sacks on their backs. Not only that, but some of them would have a pair of socks knitted by the time they got back to Clough! Males reading this will never forgive Women's Lib for ruining the capacity of modern females to endure endless hardship and engage in backbreaking work, in order to sustain the family economy, in the same manner as their predecessors did.

THE PENAL LAWS

There is also a section containing information about the area at the time when The Penal Laws were in force. Catholic religious services were illegal and priests were often pursued by the authorities. Whenever Mass was being celebrated, it had to be done secretly. Pat Hogan's Wood in Clooncagh is cited as one location, Tom Cormican's land in Gurteen and Joe Finnerty's Field in Clough are also named as places where Mass was said. 'Style an Aifrinn' is the title given to this last named spot. Once a priest called Fr. Coen was jailed due to information given by a person referred to as 'Seán na Sagart.'
A priest was hidden in Ballygreaney. A reward of £10 was offered by the authorities for information leading to his capture. However, the people of the area remained loyal and the priest was never captured.

In neighbouring Mount Hazel a priest was less fortunate. According to reports he was shot dead by English soldiers while saying Mass. A number of people present were let go with a caution.

There was a priest in Creeraun who lived in a house in a wood. The house was surrounded by trees and Mass was celebrated there every morning. When the clergyman died a hole five feet deep was found in the floor. There was food, a paper and clothes in it. It is thought that the priest used to hide there whenever the military approached. According to John Kelly of Keave a light was to be seen over the place where the house stood. Fr. Mahon lived at Raftery's house in Killuane and was protected from the soldiers in Penal times. He used to say Mass by a rock at a spot called 'Cor an Aifrinn.' According to Michael Burns his grandparents attended Mass there.

There was a good deal of unrest in later periods also and this is reflected in the stories that pupils collected. During the United Irish Rebellion several parishioners were charged with capital offences and some of them were hanged in Galway city. John Flynn, in his book on Ballymacward, deals with the activities of the Ribbonmen and those engaged in agrarian unrest at a later date. Things improved a little as a result of the British government's attempts to 'kill Home Rule with kindness' but the landlords were very powerful and owned vast estates at the beginning of the Twentieth Century. However, the tenants were more successful in demanding their rights. Cattle belonging to landlords and other large landowners were driven off the estates and often ended up far away from base. In 1920, one such event took place in Corskeagh when Patrick Raftery's animals were driven from his farm. They were found wandering near Monivea about 10 miles away sometime later. Ned Nevin from Killuane and members of the United Irish League engaged in this kind of activity regularly. The campaign was intended to speed up the departure of the landlords and to have the land divided among ordinary farmers.

LANDLORDS

William and Dennis St. George Daly of Dunsandle were the principal landlords in the Gurteen area. They were not popular and became less so when they evicted poor farmers and turned the holdings into ranches that were leased to graziers on the eleven-month system. The situation was very rigid at the time. According to the writers, no ordinary tenant could plant a tree and herds could not possess dogs. One of the herds in Corskeagh did not obey this rule. Apparently he trained the dog to go under the bed whenever the landlord appeared! When work became available on the public roads, any tenant who had a stack of corn in his haggard would not be given employment.

Tenants who failed to pay their rent on time would be evicted. This happened to a local man named Connaughton. When he was evicted his house was burned. (This was the usual procedure at that time). We are told that other tenants 'stood out' for Connaughton and that he got his land back. We are not given any details as to how this happened. The following lines refer to the event:

> Bold Dillon's eviction,
> The landlord's visitation,
> The tenants' salvation
> The Plan of Campaign.

Other landlords mentioned were: Armstrong, Reeves, Reilly and French. The tithes that were collected consisted of money and corn. (Tithes were collected by Proctors for the upkeep of the Protestant Church). Two houses belonging to landlords were burned; one in Clough and the other one in Clooncagh. The Rackrents are referred to also. This meant that if a tenant improved his house or land in any way, the rent would be raised immediately. Obviously this added to the misery and squalor of the unfortunates who lived here at that time.

ACCIDENTS

As well as deliberate burnings, mention is also made of an accidental one. This occurred about ten years prior to the Folklore collection. A large barn belonging to Tom Cormican took fire after an eight year old boy let a lighting match fall from the loft. Carts, machinery and straw were destroyed.

A number of drownings occurred. A man named Kelly was drowned at Poll Tuairín 70 years previously. The river was flooded and the man described as a 'weak minded man,' walked into it. His body lay in the waters for days and was recovered by the police who brought a boat from Tiaquin. The man in question was 70 years of age. Another 75 year old drowned in Lough na Hinch. He was Pat Connors and his body was recovered from waters that were only about 4 feet deep. This happened on March 21st. 1917 as he was coming home from Mt. Hazel after a night's visiting. Apparently he sat by a bush to light his pipe and fell asleep. He slipped into the lake and drowned. His pipe was found floating on the water close to the body. An unnamed man drowned in Clough River while working there with a horse and cart. No details are given in this instance.

WEDDDING CUSTOMS AND BELIEFS

Dowries were a common feature of life then and the amount of the 'fortune' paid by the bride's parents usually depended on the size of her future husband's holding. 'Walking the land' took place beforehand and if the situation was considered satisfactory, a substantial meal would be provided to the visiting party afterwards. The bride's mother often donated a feather bed to the couple as a wedding present.

On the wedding day, if the groom left the church before the bride, it was believed that he would die first and visa versa. Sometimes the bride would return home from the church behind her husband on horseback. Celebrations would then take place at the future home of the couple. There would be lots of music, dancing, food and drink and entertainers known, as 'strawboys' would perform for the newlyweds and their friends.

One custom described by Mrs. Dooley of Clough was the breaking of an oaten cake over the bride's head as she came in the door after the nuptials.

It was considered unlucky to get married on a Friday or on the 'cross day' (28th December?) of the year. It was equally unlucky to meet another wedding party or to pass by a cemetery on the day of the wedding. Good luck was sure to follow if the sun shone on the bride and groom. Brides wore a white hat and gloves and a brightly coloured suit. No reference is made to the groom's apparel.

MATRIMONIAL MUSINGS

If you are thinking of getting married, would the following lines help?

Marry on Monday for health
On Tuesday for wealth,
Wednesday the best day of all,
Thursday for losses,
Friday for crosses
And Saturday no day at all.

Or how about this one? It seems to be addressed to the ladies.

Marry in black, you'll wish yourself back,
Marry in white, you'll do what is right,
Marry in green, unfit to be seen,
Marry in blue, he's sure to be true,
Marry in yellow, he'll be a good fellow
Marry in red, you'll wish yourself dead.

ARTS AND CRAFTS

One section deals with some of the handicrafts that were current at the time as well as those that were practised previously. One woman made candles from rushes and lard and went around the village of Gortnalone selling them. Ploughs and gates were made of wood and were manufactured locally. The smiths provided iron spades. When making sleáns, they tempered them with steel to give them sharpness and durability. Parishioners also made wicker baskets from sally rods which of course were quite plentiful. Wool was woven and the populace used it extensively to make clothes for themselves. Lime was manufactured locally also and special kilns were built where it could be burned. Nearly all dwelling houses were thatched and each person found material in the form of straw and scallops for thatching purposes. Many of the inhabitants were able to thatch their own houses.

Horsewhips were made by a man in Monivea referred to as 'Páidín Bán.'
Apparently the majority of houses had spinning wheels at an earlier period and housewives spun the wool and then sent it to the weaver to be woven into cloth. The women used to dye the wool sometimes and many of them made beautiful patchwork quilts. A kind of detergent was produced by burning heaps of ash branches and washing the clothes in the residue of the ashes. We are told that pottery was made in Brackloon.

OTHER TALES

We are informed that the Milesians fought the De Dannan beside Sheeaune Well. It was believed that the fairies had an underground abode in this region. One story tells of an apparition seen by a local man. This individual claimed to have seen large numbers of little people dancing there. When the dance was over each of the dancers mounted a horse and rode around in a circle. They were thought to be responsible for the black boreen around the well.

Another hair-raising occurrence took place at Tobar Geal, a well in Paddy Raftery's land.

Two huntsmen were returning home one night when they saw a lady with white hair. One of them pointed his gun at her and then shot her. She fell down and the huntsmen left quickly. They hadn't gone very far when the white haired lady overtook them. She proceeded to give a severe beating to the man who had fired the shot. The other man begged her not to kill him and she stopped. However, when the gunman went home he woke up to find the ghoulish lady about to assault him. He began to scream but she paid no heed to his pleadings. The huntsman was found dead next morning and all the skin had been torn from his body!

There are sections dealing with cures, herbs and superstitions that we haven't even touched on. The material collected in collaboration with the teachers in Clonkeenkerrill and Tample is in English, while the folklore from Shanballard is recorded in English and Irish. Mrs. Hurley was in charge of Clonkeenkerrill School and Miss Duffy was in charge of Tample. Tom Murphy, whose wife lives in Loughrea, was the Headmaster in Shanballard.

Overall, there is an extensive amount of fact and fantasy in the collection. Teachers, pupils, parents, public and of course the Folklore Commission deserve a sincere word of thanks for this fine body of literature which is presently stored at the library in Island House, Galway.

GURTEEN PROVERBS

Proverbs were highly regarded in former times. If a person could quote one in support of his or her viewpoint, then that assured victory in the debate because it was felt that a proverb was not to be contradicted. The following is a selection of sayings that our forefathers were fond of using:

Soft words butter no parsnips but they won't harden the heart of the cabbage either.
Ní hé lá na gaoithe lá na scolb- a windy day is not the day for thatching.
A wild goose never reared a tame gosling.

There was never an old slipper but there was an old stocking to match it.
Is binn béal ina thost. -a silent mouth is sweet to hear.
A man without learning and wearing fine clothes
Is like a gold ring on a pig's nose.

Hard upon hard makes a bad wall,
Soft upon soft makes none at all.

Aithníonn ciaróg ciaróg eile - One beetle recognises another.
Don't go to law with the landlord or too far for a wife.
The fox never found a better messenger than himself.
Tosach maith, leath na h-oibre- A good start is half the work done.

Ná lig do rún le bun an claí go seasfaidh tú ar a bhárr- Don't share your secret with the bottom of the fence until you stand on top of it.
Fágann an bó bás muna mbíonn féar ag fás. The cow dies unless the grass grows.

Show the fatted calf but not the thing that fattened him.
Briseann an dúchas thré shúile an chait - Nature breaks out through the eyes of the cat.

To every cow its calf; to every book its copy.
What can't be cured must be endured.
Díol an bó, ceannaigh na caoirigh, ach ná bí gan capall - Sell the cow, buy sheep but don't ever be without a horse.

Ní luaithe gaoth Márta ná intinn mná óige. - The mind of a young woman is faster than the March wind.
Nollag ghrianmhar a dhéanann reiligh líonmhar - A sunny Christmas makes a full churchyard.
Nuair atá an t-ól istigh, tá an ciall amuigh- When drink is in, sense is out.

Patience and perseverance would bring a snail to Jerusalem.
Nuair a bhíonn an bolg lán, is mian leis an gcnámh síneadh. -When the belly is full the bone likes to stretch.

Níl luibh ná leigheas in aghaidh an bháis.- No herb or cure can prevent death.
A poem ought to be well made at first, for there's many a one to spoil it afterwards.
Filleann an feall ar an bhfeallaire- Evil returns to the evil doer.
Poor men take to the sea; the rich to the mountains.

Pity the man who is wrong and poor as well.
Small strokes fell the tallest oaks..

Is olc an chú nach fiú fead a ligeann uirthí- It's a bad hound that's not worth whistling for.
Don't build the sty until the litter comes.

Níl Sathairn sa bhlian nach spailpeann an grían- There's no Saturday in the year that the sun doesn't shine (?) Old parishioners believed that no matter how bad the weather was that God would send an hour of sunshine to dry the priest's vestments.

Tar éis tuigtear gach beart- Every thing is understood with hindsight.
When all fruits fail, welcome haws.

After a gatherer comes a scatterer.
Bíonn gach duine lách go dtéann an bó sa gháirdín- Everyone is friendly until the cow breaks into the garden.
There are two tellings to every story.

Is leor friochtán amháin sa pharóiste- One frying pan in the parish is enough.
Truth stands when every thing else falls.
One pair of good soles is worth two pairs of leather uppers.

Is maith an t-anlann an t ochras- Hunger is a great sauce.
Pity him who makes his opinions a certainty.
Is fear rith maith ná droch sheasamh- a good run is better than a bad stand.
A heavy purse makes a light heart.

Nuair a chruann an tslat is deachar é a sníomh ina gad- When the stick hardens, it's difficult to bend.
Wind from the east is neither good for man or beast.
Tosach sláinte codladh, deire sláine osna- Tiredness(sleepiness) is a sign of good health, sighing

is a sign of bad health.

What's all the world to a man if his wife is a widow.
You can't put an old head on young shoulders.
Is mó cor a chuireann lá Earraigh de- There are many changes in a Spring day.
A whistling woman and a crowing hen will bring no luck to the house they are in.

Ní neart go cuir le chéile- There's no strength without unity.
Capall na h-oibre an bia. -Food is the work horse.
Tis as hard to see a woman cry, as a goose go barefoot.
Ní thagann ciall roimh aois. -Sense only comes with age.
The seeking of one thing will find another.
Bean mic 's mathair chéile, mar a bhéadh cat 's luch in aghaidh a chéile- The son's wife and mother-in-law are like a cat and mouse against one another.

The mason who strikes often is better than the one who strikes too hard.
Dómnach na Failme 's Sathairn Cásca, bíonn an ghrian ag rinnce le h-áthas. The Sun dances with joy on Palm Sunday and Easter Saturday.

Sow early and mow early.
Mol an óige agus tiocfaidh sé- Praise the youth and they will follow you.
Ní bhíonn tréan buan- Strength doesn't last forever.

CONUNDRUMS

What am I? We invite you to try and solve some of the teasers that troubled our ancestors in 1937.

(1) As I went up the boreen, I met my Auntie Noreen
     She had timber toes
     And iron nose
     And upon my word
     She would frighten the crows.

Answer - A gun.

(2) Head like a thimble,
     Tail like a rat
     You may guess forever
     But you'll never guess that.

Answer- A Pipe.

(3) A roomful, a houseful and couldn't catch a spoonful.

Answer Smoke

(4) Long and narrow, thin and tall,
     Many a man it caused to fall.

Answer a gun.

(5) The beginning of Eternity, the end of time and space,
    The beginning of every end and the end of every race.

Answer The letter E.

(6) Long legs, short thighs,
    Little head and no eyes.

Answer A tongs

(7) What is under the fire and over the fire and never touches the fire?

Answer A cake.

(8) As round as an apple,
    As plump as a ball,
    It climbs over churches,
    Steeples and all.

Answer The Sun.

(9) Sidelines, starlines,
    A hand across her face,
    The picture of the Devil
    Imprinted in its place.

Answer A cow with a púicín (blindfold) on her face.

(10) What goes up a ladder with its head down?

Answer -The nail in a man's boot.

CHAPTER SIX

SCHOOLS PRESENT AND PAST

Owen Donnelly Former Headmaster of Cloonkeenkerrill

CLONKEENKRRILL PAST PUPILS

THE PUPILS AND TEACHERS OF ST.KERRILL'S N.S.

MR. MALONEY AND THE SENIOR PUPILS

Mrs. Ward with 2nd., 3rd., and 4th., Classes.

Ms. Monaghan and the Junior Classes

SETTLING IN AT ST. KERRILL'S

By

Anne Ward

When we began in 1981, we had a new school with buildings and equipment second to none. We have constantly updated our resources and we are delighted to be able to say the same 23 years later. The teachers have worked hard to ensure that pupils receive the best education possible. Pupils from St. Kerrill's have won a number of scholarships and many of our past pupils have excelled in second and third level institutions. Matthew Roche won a major award in The Young Scientist of the Year Competition in 1988. Another local man, Martin Browne is the parent of a student who won The Group Award in 2000 and The Young Scientist of the Year Award in 2001.

We are fortunate to have a Parents Council and Board of Management whose members are always ready to assist us whenever help is needed. This type of cooperation is most evident in sports and extra curricular activities.

SPORT

Hurling, football and camogie have been well catered for and we have a fine sportsfield adjacent to the school. Dedicated trainers have given their services free of charge on a regular basis in order to help our pupils. The girls have competed in several competitions and reached the finals many times. The same is true for the boys. In 2003, the boys won the County Hurling and Football finals after a host of exciting games during which they gave teachers, parents and supporters many delightful exhibitions on the playing fields of County Galway. Our past pupils have featured in County hurling and football panels.

INDOOR ACTIVITIES

This parish has had a long association with Scór, the talent competition that is run by the G.A.A annually. Even though the competition is open to children under 17, pupils from St. Kerrill's School have won many victories over the past 20 years. They have brought glory and honour to the school and to Pearse's Club. There was never any shortage of competitors in the solo singing, ballad group, recitation, question time and novelty categories.

Our ballad groups always did very well and delighted audiences on many occasions with beautiful renditions of old Irish songs. They reached the All-Ireland final in the mid- nineties and secured several Connacht titles. The Novelty actors also did well and captured many county titles. Avril Flannery made it all the way to The All-Ireland Final in 1998. This was a magnificent achievement, given that she was only 11 years old and that it was her first time to enter. Avril got a tremendous reaction from the audiences all along the way.

Perhaps the most important thing of all was the fun that the competitors and their friends experienced at the various venues throughout the country - not to mention the mishaps and the amusing occurrences on and off stage.

Gurteen pupils have participated in many other contests since the school came into existence in the eighties. These include Pioneer Talent competitions and Credit Union functions. Our Quiz team got second place in the inter schools Question Time that was conducted by Athenry Credit Union in February 2004. We are proud of the fact that our ballad group won two All-Ireland CCD Finals. (This is similar to Scor but is run by An Cumann Camógaíochta)

Our aim has always been to help create well-rounded individuals and with your cooperation we will continue to strive to do this. We have every confidence that present and future students of the school will play a constructive part in community life wherever they happen to be.

The following ladies have been most helpful in organising sporting events for our students over the years: Aggie Burke, Brid Connaughton, Marian Flannery, Olive Hynes, Mary Kilkenny Mary Burke and Eileen O'Grady.

The men who helped us were: Michael Bodkin, Noel Burke Christy Connaughton, Michael Donnellan, Gerry Flannery, Brendan Hardiman, Martin McDonagh, John and Tom O'Grady, Paul and Paddy Ryan.

SCÓR NOVELTY ACT
L-R TOMÁS FLANNERY, LINDA DUANE, ALAN CORBETT, CYRIL DONNELLAN, NIAMH O'BRIEN.

1904 - 2004 - A CENTURY OF CHANGE

By

Michael J. Kilgannon

It is easy to take the daily routine of life for granted; habit can develop its own pattern and; imperceptibly, change steals up on us. It's been an eventful hundred years for the Gurteen community much change has been shared with the wider national scene. It has been said that the past hundred years have brought more change than the 1000 years before. Maybe yes or maybe no - every generation regards itself as unique and changes, which are part of our times, may to future generations appear much less significant.

But it has been a momentous 100 years; a century of enormous advances in so many different ways. The lives of Gurteen people in 1904 were dominated by the land system of landlord and tenant, which had been in place for over 200 years. And land was a critical issue in a society, which relied for its very survival on the produce and the income it could wrest from the soil.

The break up of that system was imminent in 1904 but the signs and symbols of landlordism were still only too visible - the houses and estates of French's, Monivea, Trench (Ashtown), Woodlawn, Blake's of Vermount, Daly's Dunsandle, Stacpooles Mount Hazel- all had a presence in Gurteen and appeared destined to be a force for many years to come. Within a generation this order was swept away through the campaign of the Land League and the National Independence Movement. Farming families rejoiced - rack-renting was over and the good times had arrived. But of course the problem with farming then as now was that while the farmer may increase production both quality and quantity, he is always at the mercy of market forces, over which he has little control. Adverse economic forces in agriculture through the 20's 30's 40's and 50's imposed their own pressures on the tillers of the soil throughout the Gurteen area as elsewhere.

Not until the arrival of the E.E.C. (EU nowadays) did farming take its rightful place and provide a worthwhile living. Now other trends are exerting their influence on the agricultural scene making farming today unrecognisable from what the people of Gurteen knew in 1904.

Living circumstances have taken a huge leap forward. The comforts of the modern home were unknown to Gurteen people a century ago. Then, overcrowding, no sanitation no electricity or water were the norm. Indeed it has taken most of the century to provide these basic services. Improvement in housing conditions came only gradually with a massive leap forward in our time. Gurteen housing today is on a par with the highest standards to be found anywhere; a quick drive around the parish will confirm this.

Medicine and health care were basic and scarce in 1904. The Poor Law Union system was still going strong and the workhouses of Mountbellew, Ballinasloe and Loughrea provided a rudimentary medical service, which was only available or availed of as a last resort. Photographs from 1904 give evidence of many people who have aged before their time. Dental or optical services were still in the future. By contrast modern nutrition and health services are light years removed from the conditions of 100 years ago. Unquestionably, we are the best-fed and nourished generation that the area has ever had. We still have our health problems today but they are in a different class to what people endured in 1904.

Education has been responsible for the greatest leap forward in the lives of Gurteen people. The majority of young people in the parish today reach 3rd level standard, which has opened doors to them undreamt of by past generations. Employment opportunities at home and aboard now beckon and an education/training climate exists which will ensure a future generation of Gurteen people will compete on equal terms with their counterparts elsewhere. The local St Kerrill's National School and the secondary schools within easy reach in Mountbellew, Castleblakeney, Athenry and New Inn provide the educational platform from which young people reach towards the career of their choosing.

Much of Gurteen life over the past 100 years has revolved around the Church. Indeed Gurteen has always been a close-knit society, with echoes of a monastic past at Cloonkeenkerrill. The parish has always had a strong sense of identity, which is a binding influence for its people.

So far I have pointed to the major areas of progress in the past 100 years. However, in common with other rural communities major changes are taking place. Gurteen has always been a place of neighbourliness, friendship and concern for one another. This is a valuable legacy worth preserving. The current trend of housing development gives some cause for concern. Many new rural dwellers are not integrating into the community. This life style of course puts demands on them which do not easily allow for getting to know neighbours or for involvement in local clubs and organisations whether they know it or not they are needed; we all need each other as the Irish proverb puts it "Ar scáth a chéile a mhaireann na daoine". Our future must address this issue.

A marvel of modern times is the ease with which people travel locally, nationally and internationally. For most Gurteen people in 1904 travel was confined to the locality or to the towns of Mountbellew, Athenry or Ballinasloe. Once in a while Galway featured- then only a small sized town. The bicycle, horse and trap or sidecar decided the limits resulting in little experience outside the home area. Marriages were mainly local with bride and groom living within a few miles of each other at the most. The train at Woodlawn or Attymon brought emigrants to Dun Laoghaire (Kingstown) or Cobh (Queenstown). Customs and accents had a local flavour nurtured by local practice. Our modern travel and means of communication have brought about a revolution in our life styles. Distance is no longer a problem. The world comes into our homes via radio, television, phone and Internet. For the most part all this is very good. I wonder how the Gurteen people of 1904 would have responded to it.

Self-sufficiency was a hallmark of the Gurteen of 1904. Home produce - vegetables, meat, potatoes, oaten meal were the staple diet of the time. Purchases were few and cash resources were carefully husbanded for major items like a family wedding, the dowry being a serious consideration for the daughter of the house. Or perhaps sending a son or daughter on their way to America or keeping a nest egg for the rainy day.
Today's cash economy, where all needs are purchased would appear very wasteful to our forebears. It is a different order now but who knows what changes lie in store for future generations.

ON A PERSONAL NOTE

I enjoyed my stint in Gurteen. When I began in St.Kerrill's National School I used peddle power to get there but before I left I owned a fully fledged 'horseless carriage'.
This was marvellous on wet mornings or if pupils had to be left home for any reason.
At one stage, over 40 children from Kinreask alone attended; the remainder included children from Killuane, Ballygreaney, Cloonkeenkerrill and Colemanstown. There was a weekly visit from the priest …Fr. Jack Egan, recently deceased, with occasional flying visits from the

Inspector who seemed more interested in getting a good bag of spuds to bring home with him! I often accompanied him to Kinreask where Paddy Kilkenny R.I.P. could always be relied on to provide both quality and quantity. At one point, over 60 children were on roll in Cloonkeenkerrill N.S. which exceeds the number that now attends St Kerrill's Central N.S. This is surprising when one considers that the new school caters for the entire Gurteen area.

MY FATHER'S DAY OUT IN GURTEEN

For many years before and after 1904 a Courthouse operated in Gurteen. Why it was located there in the first place I have no idea. It was not part of the status quo in places like Ballymacward, Fohenagh, New Inn or Kilconnell. My acquaintance with the Gurteen Courthouse is at second hand through a 1953 episode involving wireless licences. This area was electrified in 1953 and most people, including my parents, bought an electric radio. Almost before the radio had time to warm up in our kitchen an official from the Post Office in Ballinasloe called asking for a radio licence. The licence had not been purchased so in due course, a summons to Gurteen Court arrived. My father headed for Gurteen on the appointed day and, en route, met Christina Morris R.I.P. (Ballymacward) who had also received a summons for the same offence.

"By the way, Mr. Kilgannon, what is the Judge's name?" says Christina.
" I believe he is Justice Skinner," he told her.

"Goodness me, Mr Kilgannon," said Christina " I hope he doesn't skin us!"
He didn't. All fined 2s/6d with 1/= expenses.

How long Gurteen Courthouse survived after that momentous case I do not know!

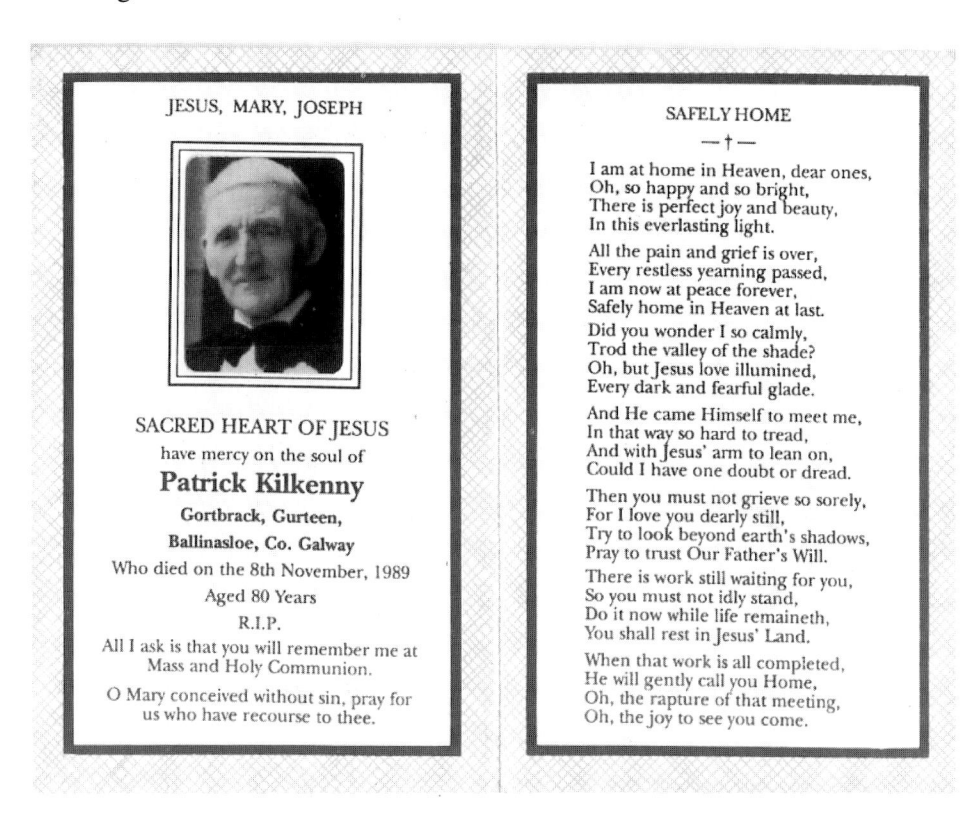

JESUS, MARY, JOSEPH

SACRED HEART OF JESUS
have mercy on the soul of
Patrick Kilkenny
Gortbrack, Gurteen,
Ballinasloe, Co. Galway
Who died on the 8th November, 1989
Aged 80 Years
R.I.P.
All I ask is that you will remember me at Mass and Holy Communion.

O Mary conceived without sin, pray for us who have recourse to thee.

SAFELY HOME
— † —

I am at home in Heaven, dear ones,
Oh, so happy and so bright,
There is perfect joy and beauty,
In this everlasting light.

All the pain and grief is over,
Every restless yearning passed,
I am now at peace forever,
Safely home in Heaven at last.

Did you wonder I so calmly,
Trod the valley of the shade?
Oh, but Jesus love illumined,
Every dark and fearful glade.

And He came Himself to meet me,
In that way so hard to tread,
And with Jesus' arm to lean on,
Could I have one doubt or dread.

Then you must not grieve so sorely,
For I love you dearly still,
Try to look beyond earth's shadows,
Pray to trust Our Father's Will.

There is work still waiting for you,
So you must not idly stand,
Do it now while life remaineth,
You shall rest in Jesus' Land.

When that work is all completed,
He will gently call you Home,
Oh, the rapture of that meeting,
Oh, the joy to see you come.

PADDY AND TERESA FINNERTY
(DAUGHTER OF OWEN DONNELLY)

THE FINNERTYS - L-R : MARTIN. ROSALEEN, NOEL
BACK: P.J.

THE BRODERICKS - MARY, SEAN AND GERARD

THE KELLY FAMILY, TAMPLE

KINREASK AND CLOONKEEN GIRLS
L-R : MARY BRIEN, GRETTA FLANNERY, KATHLEEN BRIEN,
EILEEN FLANNERY, P.J. FLANNERY, MARY FLANNERY,
LILY FLANNERY, BIDDY DEVANEY.

THE BRODERICK FAMILY & FRIENDS

MAUREEN & BRENDAN FINNERTY

CLOONKEEN BOYS
L-R   TOM LALLY, SONNY MELLODY, PADDY JOE DEVANEY, SEAN LALLY, THOMAS MELLODY, TIMOTHY DEVANEY

THE DEVANEY FAMILY
L-R   BIDDY, TIMMY, MATT, MIKIE, KITTY & MARY

STEPPING IT OUT -
BIDDY & MARY DEVANEY

MUSIC IN THE AIR
L-R :   MARY WARD, LILY
FINNERTY, MARY DEVANEY
AND EUGENE FINNERTY

COPING WITH CLASSES IN CLOONKEEN

By

John Corbett

My father often spoke of his school days in Labasheeda, Co. Clare. The teacher there was a Mr. Crowley. Crowley was very interested in his pupils and used to put them forward for various state examinations when they were in the senior classes. He was a cool customer and placed great emphasis on orthoepy and diction. For example when someone wasn't saying the word 'men' properly, he used to recite this rhyme:

> Mitty Matty
> Had a hin
> And she laid eggs
> For gintlemin.

Once when he asked a pupil why he had been absent the previous day, the latter replied:
'I had to go to the bull with Henry' (his father).
In my own time when a particular student was asked why he was late, he said:
'The bicycle had to go to Mass.'

MY OWN TIME

My first taste of school was at three and half. There was talk of a second teacher so pupils were urgently needed. Things began very well. The teacher's husband, Michael Cogavin, arrived in a horse and trap to bring us to school. To my young mind it must be something special if we were to be escorted there in a horse and trap. Alas it was short lived. Michael stopped calling for us and we were obliged to continue on 'Shank's Mare' like all the rest of the gang. This wasn't so bad however because we could share the journey with other students. We had just over a mile to go. The roads were rough and untarred then. We liked to walk on the grass margins or on top of the ditches and one of our favourite ambitions was to go barefoot. We envied those who were allowed to go unshod early in Spring. Our parents wouldn't listen when we asked to do the same so we had to be satisfied to wear shoes until May Day. For the first few days we had plenty of cuts and scars owing to the sharp stones that covered the potholes and of course there was always the danger of picking up a thorn or two along the way. The roads were gritty then and we would be covered in clouds of dust in warm weather whenever a car or lorry passed by but of course traffic was light so it didn't happen too often.

We weren't very fashion conscious then. Boys wore short pants and girls wore dresses just below the knee. Keeping shoes on us was probably quite a challenge for our parents. Old shoes were kept for as long as possible and the same was true for trousers. One boy's pants had been patched so often that it was almost impossible to trace the original material. Our clothes must have been strong because we didn't spare them when playing or fighting. As regards shoes, nearly everyone had a last and this was used often. Chunks of leather were bought and tacked on to the soles, usually by the local handyman (Tommy Broderick in our case). A double row of studs protected the soles and a steel tip was put on the heel of the shoe or boot. Sometimes goose grease was added to make the footwear waterproof. Shopkeepers prided themselves on the quality of their shoes. Wellingtons were scarce and boots were favoured as the next best thing. There is a story about a shopkeeper that met one of his customers a few months after selling him boots.

'Are those boots I sold you dry?' asked the shopkeeper.

'They must be,' replied the customer, 'Because anytime I walk near water, they take a good drink.

THE SCHOOL BUILDING

The school had two classrooms separated by a large hall. The windows were large and were high enough to prevent pupils from observing passers-by. The desks we had were plain but steady. We used chalk and square slates for writing at the beginning. Plasticene or 'marla' as it was called was plentiful. There was nothing we liked better than making little men and women or farm animals with the marla. We loved to take pieces of it and roll it in our palms. Things were even better when we had coloured marla to play with.

Later of course we had pens and pencils. The pen had a wooden handle and on to this slipped a metal holder containing a nib. These were dipped into inkwells inset in the desks and blotting paper was necessary in order to use them properly. Nibs sprained quickly through careless writing and through abuse. Often pens were used to spray pupils with ink or to create a smudge in a rival's copy. These were considered serious offences and inevitably led to the offender being caned, if caught. The cane was an ash stick obtained nearby. Usually it was a pupil who was sent to pull it and clever ones were able to doctor it in such a way as to prevent the teacher slapping too hard with it. Slapping rarely came on account of failure at lessons. It was reserved for misbehaviour and slaps were often earned justly by the culprits. Being late for class also meant a slapping. Again some of my worst memories were receiving 3 or 4 slaps on cold winter's mornings on account of being late for school. Excuses didn't cut any ice with the teacher. Mrs. Cogavin had an evenhanded approach to corporal punishment. I never remember her losing her temper and there were no 'pets.' Her own son received the same treatment as everyone else. Like most children we often dawdled on the way to or from school. In the evenings if we were late home, we would have to explain the reason to our parents. Home punishment wasn't as severe as the teacher's punishment. If we were very late we might be slapped with a strap across the legs. This was much better than being caned on the fingertips.

When I was in Infant's I had long, curly hair. One of the girls in the seat behind me used to take great delight in pulling it. I soon got tired of this treatment. At a later date I received unwelcome attention from a few of the senior boys. As a result my father sent a letter in which he threatened ' to remove my offspring from your academy unless this treatment ceases immediately.' The incident and the tone of my father's letter was a source of amusement for the class and for the neighbourhood for a long time.

Ink was manufactured in the classroom from some kind of powder and water. This mixture was used to clean blackboards too. It was black in colour but rather watery. The teacher used better quality ink from a bottle marked 'Quink'. Sheets of blotting paper were an essential part of school life. Fountain pens were a luxury reserved for affluent school goers in senior classes. Ballpoint pens hadn't yet appeared.

There were dry toilets at the end of the playground. There was a gate at the entrance of each and a door separated the cubicle from the urinal in the boys' toilet. There was a wooden seat which served us, situated a few feet over the cesspool. The toilets were attached to a high wall that separated boys' and girls' playground. There was strict segregation and if one was caught in the girls' section one was punished in the usual way. Despite this there were several incursions, especially by the boys who derived tremendous pleasure from chasing members of the opposite sex. The chases often began at the front of the school which was regarded as neutral ground; being available to both groups. Here also stood a large tank that supplied water to wash everyday wounds. Bruised knees were the most common injuries because of course the girls wore dresses and boys wore short trousers. Only when secondary school began did one transfer to long pants. Some senior pupils at primary school wore them too but these were the exception rather than the rule. Wearers were normally those who should have left but whose parents sent them during the winter or when farms weren't busy. These 'post grads' often were 17 or 18 years of age but were just a tiny minority of 'the scholars'. The majority left at 14 years and again it was only a minority who received second level education.

The playground in Cloonkeenkerrill was limited. The surface was a mixture of gravel and grass. The surface at the front of the school was of harder material and must have contained stone of some sort. There were thick walls all around the school about 4 or 5 feet high. Bushes and trees grew outside the wall on the girls' side but there were no trees at the wall on the boys' side. The field nearby had a large number of trees so these saved us from wind and weather. The school windows were big and too high for any young person to look in or out through them. A double gate between two sturdy pillars sealed our exit from the road. The view as one exited was poor but this didn't matter on account of the scarcity of vehicles. Horse and carts were the main traffic plus the occasional delivery van. Tractors were rare and any lorries that were there hardly ever passed us on the way to school. Most of them would have been taken up with turf drawing. Tommy Kilgannon's egg lorry was the exception.

GAMES

Hurling was not permitted at playtime. This ban may have been intended to protect pupils from injury or maybe it was meant to protect the large windows. There wasn't enough space in which to play hurling any way. When handball was being played, a blackboard was sometimes put in front of the end window for protection. Most of our games consisted of kicking a small ball in imitation of Gaelic football. We also had our own version of rugby. Rules were vague and variable. The idea being that when anyone got the ball all the rest brought the unfortunate individual down and jumped on top of him. The struggle continued thus until the victim released the ball or by some miracle managed to retain it until he crossed the designated line.

'Pot Hooks and Hangers' was played by boys and girls. Two people stood back to back. Each of them hooked arms with a partner. With backs pressed together, one raised the other off the ground. Then the other partner did the same. This kind of human see saw continued for as long as the parties desired.

OTHER GAMES

'Four Corner Fool' and various running games were played also. 'Buddy' was a favourite with the boys. This was a form of wrestling requiring a minimum of 4 persons. Each boy carried a player on his shoulder. The two on the shoulder wrestled and mauled one another until the player or carrier was knocked to the ground. As can be imagined the results were often inconclusive, with perhaps all 4 participants biting the dust simultaneously. Mud stained limbs and clothes invariably resulted from these contests. Surprisingly there were no serious injuries.

'Tig,' ie. Running after someone and tapping them on the back was also popular, 'London Bridge, was often played also. Two pupils made an arch with their hands and their playmates passed through it in procession. Relay races and 'catching' games were practised by boys and girls. Girls also tried out dancing steps although I think it was unlikely that they were in receipt of dancing lessons at the time.

There was a degree of rivalry between various villages. Before and after school there was good-natured slagging between them. Our rivals came from Kinreask. One would hear chants such as:

> *'Eggs and rashers for the Killuane Dashers;*
> *Hay and oats for the Kinreask goats.'*

The girls played 'Ring of Roses' but this was considered 'sissyish' by the boys.

I have forgotten most of the rhymes that we used to recite at playtime. One of them was:

> *Out of Hell, there's no redemption,*
> *When you go in you get the pension.*
> *Tupppence a day, working hard,*
> *Chasing the Devil around the yard.*

Then of course there was the well known one:

> *Admission free, you pay at the door,*
> *Bring your seat and sit on the floor.*

ON THE WAY HOME

Another distraction was the river, less than a mile from school. We loved to walk and splash in its waters especially on summer's evenings, even though some of the younger ones were probably afraid of water or of the minute quantity of fish that was to be found there. Wild garlic and watercress grew at the bridge near Daly's house and some of us sampled them even though we didn't particularly like them. The same applied to Roche's turnip pit. Here was added the element of danger because if one was caught, one was sure of an ear tweaking at least.

Vandalism didn't really exist among us. This may have to do with lack of opportunity rather than virtue on our part. There were no telephone poles or wires on our way home and no cars or tractors that could be tampered with either. Because the playground was small there was an irresistible temptation to use the large green field adjacent to it during playtime. This was strictly forbidden and offenders, if caught, received the maximum number of slaps. This was less of a deterrent than the risk of capture by the owner who didn't take kindly to his meadow being trampled on by a squadron of students.

FUEL

School fuel was provided by parents. Once a year each family was expected to deliver a cartload of turf which was housed in a small shed near the toilets. Schoolboys would help at the unloading, a job that was eagerly sought after; being a welcome break from lessons. In other cases I've heard of pupils carrying small quantities of turf by hand but I don't recall this happening in our case.

A RELIGIOUS OCCASION - CAN YOU IDENTIFY
THESE CLOONKEENKERRILL STUDENTS?

DRESSED IN STYLE
JOSEPH COPPINGER & TOM O'BRIEN

CLOONKEENKERRILL 1942-43

There was a huge open fire in Mrs. Cogavin's room. The mantelpiece was made of bricks, with a spacious ledge on top. There was a solid meshed fireguard in front of it. On cold days or if somebody got a bad wetting then those individuals were allowed to stand close to the fire. In such instances the fireguard would be opened and the pupils could stand on the platform inside.

THE RUANE FAMILY, COLEMANSTOWN
BACK ROW: L-R ANNIE, MARY, ROSE, TERESA, PADRAIC
FRONT ROW: VERA, FRANCES, KATHLEEN, MARGARET.

Generally, we sat in rows of double desks facing the teacher. She normally sat at a table unless she was writing at the blackboard. There were two presses in the corner for copies, books, and chalk. The ash cane was always kept near the press when not in use.

In the classroom we did the usual quota of Math's, English, Irish, History, Geography and Religion.

'Transcription ' was a big thing at the time. The teacher would draw neat lines on the blackboard and write a headline on it. We then tried to copy this as neatly and correctly as possible. Special 'headline' copies were needed for the exercise and these were available at school. In fact I believe all our stationery requirements were supplied at school.

LEARNING LATIN

When we reached a certain stage we were expected to volunteer for Mass serving. Some soutanes and surplices were available in church but one was more or less expected to have a soutane for oneself at least. These were white in colour and were spotless. Mass was in Latin and we used school time to learn off the responses which were more extensive then than now. We derived extra amusement from converting the responses into homemade words that bore no relation to their real meaning. For example:

Ad Deum qui latificat juven tutum meum' was converted to something like 'Laffey's cat, scoot him, shoot him, maim him'.

Miss Cloonan was surprised to learn that even after several weeks study our knowledge of Latin was close to nil. In spite of this most of us were able to 'parrot' the responses correctly. We weren't really interested in finding out about the actual meaning of the liturgy and we were satisfied if we could get through Mass without making fools of ourselves.

CHURCH GOING

In the chapel novice servers were nervous of tripping on the long surplices, which they had to wear. Another difficulty was to ring the bell at the proper time. This was more difficult than you would think because at that time the priest faced the altar and had his back to the congregation and the servers most of the time. Father Sheils had taken over the curacy when I started serving and tension was less than it had been in Father O'Reilly's time. There was something akin to a major scandal when one of the servers (Mikey Devaney, I think it was), let the cruets fall one Sunday. A telling off from priest and teacher would be administered to offenders for misdemeanours of this kind and these were sufficiently stern to prevent repetition in future. In addition one could expect a tongue lashing from one's parents plus ridicule from one's schoolmates.

The church was a very public place and misconduct of any kind would not be tolerated there. This knowledge added to the strain when one was trying to stop laughing at funny incidents that happened during Mass. Once Francis Flaherty, who was in the same seat as me, let the kneeler down with a bang. (The kneelers were made of timber and were without cushions). I don't know which of us began to laugh first but we both suffered from the giggles for the remainder of the service. Laughing in such circumstances was not enjoyable, I can assure you.

A regular source of amusement in our parish was the late Mary Finn. She generally arrived when most of the congregation had been seated. She wore a dark beret, white coat and wellingtons. She would walk down the main aisle, genuflect before the altar and then cross over to the women's aisle on the left. She would kneel quietly for a while and then at a particularly quiet time during the ceremony, without fail, she would give three loud sneezes. It is difficult to say whether it was the sneezing itself or the anticipation of it that amused us most. Apart from winter coughs or playful children there were few things to distract us after Mary's passing.

Communion and Confirmation were big events in our lives. Bishop Dignan came to Cloonkeenkerrill School to assess us personally prior to Confirmation. There were weeks of anxiety before he came, wondering if you would be able to answer his questions properly. It is difficult to say whether it was ourselves or the teachers that worried most about this problem. Confirmation veterans tried to make things worse by stressing the 'mighty wallop' that the Bishop was going to deliver on one's jaw. Girls wore white dresses and veils for both Communion and Confirmation and boys dressed in suits that were specially bought for the events. Confirmation always took place in Ballymacward then and one could relax and enjoy one self when the church services were over. I think it's safe to assume that the suits that were bought for Confirmation lasted until one was ready for long pants and had left the national school behind.

THE THINGS WE LEARNED

In History we learned about ancient tribes such as the Fir Bolgs Tuatha De Dannan, the Picts, Milesians and Celts. We also learned about the Salmon of Knowledge that Fionn McCumhall tasted while he was supposed to be minding it for Finegus. Oisin's return from Tír na n-óg enthralled us as did the Story of The Children Of Lir. Two stories from our English book intrigued me. One was about Labhras Loingsigh who had horse's ears and the other concerned a surly porter who was punished for his rudeness by being turned into a door knocker.

One of the Irish poems that appealed most to me was:
An Gleann inar Tógadh Mé.

One hero that we rated highly was Brian Ború who defeated the Danes in the never to be forgotten Good Friday at The Battle of Clontarf in 1014. Another popular figure was Roderick O'Connor, the last High King of Ireland. Of course we weren't told how ineffective he was as a ruler or military man. The history books omitted the fact that the brutal O'Ruairc of Breifne had severely ill-treated his wife Dervorgilla, thus causing her to ask another tyrant, Dermot Mc Murrough, for help. I am not suggesting that our teachers were to blame for these omissions. However, I was always somewhat surprised that faction fights weren't mentioned in primary or in secondary school at that time. We continued on our way happy in the belief that we were still close to being saints and scholars and that nearly all our ills were due to the cruelty and treachery of our nearest neighbours, The British.

In Geography we learned the names of the principal rivers and mountains. We also were expected to know the names of the main towns in each county.

Our Irish vocabulary was limited but we got a good grounding in grammar from both teachers. We were expected to pass The Primary Certificate Examination before leaving national school. As well as written work we also did a good deal of mental arithmetic. I left for secondary school before I was twelve and up to then we had not done geometry or algebra.

The only books we read were textbooks. There was no library and most households had only a limited selection of reading material. Very few had radios and those who had used them sparingly. Two batteries were needed; a 'wet' battery and a 'dry 'one. A dry battery lasted six months on average but wet ones had to be charged regularly and one was lucky to get one month per charge from it. Sunday games with Micheál O'h Éithir were very popular and because we were one of the few families to have a radio, crowds used to come to listen to the commentaries. (This was when I first sampled 'fags'; my reward for admitting G.A.A. fans while my parents were absent)

MUSIC

We also had a gramophone and listening to it was a great treat as far as we were concerned. (John McCormack, The Flanagans, The McNultys and The Moate Ceili Band were among our collection). The needles were a nuisance. They had to be changed very often. If this wasn't done the quality of reproduction became very bad and damage was done to the records also. The gramophone had to be wound up and care had to be taken not to wind it too tightly. On the other hand if sufficient winding wasn't done, the music was liable to end with a slow growl in mid-record. In some cases gramophones were used to provide music for dancing but this didn't happen in our house because my parents played the concertina and fiddle. There were plenty of local musicians who came to visit us also. My sister and myself were often put to bed, despite our protests, before some of the music sessions ended.

All in all school was a happy time. Our teachers were helpful and we had good fun even though we didn't take them or their admonitions too seriously.

SMILING FACES
(RUANES) BACK ROW: PADRAIC, TERESA, FRONT ROW: VERA & ANNIE

FROM KINREASK TO CLOONKEEN

By

Eileen Flannery

I am delighted to have an opportunity of meeting my classmates again. Over the years I've often wondered what became of them. I have happy memories of my schooldays and I remember our teachers, Mrs. Cogavin, R.I.P. and Miss Cloonan with fondness. They were good, kind people who were concerned not just with our education, but also with our well-being. I think of the bottles of cocoa/tea lined up before the fire, to be warmed for lunch. Our coats that got wet on the way to school were dried in the same manner.

The heating system was dependent on a load of turf from each family once a year. It was a great day when Dad would arrive with a load of turf as we were usually allowed to go home with him on the horse and cart. We would try to coax Dad to come as early as possible.

Cloonkeenkerrill was three miles from our house so we had a six-mile walk each day. But 'by the Grace of God,' we survived.

MORE SMILING FACES
THE FINN FAMILY, KINREASK

JIMMY KELLY WITH MARY, UNA & VINCENT

KATHLEEN DEMPSEY AND HER DAUGHTER CHRISSIE

JIM DWYER'S WEDDING

OUR TEACHERS

MRS. BRIDE COGAVIN

Mrs. Cogavin, who lived in Ballyglass, was the principal in Clonkeenkerrill from the 1940's until her retirement. Occasionally her husband brought her to school in the horse and trap but she cycled the three miles plus to school on most days. She was gentle and even-tempered. I am told that she did lose her cool on occasions but I never remember this happening. Slaps from Mrs. Cogavin were for misbehaviour and for being late for school. Nobody was exempt and she ensured that her son Micheál and her relatives received the same treatment as the rest of us. There was a large mesh guard in front of the fireplace and we were not allowed to stand inside of this. However, when the weather was bad, Mrs. Cogavin saw to it that we got a chance to stand close to the fire to warm ourselves.

She was a neat writer and did her best to get us to follow her example. She used to draw headlines on the blackboard and we were encouraged to transcribe them onto our copies, not always with the results that her efforts merited, I must add. She often said that we had 'the wrong end of the stick,' when we failed to understand the point that she was making. When our attention lapsed, she reminded us that, 'You can't whistle and chew meal' and that our lack of knowledge was, 'your own funeral.'

Religious Doctrine was important at the time and pupils were expected to know the answers in the long Catechism 'by heart.' Even though the meanings often eluded us, the lists of questions, and more especially the answers, certainly added substance to our vocabularies.

In Maths she taught us tables and helped us with mental arithmetic. She had a liking for English and History and gave us a good grounding on those subjects. We learned about the main towns in each county in Geography. She also expected us to be familiar with the largest rivers and mountains in Ireland.

She was a dedicated teacher who rarely missed school. She kept the classroom tidy and she seemed to cope effortlessly with the task of running the school. She lived to an advanced age and willed her body to be donated to scientific researchers after her death.

SHEILA CLOONAN-BELLEW

Sheila Cloonan also began teaching in the early forties. She was a young, attractive teacher bristling with new ideas and determined to get us to share in her enthusiasm. It must be said that our response didn't always live up to her expectations. Sheila was proficient in Irish and was ready to share her expertise with the senior pupils. When we began to serve Mass she tried to teach us the meaning of the responses but our indifference to Latin soon became evident and she eventually abandoned the idea.

SHEILA BELLEW WITH JOHN CLOONAN, NOEL TREACY AND MICK BELLEW

She was interested in physical education and

did her best to get us to acquire good posture. She engaged in Drama and performed well on stage. Sheila was full of vigour and often became impatient with our apathetic approach to life. She enjoyed music and dancing and supported the regular functions that took place locally.

Sheila enjoyed teaching and taught in a number of schools after leaving Clonkeenkerrill. In fact she acted as substitute teacher in the new school in Gurteen a few years ago. She is au fait with current educational developments and willingly shares her ideas with all comers. Sheila is an extremely interesting person and is ready to help whenever her assistance is required. She takes great interest in her former students and one of her greatest delights is to have them share the news of their good fortune with her. She is still hale and hearty and enjoys a singsong and a bit of fun. Her former pupils will be looking forward to her company in May.

CHAPTER SEVEN

SAINTS AMONG SINNERS

THE TRUE IDENTITY OF
SAINT KERRILL OF CLONKEENKERRILL

By

Joseph Mannion

The people of the Clonkeenkerril area have had a long and lasting relationship with St. Kerrill, their patron saint. Although most people are unaware of it, this association began in the fifth century in the time of St. Patrick. It has therefore spanned more than fifteen centuries and judging by the depth of the devotion which still exists for this holy man, is set to continue for many more.

The martyrologies or calendars of saints list the names and feastdays of many Irish saints who lived during the early Christian period. The Irish equivalents of names such as Brigid, Brendan, Kieran, Kerrill, Cuan, Benen, etc. were in common use throughout the length and breadth of the country. The compilers of the various martyrologies were faced with enormous difficulties when the festivals of two or more holy persons bearing the same name were to be recorded. This is hardly surprising given the fact that when the earliest of these calendars was compiled, more than three hundred years had elapsed since the time of St. Patrick. Due allowance must also be made for the very poor methods of travel and communication which existed during the early Christian period. Indeed it has been said of the compilers that they possessed 'but a hazy notion of the early history of Irish Christianity'. We must therefore view the details recorded about our early saints with a degree of caution and where possible, information contained in other records should always be taken into consideration when studying the life of any saint.

Confusion of details regarding saints with similar names is quite common. A mistake of this kind has been made concerning St. Cuan of Ahascragh in the seventeenth-century Martyrology of Donegal. At 15 October, the feastday which has been celebrated at Ahascragh in honour of St. Cuan for many centuries, there is a note suggesting that this was the festival of St. Cuan of Cluain-mór which is thought to refer to Cluain-mór-Maedóg in Leinster. Also worth noting at this point is the case of St. Benen, son of Lugni, of Kilbennan, near Tuam who, since the beginning of the ninth century, has been repeatedly confused with St. Benen, son of Sesenen, St. Patrick's successor at Armagh.

Similarly with St. Kerrill of Clonkeenkerrill whose festival on 13 June was first recorded about A.D. 800 in the Martyrology of Tallaght. Clearly this day had been celebrated at Clonkeenkerrill in honour of St. Kerrill - or Caireall mac Curnain as he was then known - since the time of his death some three hundred years earlier. However, when his feast day was being noted, Caireall mac Curnain was mistaken for a later saint called Caireall mac Nessain who had lived in the seventh century. This resulted in the feast day being incorrectly recorded and the resulting entry reads: 'Carilla i Tír Ross', and in the accompanying notes we find: 'Cairell in Tír Rois'.

The ninth-century Martyrology of Oengus the Culdee is believed to have been based on the Martyrology of Tallaght. In the notes attached to this slightly later work the entry at 13 June also reads: 'Cairell in Tír rois'. In the same notes there are a number of entries which refer to saints who, like St. Kerrill of Clonkeenkerrill, lived and laboured in the former kingdom of Sodhan in east Galway. For example the feast day of St. Modiúit, founder of an early church at Cill

Modhiúit, now Killamude in Ballymacward parish, is noted at 12 February while the festival of St. Conainne of Cell Conainne, now Kilconnell, is entered at 8 March. It is obvious from these entries and the previous one at 13 June that the compilers of the Martyrology of Oengus the Culdee were aware that Tír Rois and Sodhan were different places. In fact it is stated in the index to this work that Sodhan was in Co. Galway while Tír Rois was in Co. Monaghan. Since Cluain Caoin Cairill is known to have been located in Sodhan, it follows that the notice at 13 June does not refer to St. Kerrill of Clonkeenkerrill.

It is to be regretted that this error which was first made in the Martyrology of Tallaght was repeated by many later writers in their accounts of the lives of the Irish saints. This has led to the unfortunate situation where people who consult these works under 13 June seeking information about St. Kerrill of Clonkeenkerrill are completely misled. As a result, people in the Clonkeenkerrill area have been repeatedly informed over the years that their patron saint was born in Co. Donegal and that he was a nephew of St. Colmcille and the son of the king of Ossory. They have also been told that he worked on the mission fields of Scotland with his uncle before returning to his native country. Undoubtedly this information is incorrect since St. Kerrill of Clonkeenkerrill belonged to the fifth century and the details just mentioned refer to the seventh-century saint who bore a similar name. The misinformation surrounding St. Kerrill's identity is clearly the result of the confusion which has taken place ever since his festival was incorrectly recorded at the beginning of the ninth century.

There is a very important manuscript of medieval date in the Library of the Royal Irish Academy in Dublin which contains invaluable information about St. Kerrill of Clonkeenkerrill. The details contained in this document establish his true identity and the period and place in which he lived. From the text it is clear that it was written by someone living in the Clonkeenkerrill area. The writer would therefore have been in an ideal position to be familiar with St. Kerrill's background and his former importance as an early saint. We discover that St. Kerrill's original name was Caireall mac Curnain and that his church at Cluain Caoin Cairill was located in Sodhan - an early Celtic kingdom in east Galway. This ancient territory stretched from the Clare river in the west to the Suck river in the east and from the Shiven River at Mountbellew in the north to the Raford river south of Kiltullagh. We also learn from his genealogy that he belonged to the Sogain of Connacht - the early Celtic race of people who inhabited this kingdom.

Writing in the seventeenth century, the Franciscan priest Fr. John Colgan in his Acta Sanctorum Hiberniae - an account of the lives of the Irish saints - tells us that St. Kerrill was a contemporary and disciple of St. Patrick. As such, he would have belonged to the 'First Order of Saints'. We are told that he was consecrated a bishop by St. Patrick and initially placed over a church at Tawnagh in Co. Sligo. He is also listed among the disciples of St. Benen of Kilbennan, near Tuam, another contemporary of St. Patrick.

According to tradition St. Patrick introduced Christianity to Sodhan and is particularly associated with the western parts of this territory. Here he established churches at Tobar Phádraic in the townland of Corrafaireen in Abbert/Monivea parish and at Cill Eascrach in the townland of Patch in Moylough parish. He is also associated with other places including the hill of Knockroe where he spent a night in prayer and a number of holy wells in the area are dedicated to him.

In the manuscript mentioned above we are told that St. Kerrill was known as 'the second Patrick' of the old territory of Sodhan. We also learn that 'Patrick himself did not consecrate any place he knew Caireall was to consecrate'. It may be inferred from this that St. Patrick reserved part of the kingdom of Sodhan for St. Kerrill to evangelise. St. Kerrill established his principal church at

Cluain Caoin Cairill, 'the delightful meadow of Kerrill', but he is also credited with having founded a church at Cill Choirill, 'the church of Kerrill', now written as Kilgerrill. Since these two early churches were in the eastern half of Sodhan and Christianity had already been introduced into the western parts by St. Patrick himself, the eastern portion is likely to represent the area which he assigned to St. Kerrill to convert. Having thus continued the work of evangelisation which St. Patrick had already begun in Sodhan, St. Kerrill came to be regarded as 'the second Patrick' amongst his Sogain kinsmen.

A tradition recorded in the Kilgerrill area claims that St. Kerrill and the neighbouring missionary St. Connell had a dispute over ecclesiastical territory. On account of this St. Kerrill is believed to have abandoned his church at Kilgerrill. The parcel of land attached to this early foundation was known as 'the quarter of Kill Goirill' and according to the thirteenth-century Registry of Clonmacnois, was granted to the monks there about A.D. 600. The fact that this church land was so named at the end of the sixth century automatically rules out Caireall mac Nessain, the seventh-century saint, as the founder of the early church here since the grant in question was made before his time. It is also worth noting that the traditional rivalry between St. Kerrill and St. Connell over church territory could not have involved Caireall mac Nessain because St. Connell, like St. Kerrill of Clonkeenkerrill, was a disciple of St. Patrick and therefore belonged to the fifth century.

A reference to the tribute or church dues which were at one time paid to St. Patrick and St. Kerrill from the tribes of east Galway appears in the fifteenth-century Book of Lecan. From the details contained in this work it is clear that in the early stages of Christianity, the tribute from this area was shared between St. Patrick and St. Kerrill. In later times all of the dues were paid to St. Kerrill's successors at Cluain Caoin Cairill. This documentary evidence is of considerable historical value and although not recorded until perhaps the eleventh century, nevertheless, it confirms that both St. Patrick and St. Kerrill worked as missionaries in the east Galway area. It also recalls their close involvement with each other and indicates that both were patron saints of the Sogain people.

The true identity of St. Kerrill of Clonkeenkerrill is firmly established by the details contained in the various documents that have been discussed in this article. We have seen that he belonged to the Sogain of Connacht and was therefore a native of east Galway. He was a contemporary and disciple of St. Patrick and St. Benen and as such, lived in the fifth century. Having been consecrated a bishop, he continued to spread the Christian message and nurture the infant church which St. Patrick had introduced into his native kingdom of Sodhan. This led to him being called 'the second Patrick' - a title which reflects his very high standing among our early Irish evangelists. He founded churches at Clonkeenkerrill and Kilgerrill and the tribute from the inhabitants of east Galway was divided between himself and St. Patrick as patron saints of Sodhan.

When we consider the great devotion which the people of the Clonkeenkerrill area still have for their patron saint and their continuing interest in his life and legends, it is clear that St. Kerrill's influence on the Christian lives of the people of east Galway which began in the fifth century is set to continue for many years to come.

ECHOES OF MY SCHOOLDAYS

By

Mary(Sr.Vera) Ruane

Memories come drifting into my mind of my Cloonkeenkerrill schooldays in the 1940's and 50's, an era in which the established way of life seems primitive in comparison to todays high -tech standards.

Dotting the landscape of my mind in kaleidoscopic fashion, are vivid images of classmates, teachers, books, jotters, inkwells, games, annual visitations by doctors, lavatories, 'the stick,' and the process of learning the basics of reading, writing and arithmetic. Sewing and knitting classes were held on a weekly basis, to the chagrin of some. Once, I remember instructing a friend on how to break her sewing needle when she whispered that she was not happy about the task in hand. Luckily, she escaped with just a scolding after the teacher heard the needle snap! Occasionally, laughter was stifled at the less than erudite answers given by students.
'What is an owl?' the teacher asked a certain girl. Without hesitation the girl replied:
'A lad that would pick the eyes out of you'.

During cold, damp winter's mornings, fires were lit in both classrooms after coals were collected from a friendly neighbour. Later, bottles of tea and milk would vie with each other for front row places by the fire, in order to be heated in time for lunch.

Memorising the catechism questions and answers in preparation for First Holy Communion and Confirmation was a daunting task. Later the parish priest would visit and, sensing the apprehension of the class, generally confined himself to asking the most elementary questions in the book.

To this day the word 'nightingale' evokes humorous memories! During singing classes, after the tuning fork sent forth its tone, each student was asked to reproduce the equivalent sound. When this had been done we were assigned to one of two groups- the nightingales or the crows. The crows were usually dispatched to a corner in the back of the classroom to be impressed by the nightingales or at least to listen to their singing. The crows had much more fun. I know because I was one of them, since the nightingales always flew over my nest.

I savour these precious memories and would not exchange them for any experiences I might have had in a different time and place.

AT HOME AND AWAY

By

Father Vincent Lawless

I was appointed to Gurteen Parish in July 1994. I had spent the previous 4 years in Killoran. Before that I spent 33 years in Nigeria.

My grandfather, Jack Walsh was born in Laragh, Attymon. His father was a herd for the
Daly Family in the Gurteen area. His fondness for drink got him transferred to Laragh
His brother took over as herd in Gurteen. My mother, his granddaughter, lived in Laragh.

My grandfather, John Lawless from Killimordaly, married Mary Haverty. Mary died and he married Kate Carroll from Gurteen. My uncle James (Seamus), fondly known as 'Ghandi', went to live with the Carrolls and he inherited their house and farm. He went to England and the farm was sold. The Carrolls attended Tample School. I met one of the Carroll Family in Chicago in 1964 and he told me that he worked in the building of The Washington Memorial.

I was ordained in 1956. I was the first priest to be ordained in the parish of Kilconieran. Some others followed after me.

ON AFRICAN SOIL

I arrived in Nigeria in October 1957. It took two weeks to get there. They were probably the best weeks of my life. The food on board the ship was wonderful. Can you believe that 30 pints of beer cost just £1? What a pity I wasn't drinking at that time!

My first appointment was to the Prefecture of Kaduna. It is now the Archdiocese of Kaduna. It was twice the size of Ireland. My first parish was called Gawu. It was a time of great change. Those before me had sown the seed and it was my task to ensure that the work which they had begun would continue. Independence was around the corner and when it was achieved everybody wanted to send their children to school. Prior to this only the disabled were given an education: i.e. the weak and the partially sighted. Now these were the ones that were getting employment. Work was plentiful because of the large number of schools that had to be built.

The family unit was very strong in Nigeria. Parents, grandparents, uncles, aunts and siblings were all part of the same family. Each adult was expected to take care of one or two children from the extended family. As well as supporting your own children, you could find yourself paying school fees for your brother's or sister's offspring also. If you cared for a girl while she was being educated, you would be rewarded later with a substantial portion of her dowry when she married. Education was highly rated by the people of Nigeria. Each village or group of villages would approach a priest and ask him to provide a school for them. Often people from remote districts located more than 20 miles from a main road would expect to have a school in their area. This meant carrying cement, timber and zinc sheeting all the way to the school site. Women carried materials on their heads and the men transported their loads on heads and shoulders. A commitment of three to six years was essential if the work was to be completed. The length of time depended on the size of the building and the number of school going children. Bricks were made from mud. These were mixed with grass and water before being baked in the sun. They were almost as strong as cement blocks.

When classrooms became available, Nigerians began to get interested in adult education. Previously the majority of them were illiterate but as the schools developed, so did a strong desire on their part to be able to read and write.

THE DIFFERENCE BETWEEN THE OLD AND THE NEW

As the school progressed, our church began to blossom. I was struck by the contrast between the old church of St. Patrick in Ireland and the new church in Nigeria. You would never have a Mass or service without readers. Men and women vied with one another for this task. The choir used to practice at least twice a week. Bigger churches often had two choirs. What a difference between it and Ireland! Is it any wonder that so many priests are anxious to return to the missions after having visited this country? The mission churches are fully alive whereas Mass goers here lack enthusiasm and are slow to organise choirs and readers or to engage in liturgical activity.

In Ireland we celebrate wedding and birthday anniversaries but in Africa they take things a step further. I was only in Nigeria for a short time when a man came to me with a chicken under his arm. He told he was celebrating his baptism. I had baptised him the previous year. This was the first time I heard of anyone celebrating his or her baptism. I think it's unlikely that any such celebration will take place in my own parish or in the parish of Gurteen in the foreseeable future. Having said that, I look forward to meeting all my former parishioners for our big celebration next May.

MISSION TO LIBERIA

By

Fr. Gerry Sweeney

Irish soldiers, many of them from the Western Command are now working with the U.N Peace Force in Liberia. They play a key role in returning Liberia to the rule of law and ridding the country of lawlessness. They are based a few miles outside the capital Monrovia and from that safe base, they protect patrols up country and enable U.N. reinforcements to take place in an orderly manner. On the Keith Finnegan Show last week I enjoyed the interview with one of the Personnel Officers as he mentioned names and places that were very familiar to me.

Irish S.M.A. missionaries first went to Liberia early last century and have continued working there up to the present. I went to Liberia in 1975. At that time the country was peaceful and prosperous and our missionary work went ahead very rapidly. Then in 1980 the army revolted. The President and many of his ministers took control of the country. They lived off the fat of the land and in ten years had brought the country to ruin. Coups and rebellions became common place and eventually they escalated into full-blown civil war. Since 1989 there has been no effective central Government and destruction, poverty and hunger are widespread. Gangs took over everywhere and the lives of ordinary people were threatened.

There is an African proverb which says, "When elephants fight, it's the grass that suffers'. Most of the suffering caused by the warring factions in Liberia was borne by the ordinary people who had to flee their homes and farms as the fighting spread over the countryside.

The Catholic Church in Liberia played a leading part in acquiring and distributing aid via a network of churches, schools and hospitals. There was extensive damage to buildings and property. However the faith of the people is strong and I've no doubt that they will rebuild their lives and their communities in the not too distant future.

The number of S.M.A. missionaries is greatly reduced but the local church is well established. There are three dioceses with their own bishops and priests and when peace is restored, the church will emerge stronger than ever. Kpakala Francis has been a great leader during the troubled years and has received international recognition. It is my fervent hope that the U.N. troops complete the task of peace keeping and are able to open the way for the great Liberian people to get on with their lives.

My time in Liberia is over but it was a great experience. I am happy to succeed Fr. Lawless in Gurteen.

I hope that our celebration of the reunion of Cloonkeenkerrill, Shanballard and Tample past pupils will be a success and that the event will mark a special period in our lives.

MY STAY IN GURTEEN

By

Fr. Joe Clarke

Congratulations to all who are involved in organising this occasion. It is nice to get together for a happy event and to remember people and incidents.

It is true that we remember our first school days very well. The teacher and his/her skills, where we sat, our friends who may still be close, the subjects we dreaded and maybe the fights we got into.

I have a clear memory of having a brown bread sandwich to eat at lunch. We ate inside. The teacher would usually eat at the top of the class and he would have something sweet to finish up. It may have been small but it looked very large from where I sat.

In the late 70's Cloonkeen was already closed and Shanballard and Tample were waiting for the new school to be completed. The new school was a huge improvement in that it had extensive facilities. As far as I know it cost £30,000 per classroom to build.

My memory of those schools goes back less than 30 years. The changes in education and also in the community since that have been profound.

I wish well to all who are coming together to celebrate this occasion.

FR. JOE CLARKE AND MICHAEL BLEHEIN

PUNISHED FOR PRAYING
AN EXTRACT FROM AN PUNANN ÁRSA

By

Martin Finnerty

A local man, Martin Glynn, was one day passing the local charter school about his business. The Angelus bell rang and a boy, who was apparently not long in the school, took off his little cap to pray in answer to the call. A schoolmaster who observed the boy so doing walked over to the youthful offender and knocked the poor lad flat to the ground. Glynn's blood boiled; he jumped over the wall and gave the schoolmaster the bare knuckles and upended him.

Such was a most serious offence in those days. The schoolmaster was not acquainted with his assailant but gave such a description as led to the pursuit of Glynn.

A search followed for the apprehension of Glynn who was forced to avoid the penalty, and unsuccessful attempts had been made for his arrest over a long period. A Mr. French of Monivea Castle, who was like those of his class, the local Justice of the Peace, advised the friends of Glynn to get him to surrender. Glynn did so, and when brought before the local court, this Mr. French who presided at the court and was apparently sympathetic, refused informations on the grounds that the schoolmaster was unable to identify the defendant as his assailant. Some time afterwards Glynn met this Mr. French on the road and acknowledged his indebtedness for simple justice.
'Well,' said Mr. French, 'To tell the truth, was it you assaulted the schoolmaster?'
'Well, your Honour,' said Glynn, 'I will tell yourself no lie. It was me.'
'More power to you,' said Mr. French, 'You are a good man.'

CHAPTER EIGHT

LIGHT ENTERTAINMENT

A BURNING DESIRE TO ESCAPE

By

JOHN KENNY

Mrs. Duffy was principal when I was going to Shanballard School. Another teacher we had was a Mr. Clery from Clare who taught us for a while before Mr. Murphy came.
Most of us weren't interested in lessons and by the time we got into Seniors, we decided that we'd had enough. Four or five us (John Dooley, John Scarry, Jim Cunnife and myself. I'm not sure of the names of the other conspirators.) had a meeting and came to the conclusion that the school should be burned down. We figured the best way of doing this was to put the lunch wrapping papers into the fire when nobody was looking. We thought they would be sucked up the chimney and that they would start a blaze that would engulf the entire building.

We tried the papers but our plan didn't work. Our next ploy was to stay away from school, unknown to our parents. We set off as usual next day but when we had gone some distance, we stopped. Younger pupils that had been accompanying us went to class as usual. The teacher sent large numbers of students to look for us when the younger students told her what we'd done. She sent them and others to fetch us. When we saw the posse approaching we hid under a bridge. We ignored the appeal of the students to return to base and at this point we headed for the hills in order to prevent our capture. Mrs. Duffy wrote letters to our parents which she gave the children to deliver but we took them from the younger ones on the way home and destroyed them.

This hide and go seek went on for three or four days but we were forced to conform eventually. The teacher slapped us and gave us a severe dressing down. This ended our hope of escape from the classroom.

We had a few minor 'dodges' that allowed us some relief. Two of us used to ask to go to the toilet in close succession. We would then play games of handball against the gable end of the school. The games were of short duration and things went well for a while. Unfortunately a game lasted longer than usual one day and a dispute arose about the final score. While this was going on the teacher suddenly appeared. There were no further games of handball after that.

We regarded lunchtime hurling as another escape route. The teams were chosen on a geographical basis and there was always a good deal of rivalry between Gurteen and Killimordaly students. The matches were played on a pitch some distance away from the school. Sometimes there would be disputes about the scores resulting in after match affrays. Because of these we tended to ignore the teacher's whistle as she blew to summon us to class. We hardly ever returned on time and we would receive several slaps for being late. I forgot to mention that we spent more time refreshing ourselves, drinking stagnant water from a nearby well. (I often wondered since how none of us contracted some serious disease) The owner of the field where we played our matches often came in to complain about us to the teacher. For a start we didn't have his permission to use it and of course we didn't worry unduly about knocking stones off walls or leaving gaps in fences. This didn't help our case at all and Mrs. Duffy threatened to put a total ban on hurling altogether. Luckily, she never carried out this threat.

It was always a relief when someone delivered a load of turf. At the time there was only a narrow gate in front of the school so this meant that loads would be tipped on the roadside. We would be asked to carry the sods into the cloakroom in our hands. When the teacher wasn't looking we would bring the turf out again so that a pair of sods might have been brought in and out several times before being finally left in the cloakroom.

One day there was an early delivery. We all volunteered to bring the turf in but the teacher ignored our offers. We worried that we might have to spend lunchtime at the job so we made no further references to it until afternoon. Again the teacher ignored our offers. Then shortly before three o'clock, she told us to bring it in. We all rushed to do her bidding and we completed a task that normally took us about an hour to do, in less than ten minutes.

As you can see all our plans for freedom came to naught. In truth it must be said that we enjoyed our schooldays even though we were happy on the day we finally bade goodbye to our desks and teachers.

OUR YOUTH CLUB

By

Noreen Parker

Our Youth Club was established in the late 1980's and based in Ballymacward Community Centre.
The Club has continued ever since except for a short lapse in the 1990's. During the 1970's both Ballymacward and Gurteen had active Macra na Feirme Clubs with high membership. Nearly every parish at that time had at least one Macra club and some had two. Like as in many other counties Macra na Feirme Clubs began to decrease in County Galway and by 1982 the parish no longer had a Macra na Feirme Club.

After a short time it was realised that there was no recreation facility for teenage and young adult age groups in the parish. Under the umbrella of Ballymacward Community Council a Tennis Club and Badminton Club were formed. While the Tennis was a big hit during the Summer months the Badminton really took off with demand by all age groups for a game. Players came from Ballymacward/Gurteen, Woodlawn, Castleblakeney and surrounding areas.

Because of the huge interest from school going age groups in having some kind of recreation activity on a regular basis a group of potential group/youth leaders got together and Our Youth Club was born.

Sporting activities were, and are still, the most popular activities for members. These include: indoor soccer, unihoc, pool, tabletennis, darts, badminton and board games. From its foundation to the mid 1990's the Club was known as Gurteen/Ballymacward Youth Club and was affiliated to Galway Youth Federation, a branch of the National Youth Federation. While the indoor activities were the most popular, the club also competed and excelled in orienteering and outdoor activities. These took place at Peterborough Outdoor Education Centre. Light Entertainment, Drama, and Treasure Hunts got all family members involved and culminated in a very successful and glamourous Fashion Show.

The Club night has always been on Friday but in the early 1990's it was decided to have two sessions because of the increase in numbers. Club leaders completed training courses and passed on their skills to members who put these into effect at local level. The majority of members were pleased to do similar courses, thus helping to maintain and strengthen the organisation.

The Club first entered the Light Entertainment competition known as 'Tops of the Club' in 1991 and members were delighted to receive an award in their first year. In 1992 they won the Rural Club award with another fantastic show. 1993 was truly the highlight of this competition for the Club with a show comprising of Junior members (under 12 years) called CO-OPERATION. To win the overall County title was great, but to get through to the other heats of the All-Ireland final and finish second was a marvellous achievement. The 1994 show called 'The Only Way Is Up', reached the All Ireland Quarter Finals and picked up several awards on the way.

After a short break in the 1990's the Club reformed and affiliated to the 'Foroige' youth organisation. The indoor sporting activities are still as popular as ever. The Club now competes annually at the County Foroige sports/activity day and in the Soccer World Cup tournament competition. Best Actor, Best Set and Producers Special Awards have been received in the last few years by members for their Drama and Light Entertainment presentations. Club members have participated, as representatives on the National Executive and the skills they have acquired will be of great benefit to them in the future. Members have always been actively involved in organising events and in the upkeep and maintenance of the surrounding amenities in the area.

The continued success of a local Youth Club would not be possible without the dedication of its leaders and the support and co-operation of parents. It is not possible to name all the hardworking leaders and members here but you all know who they are. So please continue to support and encourage them for the future. Long may Our Youth Club continue.

Finally, I am truly honoured to have been asked to share my memories of a very successful Youth Club.

BEST ACTOR, ALAN CORBETT

CONFIRMATION TIME

A RELIGIOUS DRAMA PERFORMED BY BALLYMACWARD YOUTH CLUB

TOPS OF THE CLUB
SINEAD KILKENNY

FOROIGE ON STAGE

YOUNG SINGERS-
FIONA WARD & GERALDINE KELLY

WORK AND PLAY
TEACHERS AND PUPILS CONSTRUCT A BOAT

WORK AND PLAY
SAFE FROM SIN

WORK AND PLAY
KNEE DEEP IN MERRIMENT

WORK AND PLAY
AUTUMN SUNSHINE

SHARING A JOKE
GERARD CONNOR & EDWARD MITCHELL

SHARING A JOKE
PAUL RYAN, VINCENT CONNOR & FRIENDS

SHARING A JOKE
KEVIN FINN, JENNIFER BURKE, BRENDAN HARDIMAN & OTHERS

JAW BREAKERS AND..

Many of you will be familiar with Goldsmith's lines in 'The Deserted Village':

While words of learned length and thund'ring sound
Amazed the gazing rustics rang'd around; etc.

Some of you will probably be surprised at the vocabulary of the people of this parish in former times. Although educational opportunities were limited, some of our ancestors were proud of their proficiency in English and their colourful turn of phrase. Tommie Mitchell speaks of a Mount Hazel inhabitant, M, who was noted for his stylish expressions. M had been working to build a hovel for a couple that had a child 'out of wedlock'. When asked what he had been doing that day, he said,
' I was employed in the construction of an abode for a social outcast.'
He drove to Ballinasloe once in a donkey and cart. He spoke to the innkeeper in the following manner:
'Kindly release the quadruped and I will reimburse you for our accommodation prior to my departure'
Another time he went to Ford's Shop and left the ass and cart partly blocking the entrance. He apologised to a fellow customer thus:
'I beg your indulgence for impeding your progress. If I had anticipated your arrival, I wouldn't have driven my quadruped in such close proximity to the premises.'

The use of 'big words' wasn't confined to M however. A lady in the parish, who was teaching her children to make clothes, used to warn them to allow enough material for the completion of the garments, saying:
'It's far easier to subduct superfluities than it is to remedy deficiencies.'
A Ryehill Resident referring to the weather phrased his comment this way:
'I prognosticate that there will be a definite dissolution of the atmosphere in the afternoon.'

Sheila Bellew mentions another adage that was popular in her childhood. It was taken from a book called 'Reading Made Easy', which the local wits converted to 'Ready Me Daisy'. It sounded something like this:
'Nocturnal perambulations are perilous, especially in territories abounding with subterranean concavities.'
No doubt it helped to reduce the number of people walking near bogholes at night!
If 'Reading Made Easy' had pieces like that, one wonders what the authors would have chosen for advanced readers.
Sheila also found an elaborate version of the saying. 'A nod is as good as a wink etc. It was phrased like this:
'A spasmodic movement of the optic is as adequate as a slight inclination of the cranium towards an equine quadruped, devoid of its visionary capabilities.'
It was said that one parishioner used to speak to his donkey like this, whenever he wanted him to turn at the end of a furrow:
'Halt Edward, pivot and proceed!'
Another farmer asked a shopkeeper for 'a manual-excavating implement.' Obviously he didn't believe in calling 'a spade, a spade.' Then I suppose most of us are happy to call 'a spade a spade ' unless we trip over one in the dark.

We can consider ourselves lucky that such expressions are less common nowadays, otherwise we would all need to carry big dictionaries around with us.

CONFUSING MESSAGES

Nearly everyone has stories of apprentices being sent for 'sky hooks,' 'round squares' and 'glass hammers.' The artist, Stanley Holloway, has a monologue about being told to take his medicine 'in a recumbent posture.' He searches everywhere for 'a recumbent posture,' before he finally sits down and swallows it.

Then there was a story about a lady that went to a doctor. The Doctor told her that she had a complication of diseases and the symptoms of an ulcer. When she came home her husband asked her what the doctor had said.
She replied, 'Oh, he complimented me on my diseases and said I had the sympathy of Ulster.'

Another story concerns a man who thought that The Soldier's Song' was Ireland's National 'Antrim.' His friend pointed out his error saying:
'No, no. The Soldiers's Song is the National Anthem. The word anthem means a piece of music, whereas Antrim is a place or state of punishment where some souls suffer for a while before they go to England!'

We conclude this section with a true story about a parishioner. The Late Jack Connallen of Cloonkeenkerrill was invited to lunch one day by a neighbour. The hostess spilled some peas as she was serving him.
'I'm very sorry Jack.' She said, 'And I'm afraid I have no serviettes.'
'Tis all right A Girleen,' said Jack, ' Me teeth are bad and I wouldn't be able to eat them anyway.'

HAVING A BALL

By

John Joe Ward

My only memory of my first day at school is, when the teachers, Mrs. Walsh and Mrs. Hurley, stood at the school gate to welcome me in. The dog followed me to school and waited for me all day to walk me home again that evening. I played with 'marla' for most of the day.

I remember one Sunday evening playing 'pitch and toss' at the crossroads with a group of friends when the local teacher looked out the window of her house and saw me. I received two slaps the following morning at the school door for not being in doing my homework the evening before. She never even asked me if I had my homework done.

A friend of mine who always seemed to be in trouble with one of the teachers got three slaps in each hand on a daily basis. He often pulled back his hands as the stick was about to be drawn and the teacher would hit herself in the shins. Everyone would laugh at such an incident and then we would all receive a slap.

On my first year at school we had a big snowfall on May 10th 1943. Eight pupils turned up for school that day; some in their bare feet. At that time pupils walked to school bare foot from the 1st of April when the weather was fine. Due to the snowfall we got the day off and we went up to Broderick's field making snowmen. This gives you an idea of the amount of snow on the ground but all the snow had melted by that evening.

The school was often so cold and damp that you could write your name on the condensation. A small fire in each classroom served to keep the pupils' bottles of milk and cocoa warm on a winter's day. When the teachers stood in front of the fire to help keep themselves warm they would block the heat from the rest of us.

At that time we made 'ragballs' from a sack stuffed with hay; this worked well on fine days but in wet weather it wasn't too successful. As time progressed we decided to save up for a real football. It took about 6 months for us to save the price of it. Pupils brought in whatever savings they could manage; some brought in pennies, some two pence and some 6 pence. Finally we bought a full size football in Lohans in Menlough. We paid 50 shillings for it. That kind of football would cost at least 70 Euros now. We had some great games in the schoolyard but as also happens nowadays; the ball would often get punctured and would have to be repaired. Footballs back then were laced and would have to be opened and the bladder removed to put on the patches. The pupil with the smallest hand would have to search the cover of the football for thorns. Pumping it was always a major operation, as a valve had to be got from someone's bicycle and inserted into the tit of the bladder. It was a three-man job, as two people had to hold twines as the third man pumped. When the ball was fully inflated the tit was turned down and tied with the twine. This was pushed into the cover of the football and the fong was pulled hard to lace up the ball. It was then pushed under the lace and we were ready for action again. If the ball was flat the following day there was always a major enquiry as to who had tied the bottom twine. So as you can see there were enquires back in those days too!

I remember making my First Holy Communion and Confirmation in the same year. We walked to the Church through the bog in the summer. This was a twenty-minute journey. In winter we would have to use the road and then it took us 45 minutes to get there. I attended a mission in 1947. We walked to the Church for the morning ceremony; we got time off from school to attend Confessions at mid-day; and in the evening we were expected to be at the closing ceremonies. In all we clocked up about 18 miles. The two aisles would be packed to capacity for Confessions during the mission. Each penitent would be kept at least 30 minutes and the Missioner would roar at some of them. His voice could be heard throughout the chapel and those waiting in line would tremble with fear!

Soon after that particular mission we got a terrible storm which took slates off the west gable of the school and damaged the fascia boards. We got two weeks off school while repairs were underway. The old school at the crossroads at that time was a great place for courting couples. On the night of the storm there was a courting couple inside. The door of a pig's cabin was blown down with the storm that night and the pig got out and went into the old school. When the couple heard the pig grunting they thought it was the Devil; having heard so much about him at the Mission. They took to their heels at once and ran out onto the road in the height of the storm!

Later in 1947 we got a massive snowfall which lasted 7 weeks. We got the first two weeks off from school and when we returned we spent all our time sliding in the frozen snow. At that time it was difficult to get boots in the aftermath of the war, so pupils wore clogs. Clogs were similar to boots but were made of light material with thick timber soles and a steel rim on the underside. They were perfect for sliding for those five weeks!

The guards and priest were frequent visitors to the school. Whenever they came we were given an extended play hour. The guards would summons the parents of pupils that had been absent from school for two weeks or so. They also examined rollbooks for absentees on the days they called.

These are just some of the memories I hold of my good old school days; days I will never forget.

THE 'STRAWBOY' REVIVAL

By

Marian Spellman (Mitchell)

For countless decades, they were expected to entertain free of charge but
in the latter part of the twentieth century the customary visits by the Strawboys to the homes of newly wed couples underwent a noticeable decline.

However, all was not lost and the tradition, although somewhat diminished, had not entirely lost its appeal. With the revival of set dancing in recent years a new awareness of the value of this custom has brought about a re-birth of our traditional form of entertainment. Today, instead of the Strawboys visiting the home of the married couple, they visit the wedding reception, where they entertain the newly weds and guests alike.

This, I hasten to add, is not confined to wedding celebrations alone. The Strawboys perform at many functions around the country. Any get together is valid reason enough to invite them to display their talents.

For those of you who have never heard of such activity or indeed the term "Strawboy", allow me to enlighten you a little. Long ago it was the custom, particularly in parts of Clare and North Mayo, for a group of eight local dancers and singers to mask themselves in straw and visit any house in the locality that might be home to a newly-wed couple. The dress worn by the Strawboy groups varied. But, in general it was as follows: The four male members of the group wore waistcoats of straw with knee and ankle bands to match. They wore black or plaid trousers and black footwear. The female members of the group wore long black skirts, black or plaid shawls and dark footwear also. Nowadays, the ladies wear the traditional farmhouse crossover bibs. All wore straw hats, or hoods covering the face. This was deliberate, as it was not necessary for the assembled guests or indeed the bride and groom to know the identity of the dancers. The main purpose of the Strawboy's visit was to extend the hand of friendship and to hope that the couple would be blessed with good luck throughout their married life.

In order to keep this aspect of our tradition alive, an enthusiastic group of performers have now reintroduced the custom in this area. This talented group of people call themselves "The Ramblin' Strawboys". They hail from Westmeath, Roscommon and of course, Galway. As the song says "Where the three counties meet," you will find the most entertaining and liveliest form of song and dance that you have ever seen - with "twig-dancing" thrown in for good measure. This is just a small part of the group's repertoire.

"The Ramblin Strawboys", like a variety of venues and have been "spotted" in castles, dance halls, pubs, hotels, barns and cross roads. Their talents are recognised and appreciated throughout the western region.

The good news is that the Strawboy tradition is here to stay. It has been revived in three counties and all the signs are that it will continue to flourish. Its success proves that Irish audiences appreciate traditional material, especially when it is of a high standard. This approval in turn acts as a stimulus to those on stage encouraging them to strive for an even higher level of performance.

Finally, if you are unable to join us as we perform then, please, consider attempting the "auld" step or two yourself. For, as the old saying goes, "Tá an cultúr agus and ceol fite fuaite le saol na hÉireann".
"Cuireann damhsa ordú meanman orainn agus ar gach gaol."
"Gan dreas damhsá bheimis caillte."
"Bí linn céim ar chéim!"

THE RAMBLIN' STRAWBOYS

CHAPTER NINE

THE SCHOOL SCENE IN SHANBALLARD

Organizing Committee of St. Kerrills First Festival
Back Row (L to R) Martin Kitt, Mike Donnellan, Noel Burke, Gerry McDonagh, Paraic O'Connor.
Front Row (L to R) Eamonn Mitchell, Eileen O'Grady, Catherine Donnellan, Sean Bodkin, Mary Burke, Eoin Cunniffe

Organizing Committee of St. Kerrills Festival 1998
Back Row (L to R): Eamonn Mitchell, Noel Burke, Fr. Vincent Lawless, Joe Greally, Stephen Walsh
Front Row (L to R): Mary Burke, Renee Ryan, Martina Hardiman, Paula Naughton.

(Missing from Photograph: Sean Bodkin)

Shanballard N.S Pupils 1926

BACK ROW (L to R): Mrs Mgt. Kitt, Assistant Principal; Babe Bodkin; Lucy Hawkins; Cathy Mentane; Bridie Walsh; Katie Lyons; Kathleen Spellman; Kathy Keane; Sarah Hawkins; Pake Lyons; Mrs. Julia Duffy

SECOND ROW (L to R): Tom Walsh; Mary K. Hawkins; Bridget Grady; Kathleen Walsh; Mary Hooban; Nancy Hooban; Mgt. Walsh; Julia Hession; Tommy Melody;

THIRD ROW (L to R): Mick Grady; Joe Naughton; Eugene Melody; Ned Bodkin; Joe Hawkins; Sonny Laffey; John Kenny; Bobbie Melody; John Dooley; Mick Bodkin; Tommy Laffey.

FRONT ROW (L to R): Arabella Melody; Mary Dooley; Mary Kenny; Mary Carr; Kathleen Grady; Tess Hawkins.

St. Monicas National School, Shanballard. Erected 1896

JUST RELAXING-
MIKIE AND MAI TAKE A BREAK AFTER A GAME OF TENNIS

SHANBALEESHAL 1935

SHANBALLARD IN THE FORTIES
MRS. KITT AND PUPILS

GABRIEL CLARKE, BRIDIE SCARRY
AND THE KELLYS, CAPPALUSK

PUPILS AT WORK
LEFT: BREEGE RUANE, ANNE M. RUANE, ANGELA KILKENNY, BRIDGET O'GRADY, FONSIE DILLEEN, JOE DILLEEN, GABRIEL CLARKE
RIGHT: KITTY O'GRADY, TERESA NAUGHTON, MARGARET LAFFEY, HELEN O'GRADY, MARY NAUGHTON

WORK AND PLAY
SPORTS DAY FUN

SHANBALLARD PUPILS

SWEET SOUNDS OF SHANBALLARD

By

Nancy Coen-Cormican

I had no gift for it,
It hung out on the welter of the moor;
A black-faced country staring in

All day. Never did the sun
Explode with flowers in the dark vases
Of the windows. The fall was wrong

And there was the uplifted striking north
Before the door.
We lived in the flintlights of a cavern floor.

It was enemy country too. The rafts of the low
Fields foundering. Every day the latch
Lifted to some catastrophe, such as

A foal dead in an outfield, a calf lost
In a mud -suck, a hen laying wild in the rushes,
A bullock strayed, a goose gone with the fox;

The epic, if any, going on too long.
Nil the glory in it, null the profit;
It was too big for me and full of threat.

A place that glugged green in the vast egg
Of the weather, too littered with rains
And with minor stone-age tragedies
Like getting wet feet in the goose paddock.

This is the first part of a poem by Padraic Fallon. As a child he spent his holidays in Gurteen with his aunt, Mrs. Cormican, my grandmother- better known as 'the woman with the black clothes.' His Gurteen, ' glugged green in the vast egg of the weather, with the black-faced country staring in.' My Gurteen was sunnier. In fact the sun shone mostly around Shanballard School. Sometimes there would be a thick fog on a winter's morning when you couldn't see your hand. On the way to school, I would tell myself that the school had disappeared in the night. Just as I had convinced myself that it had miraculously vanished, the woolly outline of its familiar building would suddenly loom up in front of me. So much for dreams!

It was a happy school though. Airplanes were rare sights in those days. When the sound of one approaching in the distance was heard, Mr. Blehein would let us out to see this low flying spectacle passing overhead. His detailed explanations of the dynamics of this wonder were rather lost on us. Nevertheless our minds used to be on overdrive for the rest of the day. Although Rural Electrification hadn't yet come to us, Mr. Blehein generated his own electricity. His do-it-yourself windmill whirred like a spinning top on windy days and his house was lit up like a Christmas tree. However, on calm days, it stood there like a lazy giant, and it was back to the trusty oil lamps again. Although we didn't realise it at the time, we were probably the only children in Ireland who had first hand experience of the electricity generating process. The little world of ours revolved around a very inspiring teacher.

Books were hard to come by those days but I was fortunate. I had an English uncle who kept my voracious appetite for reading satisfied. Miss Lynch and my mother constantly swopped what seemed to me to be an endless store of books and I was the lucky librarian given the task of ferrying the reading material to and fro. My visit to Miss Lynch was the highlight of the week. She had a wind-up gramophone plus a dozen of 'seventy eight' records of Strauss music. She was a Strauss buff who knew everything about the three generations of those musical geniuses. A slice of sweetcake, a glass of raspberry and the Blue Danube sent me straight to Heaven. I visited the Vienna Woods years later on a lovely balmy Saturday afternoon and in fancy I was transported back again to Miss Lynch's kitchen with the gramophone playing her favourite piece: Roses From The South.

THEN AND NOW

When I was young there was a marked difference between the seasons. The fields used to be covered in snow, with big drifts beside the ditches. After school we delighted in building snowmen, using potatoes for eyes and mouth. The summers seemed long, hot and lazy. We spent much of our time under the bridge of the river fishing for eels that we never managed to catch. At the height of summer we dammed the river to create our own swimming pool. Our dog, Flock, used to swim with us.

One winter's day a little black and white goat arrived on the scene and we kept him. We never knew where he came from but he wormed his way into my affections and became the love of my life. We used to dress him up in jumpers and socks and he loved it. On a Spring's day while I was at school he followed the postman on his rounds and never returned. I should have known that there was a touch of the travelling showman about him from the way he paraded around in his stage clothes. We never found out what happened to him. His departure was as mysterious as his arrival. I was disappointed at his lack of loyalty but I suppose we all have to grow up sometime.

SHANBALLARD TEACHERS
MAUREEN, MICHAEL AND MAI BLEHEIN

MRS. JULIA DUFFY AND PUPILS FROM SHANBALLARD

THE MASTER- A MAN AHEAD OF HIS TIME

By

Fr. John Garvey

Much has been written in the past twenty years about the value of storytelling as a method of education and a means of communication. Children love stories as their imaginations can easily picture the scene being described. They also appreciate the time and the effort that the storyteller makes for his or her listeners.

Michael Blehein used simple examples from experience to make important points to the students in his care.

One day he was walking along the road when he spotted in the hedge a beautiful sapling, which was ideal for making a fishing rod. He wondered to himself if it was the right time to cut down such a shoot. Later that evening a traveller was passing by Michael's gate and had in his possession a lovely straight sapling. "What is the best time of year to cut one of those saplings?" Michael asked him. "The moment that you see it" the traveller said. Returning to the part of the hedge Michael discovered that the sapling was gone.

Another time he spoke of walking past a neighbour's home and seeing the woman of the house outside sitting on a chair. She held a crow-bar with one hand and a file in the other. To her heart's content she filed the crow-bar. "What in the name of God are you doing?" Michael enquired. Her reply was instant: "I can't find my darning needle".

Michael often recalled the incident of the inspector who visited a school one afternoon and asked the pupils about what happened at Ballyneety. Nobody knew but it was now three o'clock and closing time for the day. However the inspector was back first thing the following morning and asked the pupils the same question. One pupil raised her hand and gave a perfect answer. When she was asked the source of her information she said "I looked it up at home".

Michael encouraged us to be interested in current affairs, local knowledge and folklore. In addition to the various subjects emphasis was put on general knowledge. The barograph on the window traced the atmospheric pressure for the week. We had a garden in the schoolyard in which were grown vegetables and flowers. There was a day set aside after the Summer holidays when we could return and take away some of the plants. At one time we got tin whistles and learned a few tunes.

Michael took full part in the sports we played. Many a great game of handball was played against the school gable - sometimes the ball would bounce off a stone in the yard and in a completely different direction than anticipated. He displayed his fitness with his ability to stand on his head, his hands and then do a somersault. Hurling had been discontinued because too much glass was being broken but we did play football, though we had to be careful not to let the ball go over the wall and disturb the bees.
Michael drove us to the Community Games which took place in Ballymacward Sportsfield at the time where there was great excitement at getting a medal and all sorts of excuses at not.

Born in Rossport, Bangor-Erris, Co. Mayo over ninety years ago, he has spent most of his life in Co. Galway. He met and fell 'head over heels' in love with Mai Ward from Ballymacward 67 years ago. Michael taught practical things like how to assemble an engine or set up an electric plant of your own. He also taught us gardening and bicycle maintenance. At one stage he and his pupils built a boat.

Mai acted as unofficial school nurse and was ever ready to help in caring for people who were ill or injured. She has a phenomenal memory and can recall in detail events that took place almost ninety years ago.

Gurteen was fortunate to secure the services of such a talented and dedicated people.

From 1939 to 1979, Michael Blehein shared his philosophy with us and has given us many good memories. It was more than a job - it was a way of life.

John Garvey

THE MURPHYS

Tom Murphy was principal in Shanballard National School up to the late 1930s. While there he conducted a survey for the Folklore Commission. It was a bi-lingual survey and contains a vast amount of information about the parish and its history. While Tom was teaching there his wife, a native of Oughterard also helped. Prior to then she was employed as a teacher in a Dublin school. When she came here she taught singing to the children and availed of the piano that was in the school residence. Although she was a trained teacher, she wasn't paid for these lessons. Surprisingly the pupils that she taught had to undergo inspection by the Department. Another unusual thing was that her husband's salary was reduced from nineteen pounds per month to sixteen prior to the war. Mrs. Murphy was appointed acting principal of Shanballard School for a short period.

Her husband and herself left and went to Menlough and later took up positions in Corgary National School, near Mountbellew. He was principal there and she also got a teaching post. She has a great affection for the parish of Gurteen and remembers many of the colorful characters that attended school there. She tells the story of a local inebriate who was picked up by a landlord on the roadside one day after the former had collected his pension and spent it on drink The Landlord, (Lord Trench, I think it was) arrived at her door and wanted to leave the drunkard with her. He had tried unsuccessfully to get the man into his own house previously. She refused to do the landlord's bidding. The landlord then asked for a chair. He put the man sitting on this and left. When he had gone the inebriate immediately came to life and returned to his own house. She was of the opinion that he was far less drunk than he appeared to be and only maintained the facade to avoid a confrontation with the landlord.

She talks of a fire that started near Cormican's House and spread over the entire area resulting in a great loss of the turf that many people had hoped to harvest. Most teachers had turf then and Murphy's turf suffered the same fate as the neighbour's turf.

She is now in her nineties and was a regular bridge player up to a short time ago. She lives with her daughter in Loughrea and is a very pleasant person who is ready to share her experiences with those who visit her.

GOOD OLD SODS

By

Ollie Ruane

Shanballard was a two-teacher school. My first day in school was to Mrs. Kitt's class. Mr. Blehein was the Headmaster. There was no school transport in those days. I walked about 2 miles to school. In Summer, we usually walked to school without shoes. There was no electricity in the area at the time so our lessons were done by the light of an oil lamp. Our headmaster, Mr. Blehein had a wind generator in his back garden that provided him with electricity. Sport in our school consisted of football and handball. One time our teacher tried to get hurling going but only one or two had proper hurleys. The rest arrived with an assortment of sticks with knobs on them. Our teacher said it was too dangerous so the hurling was called off for the time being.

The school was heated by an open turf fire. Each family with children going to school brought a load of turf. When turf ran out we used to bring two sods each under our arms to school in the mornings. On our way home in the evenings, our gang - the Corskagh and Carhoon group parted company with the Shanbalishel/Cappalusk crowd at what we called the head of Corskagh road. Most of the time we parted on good terms, but on odd occasions gang warfare broke out. It usually started if there was ammo such as fresh scraws after the council edging the road or snow.
'Cowardy, Cowardy bastard, stick your head in mustard' or
'Hay and oats for the Cappalusk Goats,
eggs and rashers for the Corskagh slashers'

These were usually the opening shots. Next morning the battle was all forgotten and we were the best of friends again. One day we saw an object with a long tail passing overhead while we were out playing. The Master told us that it was a jet plane- one of the first to fly in this country. When we returned to class he explained to us how it worked and how it differed from an ordinary plane. I was proud to be able to tell my mother all about it when I got home that evening.

We learned many valuable lessons from Mr. Blehein. He taught us to respect ourselves and others and to be helpful to those who were less fortunate than ourselves. I always remember the expression that he used:
'There but for the grace of God, go I.'

Ollie Ruane and Friends at M&N Studios

CHAPTER TEN

HOW THE SENIORS SEE IT

THE ROUGH AND THE SMOOTH

By
John Joe McGann
(Compiled by his Granddaughter Gráinne Lally McGann)

The following article contains a brief account of the memories my grandfather, Mr. John-Joe McGann, has of his time in Shanballard National School, and of life in the locality in the early 1900's. Although his name was John Joe, he was generally called Joe. I have used this name throughout the article.

Joe first went to school in 1917 at the age of seven. He said that they didn't go to school so early age then because of the long distance they had to travel. He remembers his first day as if it were last week. On that momentous day someone tried to get him to drink a full inkwell! Thankfully, someone came to his aid and he was spared the unpleasantness of the 'ink drink.' He later found out that the student in question was Mick Dooley. (Joe did not see Dooley until between fifty and sixty years later. He was passing by a public house one day when a man rushed out to greet him. It was the same Mick Dooley and Mick reminded him of the inkwell incident.) When he went out to play he was picked up by a "big strong chap" who kept swinging him around until he got a reel in his head. Joe couldn't stand up, much to everyone's amusement! {This turned out to be Stephen ('Staff') Reilly.

Joe and his sisters had a long distance to walk to school. It was inevitable that they would be late sometimes. His teacher at that time, a Mrs. Duffy, whom he remembers fondly, never marked them absent because she knew they'd arrive at some stage! During the Summer, pupils didn't wear shoes. Someone in the house bought several pairs of clogs. These were for winter wear. The clogs turned out to be useful because if they were late, Mrs. Duffy would send someone out to check for the noise of the clogs!

MR. & MRS. JOHN JOE McGANN

Joe took part in everything that was going on in the school - good and bad. This included a lunchtime excursion down the road to "Biddy Connell's". Biddy's place was only a short distance from school. One day Joe and his friends saw a cake left on the windowsill to cool. It was not left there long - suffice it to say they all had a lunch of freshly baked bread, all except Biddy that is! She learned from her mistake and Joe never noticed anything left to cool on the window after that.

Another teacher that Joe remembers was Ms. Mahon from Ballymacward. Her mode of transport at the time was a bicycle. One morning she was very late. When she turned up she was in the company of the Naughton children from Carhoon. Seemingly her bike was not in working order. She had walked from Ballymacward to Naughtons (across the fields) because she knew that they would be familiar with the short cut via Corskeagh to the school. Ms. Mahon later married Joe Kitt. She and her husband bought what used to be Lynch's land and house. The house was close the school -so no more long cycles were necessary.

Joe and his family moved to Carhoon from Lenareagh in the early 1920's and went to a new school but he remembers hearing about the hobby that the new teacher in Shanballard had - beekeeping! Mr. Bleahene, the school principal, used to bring some honey to the pupils in the school. (This was probably why Joe remembers it because he always liked honey and still does.)

While he was a young boy growing up, Ireland was, as he puts it, "in pieces". The old I.R.A. was particularly active here and this was why the 'Black and Tans' were sent to the area. (It seems someone had reported seeing IRA members in the vicinity). According to Joe this so-called 'police force' had some strange ideas about enforcing the law. Keeping the peace didn't enter their minds at all. He relates how the Black and Tans arrived in Cloonkeen in the dead of night and entered houses there (no locked doors back then!). They went straight to the bedrooms. They proceeded to rub the jaws of the people they found in bed. The purpose of this exercise was to ascertain whether the jaw was coarse - if it was, then that person was old enough to shave, and therefore old enough to take up arms against them. These unfortunates were taken out and considered themselves lucky if they escaped with a severe beating.

On another occasion the Black and Tans came to beat up a certain individual. Joe tells of one 'chap' that was taken out of his bed wearing nothing but his shirt! He was strongly built and was well able to fight but of course he was outnumbered on this occasion. The Tans got ready to give him 'a good hiding' but he was too quick for them. He made a dash for it and escaped, leaving them nothing but his shirt. He headed for the nearest bog, which he knew far better than they did. He burrowed into a rick of turf and hid there until morning. He returned home next day, hoping that the Tans would have gotten fed up waiting for him.

A WEDDING AT MCGANNS

Another memory Joe has is of the family of a young policeman. One morning on his way to school with his two sisters, Annie and Katie, an old woman came out of a house as they passed. She called out in a pleading voice:
'I want you to come in and say the Rosary. I want you to say a prayer for my son. He's after being shot.'
They followed her into the house. Inside they saw three children and a young woman all of whom were strangers to them. They were all terribly upset. Joe learned later that the older woman's son was a member of the R.I.C.-. the police force set up by the English Government to keep law and order in Ireland. Most of its members were Irish. The R.I.C. Men were given an ultimatum - Resign or be shot. This particular man decided not to resign. He felt that if he did so he and his family would go hungry and end up destitute. The IRA carried out their threat and had him killed. His family had no other option but to come to live with his mother because they had nowhere else to go. This incident occurred, as far as Joe can remember, in 1918. He also remembers that they stayed there for some time. He used to bring two of the children to Mass. To make matters worse, the surviving family members were boycotted owing to the fact that the policeman had not resigned.

Joe has many other memories of that turbulent era. Like the rest of us, he is thankful that things have changed for the better in Ireland and that we can live our lives free from fear and physical hardship, unlike the inhabitants who lived in this parish when he was a child. He has been in good health for most of his life and although he is in his nineties, he takes a keen interest in current and sporting affairs.

GRAD YOUNG COUPLE - GRAINNE LALLY-MCGANN AND HER HUSBAND PHILIP

LOOKING BACK OVER NINE DECADES

By

Tommie Mitchell

Gurteen is the sister (Junior) parish of Ballymacward. While the quality of land is average, there is good and bad land to be found within its boundaries. The people are hardworking and industrious and have managed to have a comfortable existence down the years. There was always a strong Nationalist view held by its people and in the Land League years, local tenants were prominent in the struggle to remove the landlords' grip on tenant farmers. Some faced arrest and imprisonment for activity of this kind. The younger generation has but a scant knowledge of what their ancestors went through to eke out a living. It was good management and hard work that enabled them to do so.

SPORT

There was a strong tradition of hurling in Gurteen. Teams from here were able to compete with teams from parishes twice their size. Handball was another game which was played in the parish. A ball court was built here in the early 1900's. Some of the handballers were very proficient and played at county level. A good many of those sporting men emigrated to America and joined clubs in their newly adopted homeland. Many were renowned for their hurling and football skills.

TOMMIE MITCHELL AND HIS GRANDSON SHANE

A change has come over rural Ireland for some time past. The handball court is lying idle and the sound of the handball is no longer heard. It is my belief that the skills displayed on the hurling field are not as good as those of former exponents of the game. Hurling is a sport confined to Ireland and is one of the fastest and most skillful games when properly played. Handball is also a very fast game. It's played worldwide. It is a treat to watch handball or hurling competitions.

It would be my hope to see the youth of the parish reviving the skills of hurling and handball. Once there were two separate hurling clubs in the parish but they combined several years ago to form "Pearse's". This is to be admired when a better team is the result. However in the case of handball, when I see the two handball courts lying idle - one on each parish, there's a lack of commitment somewhere. Handball is one of the best games for young people who are anxious to keep fit. The great boxer, Jim Corbett (of Irish descent) from the U.S.A., who was World Champion in the early Twentieth Century, claimed that it was the game of handball that kept him fit in his boxing days. Being interested in all aspects of sport, is both excellent mental and physical therapy for people of all ages. I think it's time we brought back the crack of the handball and the skill of the caman to delight players and spectators alike.

Gurteen has a proud place in the pages of Irish history. During the Anglo-Irish struggle 1916-21 strong national sentiments were evident here. One of its sons was working as a priest in Galway.

He was called out on a bogus sick call and was murdered by the Black and Tans. His body was buried in a bog drain in Barna and wasn't recovered for some days. Fr. Michael Griffin was a brilliant young priest and the people of Gurteen built a chapel in his honour that was to become an architectural gem. It was designed by W.H. Dwyer and Co. Dublin

EDUCATION

Education wrought a great change in the lives of people. The schools in Clonkeenkerrill, Shanballard and Tample replaced the hedge schools that served the parish prior to the Education Act of 1831. The population was much bigger then and after the Famine many people emigrated. It was a great advantage for early emigrants to have 'a bit of learning' when they arrived in America.

There is less emigration now. Living conditions have improved greatly since I was a child. Families are smaller and there is a degree of affluence that my generation would have found it difficult to imagine. The roads, the church and the appearance of the village have all changed for the better. It is my dearest wish that this trend will continue and that future generations will not have to endure the hardships and privations that we had to face when we were young.

TOMMIE & KATHLEEN MITCHELL
AND THEIR GRANDSON CORMAC KEANE

THE MITCHELL & CORBETT CHILDREN

STYLISH TRANSPORT
THIS VEHICLE WAS USED FOR FILMING ON JIM BURKE'S FARMYARD

A FINE OLD SOLDIER- A BRIEF ACCOUNT OF JIM BURKE'S LIFE

Jim Burke has the honour of being the most senior past pupil of Clonkeenkerrill National School. Jim lives with his sister, Teresa, at Cuddoo, Colemanstown. He began school at the age of four in the company of his brother who was two years older. They had to walk 3 miles each way and of course, like all the others, brought their books and lunches with them. Life wasn't easy for him or his family but you would find this hard to believe when you come in contact with Jim and his sister.

Disaster struck in February 1930 when Jim's mother died. She left six children, the youngest one about a year old and the eldest just twelve. Jim's father wasn't able to cope. He had 28 acres of land and it would have been impossible to rear six children on such a small holding. This meant that the family (2 boys and 4 girls) had to be separated. Some were taken by relatives and two ended up in Lenaboy House in Galway.

The trouble didn't end there. Jim's older brother, Martin complained of a severe pain in his leg one evening and was taken to hospital. He died a few days later and no real explanation for his death was given. He was thirteen at the time.

Happily things changed for the better. After a few years the young girls returned from Galway and were reunited with their father. Jim had stayed with his father all this time.
His grandfather also lived with them and helped as best he could with the family chores.

When he went to school Mrs. Walsh was principal. He spent two years or so in Clonkeenkerrill before moving to the newly built Tiaquin School which was much nearer to him. Other members of the family went there also.

It would be difficult to meet two more hospitable people than Jim and Teresa. It's one of those houses you don't leave without the tea and you are always invited back to visit again.

In 2003 the house was selected by a company as part of the location for a feature film. The film was called 'Waiting For Dublin' and concerned a political fugitive who was being pursued by the authorities in the forties. Several scenes were shot close to Burke's house and a vast array of technical equipment was used. An old fashioned door and replica chimney were installed on the premises. Traps, sprayers and old-fashioned cars were also supplied by the company. These were kept in Burke's yard while filming was in progress. Huge numbers of spectators came to observe the proceedings and security guards were placed at the head of the road to protect the equipment and to prevent unauthorised entry. Frank Kelly (Fr. Jack) from the 'Father Ted' series was one of the main actors in the film. Shooting was postponed due to financial considerations but it is thought that it will recommence shortly.

Many people would find this scenario upsetting and would probably refuse to allow filmmakers to intrude on them. Not so Jim and his sister. They cooperated with them in every way possible and being young at heart seemed to enjoy the whole thing thoroughly.
We wish Jim and Teresa the best of luck and we look forward to meeting them at the reunion. We are confident that a special place will be reserved for them whenever 'Waiting For Dublin' is being premiered.

FROM CAPPALUSK TO COLORADO

By

Paddy Scarry

I appreciate your invitation to the Reunion but due to poor health I am unable to travel at this time. I have had heart issues for many years and got a massive heart attack in 1979 as well as open heart surgery in 1988. I am very disappointed since I would love to see some of my old friends such as the Kenny's, the Hynes, B. Kitt, the Naughtons, the McGee's, N. Kelly and many others whose names have escaped me now. I'm sure some may have also passed away by now.

PADDY SCARRY AND GRANDCHILD

I thought I'd take this opportunity to give you a little of my background for the past 79 years as best I can remember it.

My name is Patrick J. Scarry or Paddy as I was often called. I was born on April 24th 1924 in Cappalusk, Gurteen. I was the second oldest of six boys. My other brothers were John, Tommy, Michael, Martin and Vincent. I am the last surviving brother.

I have some memories of attending school in Shanballard. I was six years old and Mrs. Kitt was the teacher and Mrs. Duffy was the principal. As we went into higher grades, Tom Murphy was our teacher. I can still remember how tough he was on us. I remember standing at the little bridge above Cormicans watching him enter the school. If he wore his blue jacket and gray pants it was a sure sign he was in a foul mood. Whenever I saw this, I knew I was in for a few slaps.

After Shanballard, I spent a short time at the technical school in Mountbellew. Some time after that, I went to work for James Corbett for a couple of months. He was a very intelligent man and a great historian. He could engage in conversation with anyone. I also worked at Kyne's in Gurteen. I spent from 1942 to 1946 at St. Mary's Dominican House studying to be a religious brother (or perhaps looking for three square meals a day). Michael Carr and Martin Connors from Tiaquin attended along with me. After I left the monastery, I worked at the Genoa bar in Galway for Joe Malocca for four years. I really enjoyed working there and my life in Galway was good. Unfortunately the money was not sufficient to live on. After a great deal of thought, I decided to emigrate to America in 1950. After a couple of days in my new country, I got a job as a mail handler for the Pennsylvania Railroad where I remained until 1957. I then got a job

SCARRY FAMILY WEDDING

with Con Edison (the gas and electric company). I retired from Con Edison after 31 years. Con Edison was a great company with good benefits for their workers. I got married in 1957 and started a family shortly thereafter. I married a wonderful woman, Theresa, from Clogher, Co. Tyrone. We had three wonderful children - Patrick Joseph Jr, Ann-Marie Theresa and Michael Daniel. Patrick and Michael are married and living in Colorado and Georgia. Ann-Marie is single and living near us in New York. We became proud grandparents for the first time this last July. Michael and his wife Heather had a beautiful little girl named Hannah Ashlynne.

Paddy Scarry 1950

One big change in my life worth mentioning is that 25 years ago I became a member of the Pioneer Total Absenteeism Association. I saw the light (literally) and gave up drinking and smoking when I had the massive heart attack in 1979. My wife is also a Pioneer and we belong to a very nice group here in New York.

My wife and I spent much of our vacation time throughout the years taking bus tours all over the United States. We've been to most of the 52 states and Canada.

I hope I haven't bored you with this little bit of my history. Even though I can't be there physically, I will be with you all in spirit.

SONNY CONNAIRE AND THE LONG ROAD

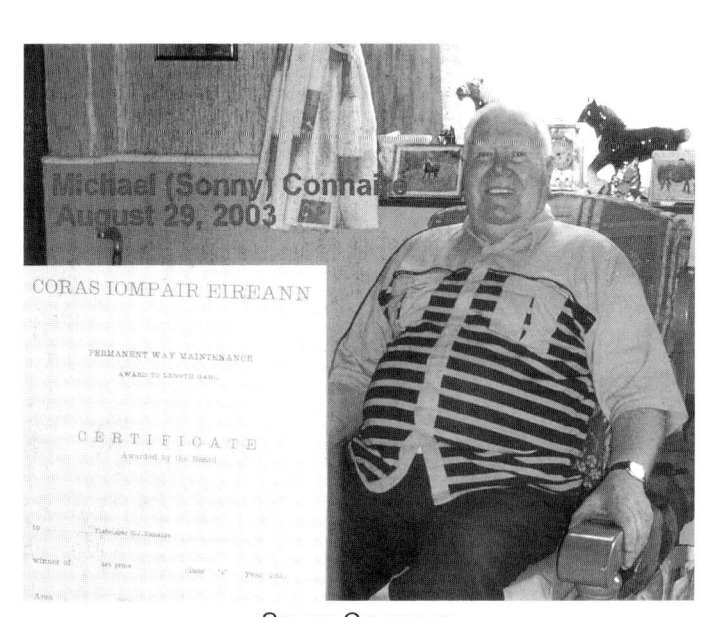

Sonny Connaire lives in Killimordaly and is one of the senior surviving pupils of Shanballard National School. Sonny spent a lot of time attending fairs throughout the country. Like most of his contemporaries, he did so on Shank's Mare.

Sonny tells an interesting story about his grandfather. The latter came in after work one evening and had his tea. After tea he donned a new shirt and announced that he was going to the fair in Spiddal. He set off on foot from Killimordaly. He met a friend in Oranmore who was also bound for Spiddal. The man had a horse and trap so this meant that Sonny's grandfather could travel in style for the remainder of the journey. They arrived at the fair in the early hours of the morning. Sonny's grandfather purchased two animals, a cow and a weanling. He was obliged to drive the animals along the same route as he had travelled the night before. When he got as far as Derrydonnell, the cow lay down on the roadside. He realised that she was going to give birth to a calf. Luckily, a friend of his lived nearby and he took the animals into his farmyard. He offered to keep Sonny's grandfather for the night but the latter refused. He continued his walk and entered the railway line near the town of Athenry. He remained on the tracks until he reached Cloncagh. The family members were just getting out of bed when he got home. His wife advised him to get into bed to rest but he didn't take her advice. He got the ass and cart and went to col-

SONNY CONNAIRE

lect his three animals.

The grandfather had six pounds in his possession before he left for the fair. As I mentioned, he bought a weanling and a cow that produced a calf in transit. He still had two pounds left when he got home.
One can only wonder at the stamina of people like that.

Sonny says that such feats were common even in his own time. He likes to trade in horse and ponies and although he isn't as mobile as he used to be, his interest in them is still as strong as ever. He worked on the railway line for most of his life and received a special award for his services in the sixties. He is a very sociable person who is ready to share his experiences with anyone that calls to visit. Sonny's house is noted for hospitality and there is no shortage of visitors. He has a very positive outlook and hopes to renew acquaintance with his old friends at the reunion next May.

CHAPTER ELEVEN

MATTERS MEDICAL AND ASTRONOMICAL

ENGINEERING THE FUTURE

By

Peter McHugh

What does an engineer do anyway? Irish Universities and Institutes of Technology, like their counterparts around the world, have been turning out different kinds of engineers for years and everyone knows that a civil engineer designs and builds roads and bridges, a mechanical engineer designs and builds machinery, an electronic engineer works with microchips and uses them in products like mobile phones and computers, and an industrial engineer figures out how a factory should be organised to mass produce millions of products, be they phones, computers, cars, or whatever, in an efficient and cost effective way. Certainly this is the traditional view and would have been true enough for quite a long time. But as we all know, things change, "time and tide waits for no man" and the modern world is presenting problems that we really didn't have to face before and that demand people with new kinds of skills to solve, and in particular, people with skills in a number of different areas. Issues such as increasing urbanisation, the environment and health are presenting bigger and bigger problems for society and engineering and technology have to, and are, evolving to meet the new needs. To educate people to be able to deal with the problems of tomorrow, new types of engineering courses are being developed that are based on multi-disciplinarity. For example, to deal with the increasing importance of industrial relations in industrial development, courses combining engineering and management (management engineering) are offered; to deal with developing infrastructure that is environmentally friendly, courses combining engineering and environmental science (environmental engineering) are offered; to deal with developing technology to improve health, courses combining engineering, biology and medicine (biomedical engineering) are being offered. I work as a lecturer in the mechanical engineering department at NUI, Galway (or should that be UCG - the name changed some years ago but it is difficult to get it out of the head!) and I have been involved in the development of the biomedical engineering course there. One of the main reasons NUI, Galway decided to develop such a course was the strength of the industrial base in the West of Ireland who would employ graduates.

DR. PETER MCHUGH AND JAMES MCGARRY AT N.U.I.G. WITH THE SEMENS YOUNG ENGINEER AWARD 2001

It might interest people to know that Ireland is the European capital of the medical device and healthcare product industry, in particular the West of Ireland. Towns like Castlebar, Sligo and especially Galway, are the European bases for most of the major multi-national companies who manufacture medical devices for the treatment of cardiovascular disease; including companies like Boston Scientific, Medtronic/AVE and Abbott. This is a multi-billion dollar industry worldwide and devices made in the West of Ireland find their way to operating theatres all over the world. In saying medical devices I am not necessarily referring to the humble syringe or surgical knife, vital though they are to medical treatment and to the local economy where they are manufactured, no indeed, nowadays medical devices really mean high-tech products that require huge investment in terms of design and production, and that make significant contributions to advancing medical treatment and improving the quality of life. One example of this, which is particularly relevant to Galway where thousands of these devices are produced each week, is the angioplasty balloon catheter for the treatment of heart disease, Ireland's number 1 killer. When introduced in the 1970's angioplasty was a revolutionary treatment for helping to prevent heart attacks and, if the diagnosis is caught in time, to greatly reducing the necessity for bypass surgery. To treat blocked arteries in the heart, instead of major bypass surgery, angioplasty involves the surgeon inserting a very thin plastic catheter tube into an artery in the thigh and guiding it up to the heart by using X-ray. The tip of the catheter is in fact a tiny balloon, initially at most a millimetre wide. When the balloon meets the blockage it is inflated up to a diameter of about 3 to 5 millimetres (depending on where the blockage is) and the blockage is opened up. Frequently, to prevent the artery from re-closing, a second catheter is introduced with a tiny coil of wire at the tip called a "stent", compressed onto a balloon. When this second balloon is inflated, the stent expands, and stays expanded, holding the artery open. The stent remains a permanent implant in the heart. This procedure has proven extremely successful and has resulted in very many lives being saved, and is far less traumatic for the patient than heart bypass surgery. The scale of usage is huge, for example when stents were first introduced in 1994, 1 million were used internationally in the first year alone.

At NUI, Galway we do research with the medical device companies to design new products and improve existing ones. This work of course includes a vital input from cardiac surgeons, and to see how the products are used I have been present at a number of angioplasty procedures as an observer. It was a humbling experience to see the cardiologists at work and to watch them save lives. However there was a great sense of satisfaction realising that the treatment wouldn't be possible without the input of the engineer in terms of designing and producing the device. I was trained as a mechanical engineer in the traditional way and I never thought I would end up in an operating theatre (be it as an observer) but I am happy to be moving with the changing times - as a famous US businessman used to say "Every few years you must re-invent yourself!"

The angioplasty device is a perfect example of a product (and industry) requiring a new breed of engineer and technologist for product design and manufacture - a biomedical engineer with multi-disciplinary skills. First of all it is obvious that these devices require very careful mechanical engineering design. The very thin small bore catheter tubes have to be designed to be inserted up to almost 1 metre inside the body - they can't be too stiff or they might puncture the soft arterial wall - they can't be too flexible or they will buckle while being inserted - getting the balance just right and repeating it exactly in mass producing millions of devices is no mean engineering feat! Likewise, the metal stents have to be flexible enough to follow the contours of the heart on the way in, to allow them to be placed correctly - but they have to be strong enough to stay expanded and hold the artery open permanently - and at the same time the wires have to be small enough not to disrupt normal blood flow after implantation. Getting it all just right is a delicate balancing act. Stents are normally made from stainless steel and the wires end up being less than one tenth of a millimetre wide, no thicker than a human hair! This is cutting edge engineering technology, challenging and fascinating, and made all the more rewarding when you know it is saving lives. But knowing how to design and produce very thin tubes or very thin metal wires is only the start of it. The designer must be fully acquainted with where the device is going. He/she must know the anatomy of the heart and the arterial system - all the twists and turns the catheter is likely to meet on the way to its destination - and also the strength of the artery wall so that the catheter can be designed not to puncture it. He/she must also become familiar with surgical techniques because it will be the surgeon who will be using the device and he/she has to be happy with it to use it effectively. And then there are other questions. Here we are talking about inserting plastic and metal into the body and implanting them permanently. How will the cells of the body react to the presence of the implant? Will the material poison the person? Will it cause infection, etc? How can all this be found out at the design stage? To find out if the device will be "biocompatible", he/she must learn biology and how to do biological experiments.

NUI, Galway was the first university in the country to introduce a degree in biomedical engineering five years ago, by developing the existing mechanical engineering programme to include anatomy, biology and surgical methods, and including visits to, and demonstrations in, hospitals to see first hand how these products would be used. More recently other universities in the country have followed suit. This is typical of what is happening internationally as this new discipline of biomedical engineering grows, and is driven by the explosion in the medical device industry worldwide and the need for trained designers and technologists with sufficient multi-disciplinary skills to hit the ground running once employed.

The main reason for the explosion in the industry is the fact that the population in the western developed world is getting older. People living longer and fewer children being born. Dealing with longevity issues and treatment of diseases normally associated with the middle age and post middle age, such as heart disease and cancer, has lead to the development of the medical device industry - there is nothing like a problem (and a potential market that can be exploited to make a profit) to focus the mind!

New courses like biomedical engineering, because of their futuristic outlook, are attracting great students from the Leaving Cert., and so may it continue. But it is important for people to realise that maths and science are vital for this kind of career. Figures indicate a drop in the take-up of these subjects in secondary school in Ireland. This is indeed a tragedy as it means that there will be fewer engineers and technologists produced at the other end. This will affect the economy, as it is well recognised, and patently obvious when one thinks about it, that it is the application of science, engineering and technology, in terms of conceptualising, designing and producing new products and generating new markets, that is the root of industrial and economic growth.

Even though at the time of writing we seem to be in somewhat of an economic downturn, and people complain about the government and public finances, it has to be said that the government have done a lot for the universities and institutes of technology in the last few years to equip them to teach new courses and to develop spin-off research programmes that help Irish industry. Ireland can now hold its head up and say that it has university research facilities that are the equal of the best in the world. This is great for our students and for our economic development.

In passing I want to mention my own first cousin, Brendan Hopkins, who had settled in Castlebar and who recently died tragically. Brendan was fascinated with gadgets of all kinds and as a regular visitor to our house when I was a boy was in his element helping out my father Eddie in his car battery workshop. Brendan was one of the most compassionate individuals anyone has had the privilege to know and his community spirit, as demonstrated by his outstanding contributions to life in Castlebar through the credit union, training the local athletics team, giving blood, involvement in the Alzheimer's association, etc., is a model to anyone.

Finally I want to mention two people who were close neighbours of mine, who I had regular contact with up to recent years and who left a big impression on me.

I have the fondest memories of Joe Greene and of numerous visits to his house. His positive and exuberant character gave me hours of enjoyment, his enthusiasm and genuine wonder for things new was extremely refreshing. Joe will be remembered by many people in different ways but one abiding memory for me was when I was a student myself - I was doing a doctorate in engineering in the USA which was a bit unusual at the time - I will always remember his enthusiasm, his encouragement and his genuine desire to know what it was really like, what it was all about and what it might lead to.

In closing I must mention Jack Halpin, my next-door neighbour for many years. Jack was one of the most interesting individuals anyone has had the privilege to know. He was a man ahead of his time and listening to him tell of his life experiences was enthralling. His desire for travel seemed limitless and his courage and stamina to make long trips, including a number to Australia, in his later years would put many younger people to shame. He never seems to let the years confine him and I will always remember conversations where he would be describing his next trip and what he would do and who he would visit. Travel was a topic of commonality between us as I did a fair bit of travel throughout my 20's, although still relatively small by his standards.

A HOLIDAY IN THE SUN

By

John Corbett

Many will have heard the joke about two Irishmen who built a turf-powered rocket with which they intended to land at night on the Sun. The truth as everyone knows is, that night does not happen on this distant orb. With current technology, we could reach the sun in about 12 days but despite what the characters in the joke think, there are four good reasons why we could never land on it.

(1)   It isn't solid.

(2)   It is far too hot. The temperature at the Corona or outer edge is at least 10 thousand degrees while the core is calculated to be in excess of 20 million degrees Fahrenheit.

(3)   The human eye would not be capable of withstanding the brightness of the sun. Even at an average distance of 93 million miles, one shouldn't look directly at it and under no circumstances should one point field glasses or telescopes in the direction of the sun.

(4)   If we could ignore the previous three factors, the human body would not be able to survive the pressure. On the Earth our bodies are subjected to 14.7 pounds per square inch of atmospheric pressure but the sun's pressure is 28 times greater than this.

THE REALITY

Having said all that, have you ever wondered what the sun is really like?
From our perspective, whenever we're lucky enough to see it, it appears much smaller than the average football as it floats above the clouds. The reality is different. Its diameter is 865,400 miles. A million planets the size of the Earth would fit into it and there would be still lots of room to spare. All the elements that exist on our planet are to be found there but because of the high temperature, they exist in the form of gas. Although we receive only a tiny proportion of the sun's output, it provides us with the lion's share of our heat, light and energy. For example, the turf or coal in our fires and the petrol and car fuel we use, are actually releasing the energy which comes from the sun and which has been stored beneath the Earth's surface for millions of years. Without its heat, our crops couldn't grow and life here would be impossible.

The rays of the sun help humans to become happy and healthy and most of us feel much better whenever it brightens the sky. However, in recent years we have reason to fear it. Because of our careless lifestyle, we have destroyed much of the blanket of Ozone gas that protects us from the harmful ultra violet radiation coming from the sun.
This destruction is the result of the large quantities of CFC gases emanating from our cars, fridges and aerosols. Attempts have been made to persuade us to reduce these but by and large we have ignored them. A recent survey has shown that a vast quantity of the Ozone layer was destroyed during the past year. Even though we realise that we are harming the atmosphere, we are reluctant to cut back on the luxuries to which we think we are entitled. If we continue to ignore the danger from solar radiation then we can expect a big increase in cancer and other life threatening diseases. It would be nice to think that we will take positive action to deal with this problem and that we can establish sunbathing as the pleasant and beneficial activity which it once was.

KEEPING THE SUNSHINE IN OUR LIVES

It is obvious that life on our planet depends very much on conditions in the sun. If the heat from it were just 12 per cent stronger than it is, then it would cause our oceans to evaporate and life on earth would quickly disappear. The fact that the Earth spins
on its axis at 1 thousand miles per hour, while it orbits the sun at a speed of 66 thousand miles per hour, ensures that we keep a safe distance from this large gaseous ball. Surprisingly, we are much closer to the sun in wintertime than in the summer (over 3 million miles nearer), it is colder in this part of the world because the rays of the sun which strike us are more slanted and give much less heat.

Everyone has heard of the 'Greenhouse effect' whereby heat becomes trapped in the atmosphere causing the ice caps at the poles to melt and which it is claimed will lead to overheating and a worsening in the Earth's climate. Like the Ozone problem, the situation will improve if we change our habits and reduce pollution.

Although the sun is the dominant force in the solar sphere, we play an important role in the relationship between Earth and Sun. In the past, life on Earth has been threatened by asteroids and meteorites which have crashed into us from space. Some scientists think that these crashes happen at regular periods every 26 million years or so. They claim that the Sun has a twin star orbiting it and when this approaches its sister star, it throws the asteroids out of position and makes them collide with us. They have named this, as yet undiscovered object, as Nemesis, saying that it is probably smaller and darker than its twin. Like the mysterious Planet X which is being sought by astronomers since the 1970's, the existence of Nemesis is just speculation. (At the time of writing Scientists claim to have discovered a new planet orbiting the Earth two billion miles further out than Pluto. It is smaller than Pluto and they have called it Sedna after the Innuit goddess of the sea. No doubt we'll be hearing more about this in the future. Many Astronomers want Pluto itself relegated to a planetoid or lesser object and if this happens, we will have lost a planet in place of gaining one.)

Generally speaking most people accept that the Dinosaurs and similar creatures have been wiped out as the result of a dramatic change in atmosphere caused by the impact of a heavenly body. However, it must be admitted that not all experts accept this explanation. Some claim that the atmospheric changes may have occurred due to disturbances on our own planet such as volcanoes or tidal waves etc.

Last year observers reported that a relatively large asteroid is due to collide with the Earth in February 2019. The good news, say scientists, is that collisions of this kind can be prevented by using nuclear weapons or by a melt down process utilising modern technology. Whether this is so or not, hopefully, we may never find out. Although our sun loses 4 million tons of heat and energy every second or so, we can expect it to last at least 5 thousand million years. Unless there's a major breakthrough in technology resulting in increased longevity, none of us will need to worry about what will happen to the sun at the end of its reign so until then I'm afraid we'll just have to keep our night landing options on the sun on hold.

INTERESTING FACTS

The sun is just one among countless billions of other stars which are scattered throughout the Universe. It travels at 140 miles per second and brings the Earth and the other 8 planets with it on an orbit that takes 250 million years to complete. The sun revolves on its axis approximately once every 25 days compared to once every 24 hours for the Earth.

THE AURORO BOREALIS

The solar wind is a stream of electronically charged particles coming from the sun. These are usually deflected into space but are sometimes captured by the Earth's magnetic field. The resulting collisions with terrestrial atoms create spectacular visual displays called the Aurora Borealis. These generally take place 50 - 75 miles above ground but can be 600 miles high: therefore they can be seen over a wide distance. The Northern Lights or Aurora Borealis can vary in colour and duration but are usually strikingly beautiful. The best places to view them are at the Earth's magnetic poles but they can also be seen from Ireland and Britain. The best times are on starry nights between 9 p.m. and midnight and Spring and Autumn are the best seasons. The year 2000 coincided with a rush of activity involving these famous celestial night-lights, the likes of which had not been seen since 1989.

CHAPTER TWELVE

MORE VIEWS ON LIFE AND EDUCATION

A DAY IN THE LIFE OF MY EDUCATION

By

Sean Connaire

At the age of six years, I had to walk three Irish miles to school in rain, hail or snow storms. I lived in the parish of New Inn and had to travel through the parish of Killimordaly and into the parish of Gurteen. The journey was long and hard on a six-year-old who wore no shoes from March to October and who only had poor quality clothes. We were never short of an appetite and often tucked in to our lunches before even arriving at school.

I used to leave home at 8.15 a.m. and arrived at school at approximately half past nine. If you were unfortunate enough to be five minutes late, you got slapped. (It was an accepted rule in those days). It was a two roomed classroom manned by Mrs. Kitt and Mr. Blehein, both of whom were strict but fair.

One of my happiest memories is of the last day before the summer holidays. The Master would organise a Sports Day which was held out in Cormican's Hill. All the pupils took part and it was most enjoyable. We had tug-of-war, egg and spoon races, three legged races, a hundred yards race and numerous other activities. Money was scarce and I'm sure the Master's salary wasn't very big but Mr. Blehein gave prizes ranging from six pence to half a crown to the winners of the various competitions. A half crown was a substantial prize and as I recall it was won by the late John Ward of Beechill on at least one occasion.

The following people from our area went to Shanballard School: Mikey Ward and his sisters, Mabel and Bernadette from Beechill, Dennis and John Ward, Bernard, Eithne and Anna Kilkenny from Streamsfort, Bobby and Bertie Kenny, Joe Melody and my sisters, Mary, Phil, Kitty, Ann, Josie, Teresa (Bobby) and my bothers, Paddy, Peadar, and of course myself - a large flock if I do say so myself.

On our way home there was never any hurry on us and we took part in numerous games and devilment and I dare say quite a few fights as well.

A MISSED DAY- NOT TO BE FORGOTTEN

On a beautiful, fine summer's day in June 1948, as eight of us trudged to school in Shanballard, late I may add, we decided that as we were in trouble anyway, we would skip school and spend the day in Tom Walshe's clough - a place where stones were quarried. It was about 10 feet deep and a great hiding place or so we thought. We went down to the bottom of the clough and spent our time playing games and telling stories. All of a sudden a shadow appeared between us and the sun. When we looked up there was Mrs. Kitt, our teacher, armed with a long stick She shouted at us to come up at once and gave us a severe lecture on the stupidity of our behaviour. She drove us down to school before her like a flock of sick sheep. On the way she told us that Tom Walshe had seen us enter the clough and had reported us to her. If wishes could kill, Tom would be dead that day. Some of us were sent to Mr. Blehein and Mrs. Kitt dealt with the rest of us herself. Each of us got 'six of the best' and our hands were warm and sore for the rest of that day at least. We would have loved to see Tom Walshe get 'six of the best' too but I'm afraid that our wishful thinking had no effect on him at all.

KILLIMORDALY VERSUS GURTEEN

There was always tremendous rivalry between the people of Killimordaly and Gurteen. Nowadays it's usually evident in Camogie and Hurling but it was of a more serious nature long ago. Back then there used to be Shillelagh Fights between the two groups. A large throng would assemble on the border of the parishes and a full-scale fight would ensue. It was so common then that it was an eagerly anticipated event and as far as I remember there was a kind of Shillelagh Championship. After a punishing contest, a ceasefire followed and the participants would retire to the local pub for refreshments- all enmity between them apparently forgotten!

There were some strong individuals in the neighbourhood when I was growing up. Lifting heavy objects was no problem to them. Two-hundredweight bags of corn and manure had to be loaded and unloaded. One man near us brought a five hundredweight bag of wheat upstairs on his own.

Of course it wasn't only men that did things like that. The Late Mrs. Silke set off on a two and a half-mile journey to collect a harrow. The harrow was a four by three-foot oaken implement and she was able to carry it on her back. On the way home she went into labour and she gave birth to her baby, unassisted. She went home then and fixed up the baby. When she had a short rest, she returned to collect the harrow. Mrs. Silke had a large family and her husband had died a short time previously.

It's doubtful if modern schoolchildren would have seen or heard of such events or even if they did, they would find it very hard to believe them.

MY DAD- PETER KERRILL GAVIN

By

John Gavin.

PETER KERRILL GAVIN

Peter was born in a townland called Ballygreaney. He was looked after by his grandmother Mary. The house that they lived in was very small and originally had a thatched roof, but later it was covered with sheets of corrugated metal and when rain fell it was almost deafening. At the age of eight years he attended a small school in Gurteen. In those days times were very hard and a small boy living with his grandmother had to pull his weight and do lots of chores. I suppose this helped him with what was to come as later he was sent to an industrial school at the age of twelve years and had to stay there until he was sixteen. The time he spent at Letterfrack will never be told as he took any memories he had of that place to his grave. He would never discuss anything about his stay there.

After leaving Letterfrack Peter worked at a place called Carnacon house in Ballyglass until his twentieth birthday; after that we don't know where he was, but he surfaced in England where he met and married his wife Mary in 1942. They had five children who never went hungry for love or anything else. He made sure we never lacked the necessities and worked hard all his working life. He often thought about Ireland and all the hardships he encountered as a young boy. The fact that he still adored his country of birth bemused me until I came across on holiday. That's when I fell in love with its people and its beautiful land. The memory of my dad singing the old Irish songs and smiling broadly as he listened to John McCormack on the old gramophone will live inside me forever.

MY AMERICAN EXPERIENCE

By

Brendan Hynes

BRENDAN HYNES

Shortly after arriving in the U.S. I was drafted into the army and sent to Fort Benning, Georgia for basic training. My biggest surprise was seeing the discrimination in the South where there were separate facilities for blacks and whites. After basic training it was back to Fort Nix, NJ for more training. I was then assigned to an Ordinance Detachment in Germany for the next two years.

The G.A.A in New York was a great organization and Gaelic Park was a popular meeting place for U.S. immigrants. While I was stationed in NJ, I was able to play hurling with the Galway team. After returning from Germany, I again started playing with Galway and a lot of new players were arriving. Some teammates in those years included Kevin Shaughnessy (Castlegar), Martin Murphy (Carnmore), Mike Sweeney (Loughrea), The Stally brothers (Ballinakill), Paddy Lally (Colemanstown), Paddy Ryan (Gurteen), Fr. Nick Murray (Ballymacward), Fr. Tom Tarpey (Ardrahan) and Mattie Duggan (Claregalway) to name but a few.

In the 1960's Galway had a great run. Only two losses in four years. New York's Gaelic Park and the Irish Dance Halls were great meeting places for the Irish in those years.

Moving North out of the city in the 70's to Putnam County, I got involved in promoting Gaelic football and the team went on to win the New York Minor Football Championship in the 80's.

The town of Carmel in Putnam County has a population of approximately thirty five thousand and a local town government. I was nominated to run for Highway Superintendent in the town government and was elected and re-elected in the 1980's. I also was an independent business owner, running a bar/restaurant in both the Bronx (the Greenleaf) and in Putnam County (The Irish Centre).

In Putnam County, I actively pursued Cultural and athletic interests. I was founding President of the West Put Gaels Gaelic Football Club as well as a former president of the Emerald Association of Putnam County and the Irish American Association of Northern Westchester and Putnam Counties. I also served as Grand Marshall of the county's St. Patrick's Day parade in the 1980's.

My wife of thirty eight years, the former Anne McDonnell from Mayo and I, have raised four children who have been able to pursue professional degrees and participate in various Irish cultural activities. My son, Kerrill, has a BS in engineering and is a licensed Professional Engineer with the NY State Department of Transportation. He also coaches the underage Gaelic football teams. My daughter, Kathy, holds a BS and MS degrees in Biology and is a college professor of Biology in New Jersey. She also teaches with a local Irish Dancing school and has her own traditional Irish music school. My son Kenneth has a BS and MS degrees in Engineering and is a Major with the US Army Special Operations. My daughter Deirdre pursued BS and MS degrees in Mathematics and currently teaches and coaches for St. Joseph's School in Connecticut. We have eight grandchildren.

I look forward to meeting all my old friends in Gurteen in the near future.

BRENDAN HYNES IN UNIFORM

TAMPLE CLASSMATES AT THEIR OLD SCHOOL

CHAPTER THIRTEEN

LEARNING LOTS IN TAMPLE

MEMORIES OF TAMPLE N.S.

By
Maura Carr

On my first day in school, my teacher to be, Mrs. Clancy was absent and I was brought to the senior's room by Miss Duffy. I did not want to go home at two o'clock when my father came to collect me. Obviously that was a good indication of the welcome I had received and how I settled into Tample School on my first day.

Tample was a two-teacher school until the late sixties. We had the privilege of having wonderful teachers in Mrs. Clancy, Miss Duffy, the principal, and later Mrs. Bellew. Those of us who left national school from the early seventies until the school closed in 1981 were the products of a one-teacher school. How daunting it must have been for Miss Duffy and later Mrs. Lyng to have the burden of responsibility for the education of approximately twenty children all at different levels.

Despite her imminent retirement, Miss Duffy embraced the change in the school curriculum in the early seventies. While there was a major emphasis on the three R's. Miss Duffy widened our horizons with nature study walks, physical education, arts and crafts. We even learned some dancing - The Siege of Ennis and The Walls of Limerick. More importantly, Miss Duffy gave us the opportunity to learn French by listening to tapes. She came to school early to teach Algebra to those who wanted to improve their knowledge of Maths. Our transition to second level was easier as a result of the additional tuition in national school.

In 1969 the world saw the American Astronauts land on the moon for the first time. Miss Duffy took all the pupils to her sitting room in the school residence nearby to watch that eventful moment. There was always intensive preparation for First Holy Communion, Confirmation and the visit of the Diocesan Examiner and we were usually treated to sweets and time off from school afterwards. While Miss Duffy could be described as a strict disciplinarian, she never shied away from rewarding us for good behavior.

MAURA CARR WITH THE QUIZ TEAM AT ST. CUAN'S COLLEGES (3RD FROM LEFT)

Conditions in Tamale were similar to other rural schools of the time. There was no central heating, running water or flush toilets. Parent gave loads of turf throughout the year to heat the open fires. Pupils helped to take out the ashes and keep the fires going. We were allowed to go up in turns to the fireplace to warm our hands. We needed to thaw out on frosty mornings, otherwise we could not hold the writing pens between our fingers.

The kettle was boiled by placing it on the open fire and I can still remember the smell of the cocoa when the boiling water was added to it. We brought a simple lunch to school. We had a choice of tea or cocoa in wintertime. In summertime we brought bottles of milk, freshly milked in the morning.

There was no school transport scheme then. We were carried on bicycles or in the pony and cart.

As we got older, we walked or cycled. It is with gratitude I remember getting a seat from the late Mick Bellew or John Lyng. Mick used to be taking his wife, Sheila, to school and John would have been driving to work.

We got to know all the neighbours en route and relied on them to fix our bicycles when we got into difficulty. We had many pleasant chats with the late Seamus Cogavin, Paddy Connor and Ned Burke. Ned lived closest to the school and he always helped to keep the school grounds in order. Another past pupil reminds me that it was Ned who cut the canes for the teachers. I know that Ned being the nice gentleman that he was, wouldn't have liked to see them being used on us. Ned invited us all to his Station parties. He and his sisters entertained us in style. Likewise Paddy and Maura Connor. We loved those invitations.

Going home from school took ages. We had opportunities to watch Paddy Connor use the meal crusher. Further down the road we examined the swallow hole in Mickey Hoban's land. In times of heavy rain we had flooding in our land in Ballyglass and we liked to go in there to investigate. Thankfully, we arrived home safely despite the many distractions en route. As children, time seemed to stand still for us. Indeed many attempts were made to "put the clock forward" unknown to the teacher. Oh now what we'd give to have the choice of "putting back" the clock.

PUPIL ASKS THE QUESTIONS
OLIVER KING INTERVIEWS MRS. LYNG N.T.

RAYMOND, AIDAN & KEVIN FINNERTY

SABINA FINNERTY AND FAMILY

THE DUFFY DYNASTY

Right through the twentieth century and extending to the centuries on either side, there is one family synonymous with primary education in the parish of Gurteen. The Duffy family was involved in teaching in three parish schools from 1887 when Mrs. Kate Duffy was Principal in Scoil Éanna, Tample, up to 2002 when Mrs. Pam Griffin-Lyng retired from her teaching post in St. Kerrill's Gurteen.

Scoil Éanna, Tample, was officially known as Gurteen School. Cloonkeenkerrill School was St. Kerrill's; and the new school built in Gurteen in 1981 is also called St Kerrill's.

Two of Mrs. Kate Duffy's three daughters - Teresa and Margaret (Daisy) followed into the teaching profession. Her third daughter (Babs) married Lawrence Griffin of Gurteen and four of their five daughters, Kitty, Pearl, Pam and Claire also became primary teachers. Gabrielle pursued a career with Aer Lingus. On Mrs. Duffy's retirement in 1925 the principal-ship of Scoil Eanna passed on to Daisy; meanwhile Teresa took over the helm in Cloonkeenkerrill. In 1974 after Daisy's fifty years of service, her niece Pam Griffin-Lyng returned to her Alma Mater and accepted the difficult task of running a one teacher school where there were thirty six pupils from junior infants to sixth class. She subsequently transferred to the new school in 1981 and continued to teach there until she retired, having served forty-eight years in the classroom. Forty four of those years were spent in her own locality since she was also an assistant in Clonkeenkerrill from 1958 until her appointment in Tample; and so Pam has the distinction of having taught in three of the four parish schools. Indeed, the Griffin family did not inherit their pedagogic genes from their maternal ancestors alone. Lawrence Griffin's grandfather, also called Lawrence, was the first teacher recorded under the National School system in Gurteen, where he had previously run a hedge school in the mid-eighteen hundreds.

In its ninety-four years of existence, Tample was served by only three Principal teachers all of whom belonged to the Duffy family; and all female which was quite amazing in the male dominated society of the time. Only one male teacher taught in the school as far as we know. This was Senator Micheál Kitt, who stood in for Miss Duffy for a month in 1969.

Teresa Duffy-Hurley served as Principal in Cloonkeenkerrill until her untimely death in 1944 leaving three young children who were regularly mothered by Daisy in her home in Tample, while their father William was away on business trips. Victor, Margot and Hazel all qualified as second level teachers.

Influence and dedication are commodities that cannot be quantified and it is impossible to exaggerate the significance of the contribution made by three generations of the Duffys to the education and formation of the local population. The fourth generation is still carrying on the tradition of imparting knowledge in the persons of Ronan McMahon, son of Margot Hurley-McMahon, Lawrence Dooley, son of Claire Griffin-Dooley; and three members of the Lyng family, Jan, Michael and Lorcan.

FOUR GENERATIONS AT TAMPLE SCHOOL

By

Breda Noone

The first entries in Tample School register are dated 1888. Among those named, probably on transfer from the old school, was Pat Burke of Tample then aged eight. In 1911 Pat married Maria Coen of Clough who was also registered in the school in 1891. From that union emerged three generations who were to attend there up to the time of its closure in 1981.

Pat and Maria parented nine children. A daughter, Sabina, was enrolled on the first of July, 1923. She married Frank Finnerty of Clough Cross. All of their eight children attended Tample School including their eldest son, Micheál, who was registered on the 27th April, 1949. Micheál and his wife Angela had three sons, Kevin, Raymond and Aidan and they too started school in Tample in 1976, 1978 and 1980 respectively.

Paddy, a son of Pat and Maria, continued a parallel lineage. He was enrolled on the 7th of May, 1928. The eldest of his four sons, Noel, followed on the 4th of September, 1961. The eldest of Noel's children, Ita, is the last name on the school register. It was entered on the 14th of April, 1981.

In addition, Mary (Mentane), Paddy's wife, mother of Noel and grandmother of Ita, was also registered in Tample on the 23rd of June, 1938.

Beginning with Pat in 1888, a total of 27 of his descendants attended the school while it was in operation.

PAT & MARIA BURKE

RIDING HIGH ON SHANK'S MARE

By

Bridget Dilleen/Sullivan.

I would be lying if I said that I remember my first day in school or even my first Holy Communion day but there are many other memories that I recall from my school days in Tample National School. The school register confirms that I entered Tample National School on 22 June 1954, register number 709.

Recycling is big nowadays but my mother knew all about it before it became fashionable. When we were young we had hand made, hand me down recycled dresses, jumpers and coats, all made by my mother from larger clothes, received from parcels from my aunts in America and England. Wellingtons were also passed on from one to another and if you were at the end of the family they were well worn when they reached you. My brother Seamus was the lucky one, he was the oldest. Our schoolbags were made from heavy material with one shoulder strap. There was no uniform in those days but we wore one even though we didn't realise it because we had the same clothes week after week. After school we would have to change in order to save our school attire. Going to school barefoot was rather a novelty and we did this occasionally. We went barefoot during summer holidays when the weather was good. I don't remember much bad weather when I was young except for the odd severe thunder and lightning storm.

Tample School is approximately one and a half miles from Gurteen and in my time the road was very rough. I have a faint recollection in the early 1960s of improvements being made to it, with workers using diggers, steamrollers and chippings. The realignment of bad bends took place but it is much the same now as it was then except for the surface quality. We had bicycles towards the end of our school days but we usually had to walk unless we were lucky enough to get a lift on the carrier of the bicycle from older members of the family. There was also a short cut through the fields from Paddy Carr's field via Mentanes, Rafterys and out close to Grady's house. The Shanballymores also took this route, entering the fields near the bridge at Markey Carr's house and walking along the river. We were always warned not to skate on the river during heavy frost or at the pond between King's house and Mary Griffin's lane when they were frozen over. Of course we always did what we were told not to do.

Tample School was a two-teacher school, with boys' and girls' playgrounds. The rooms had big high windows and an open fireplace. There was always a fire but the teacher benefited more than the pupils did from it. Every family had to bring a cart of turf for the school year. This wasn't a problem as we were surrounded by bog. When you were about to begin school, you went on the last day or two before the school closed for the summer holidays. Of course when we got sweets on the day of the summer holidays and when we went back in September we expected sweets again at the end of that first day.

Children today think that we had a very bleak childhood but nothing could be further from the truth. We had a wonderful childhood without televisions, computers, microwaves videos and digital this and digital that. The seats were timber benches with an inkwell in the middle. I particularly loved the chalk and slate. The chalk was white. I used to go to Simon Finn's house, his being the nearest slated house (now Molloys), looking for an old slate to write on with the chalk that I brought home from school.

My teacher in the junior class was Miss Maureen Keane from Attymon. I had Miss Duffy in senior class. I'm sure I speak for all past pupils when I say that we had the best teachers any students could have had in those days. They taught everything from reading, writing, knitting, sewing, singing, tin whistle playing, geography and history and they had a profound interest in the pupils even after they left the national school. Miss Duffy was an exceptional teacher. She was strict but fair. If you forgot to bring your lunch to school she would take you to the teacher's residence and give you a sandwich at lunchtime. She also spent hours preparing children for scholarship exams after school, without payment. This shows her commitment to her pupils. Many children in the locality benefited from her teaching talents because she enabled them to receive scholarships that put them through secondary school. Children from outside the area were also sent to our school because of the quality of the teachers. The traveling community used to pitch their tents around Molly Mannion's and I remember they used to come to school for a few weeks, particularly before first Holy Communion or Confirmation time.

We had religious examinations too and of course the Primary Certificate was a big thing. I also remember having medical examinations and myself and Ann were sent to Portiuncla Hospital to have our tonsils out following the school medical check.

When the Station Mass was held in a house in the morning, the children would be brought in on the way home from school and given cake, minerals and biscuits. It was such a treat. I remember being in Ned Burkes, Gradys and the King households after a station Mass and the display of food and fancy china was breathtaking.

After school there were always jobs to be done. These were: going to the well, weeding ridges of vegetables, going to the bog or helping at the hay. The worst job of all was picking stones in a newly reseeded field. It would break your back and it was hard for my father to get us to do it. He used to promise to give us money for Lady's Day in Athenry on the 15 August if we had them all picked by then. We had mostly home grown food and probably the only items that were bought in the shop were sugar, tea, flour, bread soda and John Player cigarettes for my father. If you had hens you sold the eggs to pay for your purchases. You daren't break the eggs on the way to the shop or lose the change on the way back.

SWAPPING NEWS
The Irish Press newspaper was bought daily and the Sunday Press was bought coming home from Mass in Kyne's shop. Markey Carr got the Sunday Independent and every Monday evening we swapped papers with him. We read his newspaper and he read ours- recycling of another kind, I suppose. Visiting Markey Carr's house was always a pleasure because they always had gorgeous fruitcakes. They were also involved in the hatchery business. They used to have eggs in an incubator and Maureen used to turn the eggs and listen for the tapping of the shells before the arrival of the chicks.

Another job we had to do was bring the turkey hen to the cock. This was a very responsible job. The turkey was put into a meal bag with its head out and strapped to the handlebars of the bike. We had to cycle to Molly Mannion's house or to Molloys further on the road. The lady of the house took the turkey hen and went off with it. She returned after a while. Off you went home with the turkey again. I don't think we realised what had gone between cock and hen at all.

Having the post office attached to our home had its advantages and disadvantages. There was always the possibility of somebody giving you money for sweets or on the other hand the teacher,

Miss Duffy, might come to the post office on her bicycle after school. In that case you would hide behind the wall until she was gone in case she saw you. There was always the danger that your presence might remind her of your misbehavior in school that day. I was always afraid that she might tell my mother of the goings on.

In these days it seems to be fashionable to write books or articles deploring one's inadequate and horrible childhood. Thank God that type of scenario wasn't mine at all. I am eternally grateful for having excellent parents and teachers. It is only now that I appreciate the sacrifices they made for us. I thank them for all they have done for us.

After my years in Tample National School, I went to New Inn Vocational School. This was a considerable distance from my home in Gurteen and I was able to travel to New Inn, through the generosity of Miss Duffy's niece, Mrs. Clare Griffin/Dooley, N.T. She was teaching in New Inn National School at that time. Thank you Claire for all your help.

I am married to Sean O Suilleabhain and I live in Ballinamore in Lovely Leitrim with two grown up sons and a grandson. I would like to take this opportunity to thank the organising committee for having a School Reunion and I congratulate them for their efforts. I look forward to meeting all my school friends again and hearing about their lives and the lives of their children.

Finally spare a thought for teachers, past pupils, friends and neighbours who have gone to their eternal reward. May their souls Rest in Peace.

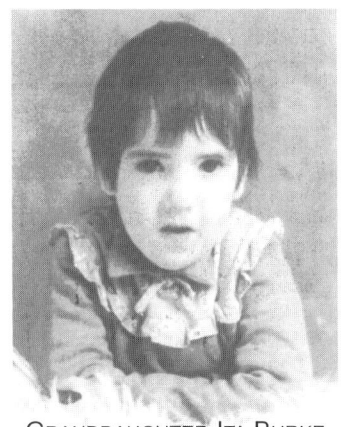

MARY BURKE & FAM

GRANDDAUGHTER ITA BURKE

THE CARR FAMILY

THE LATE PADDY BURKE

TAMPLE SCHOOL AND AFTER

By

Michael O'Flaherty

MICHAEL O'FLAHERTY

I was born in February 1948. I'm not quite sure what age I was when I came to Gurteen to live with the McGann family. I attended Tample School until I was 15 years old. I have good memories of my school days. There were two teachers in the school Miss Keane taught the younger children and Miss Duffy taught the older ones. I can remember during the Winter months when each child brought two sods of turf to school so that the fire could be lit to keep us warm.

During my stay at McGanns, a lady called Miss McCormack (whom I later found out was a Welfare worker) used to call regularly to see how I was getting on. Annie Kenny, Mrs. McGann's daughter, used to bring me to school on the back of her bike occasionally. I used to have two boiled eggs in each pocket to keep my hands warm in cold weather. I must mention that I was terrified of the turkeys on the farm at that time.

On some Sunday afternoons, Cyril and Paul Hardiman (R.I.P.) and myself used to go to the pictures in Athenry or Monivea. I remember seeing 'Doctor in the House' and 'Paleface' starring Bob Hope and Jane Russell.

I was about 15 years of age when I went to Headford. I began to work for dairy farmers there. The hours were long. Milking began around six in the morning and there weren't many idle hours between then and bedtime. I stayed there until I was 24 years old.
The Moran family who lived there were one of the first families to have a television. Around six o'clock in the evening Mrs. Moran used to allow us to watch it. Our favourite childrens' programmes were: 'Rin Tin Tin', 'Combat' (starring Vic Morrow), 'The Fugitive' and 'Car 54'.

As I grew older, I went to dances in Glenamaddy, Cong and Claremorris. We went to the local marquees in the summertime. I remember seeing Dermot O'Brien and his band at a dance in Headford. The hall was small and was packed to capacity.

It was during my school years that I became interested in the game of hurling and from then on and to this present time, it is my favourite sport. At the moment, I am very much involved with the G.A.A. as a Referee and a Club Mentor of St. Mark's - our local club.

In 1972, when I joined the Army in Renmore Barracks, Galway, everything was very new to me. Discipline was the main thing that was stressed in our training and when I look back now, I realise that it didn't do us any harm. I was sent to Dublin to participate in a Cooks Course for six months. During my time in Dublin, I met a girl named Ann and after I returned to Galway, we kept up the friendship. We married in 1975 and I moved to Dublin where I was stationed in Collins Barracks. In 1980, I served a six month's tour of duty in the Lebanon.

I continued cooking in the Army for 19 years and then I took charge of landscaping the Army grounds. During these years we had two children. I retired from the army after 25 years in

1998. It was an enjoyable and eventful period in my life. I now work part-time in Clondalkin Police Station, and in the afternoons, during school term, I referee matches, and in the summer months I do some landscaping.

To finish my story, in 1998 the most wonderful thing happened to me. I was reunited with my mother and I spent a wonderful 10 months getting to know her before she passed away.

I look forward to meeting my friends and schoolmates. I'm sure we'll have lots of interesting stories to share with one another.

SNIPPETS FROM MY SCHOOLDAYS

By

Sheila King-McKiernan.

I walked to school with my brothers and sisters and met Mary Griffin every morning at the top of the road where we joined a huge crowd on the way to school. Our way home we liked to mess with the pump and sit at Grady's gate talking to Kathleen Hynes. The weather never bothered us. I remember squelching the tar of the road with bare feet. I also recall the erecting of E.S.B. poles and the dredging of the river. We were fascinated as we watched the huge machines that were being used then. I had a happy time with Miss Keane but Miss Duffy always created tension. In cold weather we exercised and drank cocoa. Miss Duffy encouraged me to further my education. I got a special prize for "never missing" a day at school and I won a County Council scholarship.

CHAPTER FOURTEEN

FARMING, FODDERING AND FORGEWORK

FROM BELLEVILLE TO BALLYMAC

By

Gerard Flaherty

It was February 1944 when my late grandfather and grandmother and some of their family moved from Belleville, Monivea to Mount Bernard. Ned, as he was known, was a very good tillage farmer - his specialty was potatoes. The late Paddy Bodkin often told me of asking Ned if he had 'all the potatoes sown yet' and the reply he got was "I will be putting up the first spray at the end of the week'. Many people would go as far to say that Ned Flaherty and Michael Dolan of Hampstead - who moved there from Brierfield - were at the top of the class as regards tillage in the area.

The farm in Mount Bernard was a rugged one and was covered with furze and stumps of trees. Using 'elbow grease' and manpower Ned got rid of the furze and very soon the farm was in prime condition. When picking potatoes, "croobing' was his favored method. This meant going down on one's knees and scooping the tubers free from clay after the drills had been split with a plough. He used a bag, tied around his knees to protect him from the weather and the damp ground. He had a rule that once he started croobing a drill, he wouldn't stop until he had finished that particular one, no matter how bad the day turned out. As a result he was often drenched to the skin by the time he finished. My father told me that instead of removing his clothes he would stand by the fire to dry them. Sometimes they were so wet that there would be a massive cloud of steam in the kitchen as he stood by the fire. Despite the large number of wettings that he got, he was rarely sick and he continued to work like this until shortly before his death.

He did plenty of hard work in the bog too. When the turf was cut, he would make into large piles to dry. My father used to be busy with the crops so Ned would take on the turf -footing on his own and he wouldn't rest until the job was done. When he had it footed he would start to bring it home and it was only then that my father would join in to complete the drawing of the turf.

Ned had no formal education, he told the time by the sun, but this never seemed to hold him back. Diplomacy was not a strong point either. Ned spoke his mind and said what came in to his head no matter who was listening.

BRINGING TURF HOME 1944

He had a filly to sell in Athenry. He sold the filly and the buyer asked him to hold the animal for a while. He did as he was asked but the buyer never returned. That night he went to tell Mrs. Kyne of Ballymacward of his disappointment.
He said 'He is a bloody fine blackguard Mrs. Kyne. If I caught him I would hit him with what I have between my two legs.' (He was holding the bridal between his legs at the time). But Mrs. Kyne did not know that.

Another time the late Mrs. Mitchell of Killuane was praising the great dry spell in May when Ned was going to the bog. She said, 'Isn't it great dry weather Ned, a great year for turf'.
She was answered with, 'You can't eat turf Mrs. Mitchell'- meaning that although it was good weather for turf, it wasn't much good for growing crops.

My grandfather was not long in Mount Bernard when he got a visit from the Parish Priest Fr Naughton accompanied by Mr. Tiernan, who was principal of Liscune N.S. Fr Naughton welcomed Ned and my grandmother to the Parish and wished them well in their new farm.
Then he asked, 'Where are you going to send your children to school?'
Ned replied, 'Wherever the children of the village go to school'.
Fr Naughton said, 'They go to Cloonkeen but I want you to send yours to Esker'.
'I came back here to have a road to walk on when I leave my house and I'm not going to send my children to school through the fields again, Ned said.
'Well then', said Fr Naughton, 'You will want your house blessed and if you don't send your children to Esker I will not bless it, or say Mass in it'.

A WELL EARNED REST - MACRA NA FEIRME WORKERS TAKE A BREAK

Ned replied, 'I never asked you. When I want my house blessed I will get a priest somewhere and I am sending my children to Cloonkeen'. Patrick, Kitty and Frank went to school in Clonkeen and from what I heard they enjoyed their stay there.

Farming has changed completely since my grandparents made the journey from Belleville to Mount Bernard. The only lorry in the area at the time was belonging to Paddy Coen of Attymon. Paddy hauled the turf from Belleville to Mount Bernard. Eggs reared a lot of families that time as there was a big demand for them in England and the local shops bought them for export. My grandmother had in excess of 300 hens and knew every one individually. She collected the eggs every day, washed them and put them into crates. On Saturday, no matter what the weather was like, hail, rain or shine, my grandfather would stop work at 1pm, go into the house, get one of the young boys to feed the horse and put him under the trap. He himself would shave, eat the dinner and load up the eggs to go to Kynes in Ballymacward. In later years James Kynes got a van and he came to collect the eggs on Saturday. James would be followed back to the shop by my grandfather and grandmother in the horse and trap. Granny would do her shopping for the week from the egg money and she nearly always had money left over. Ned would go into the bar and have a few drinks while she shopped and chatted to Mrs. Kyne, Nonie Hansberry and who ever else was there. My late father often said that no matter how bad times were they always had plenty on the table. His father and mother, like lots more at the time, were self sufficient. They had their own potatoes, turnips, cabbage, bacon, butter, milk, eggs and had a chicken for dinner every Sunday. Ducks and geese were also kept for special occasions throughout the year. One often wonders how we have lost the art of self-survival nowadays. Our grandparents were able to provide most of their own food but we can now only obtain ours by going to a supermarket and getting it from a freezer or a shelf.

MAKING HAY

A FARM WITH THE POST OFFICE STUCK ONTO THE HOUSE

By

Bridget Sullivan

The Post Office came to our house from Lawrence Griffin, (now the residence of his daughter Clare Griffin/Dooley) in 1941. Until my sister Mary was able to operate the business, we had many people working in the Post Office. My memories are mainly of the time Peggy Griffin R.I.P. worked there.

Peggy cycled to our house every day and spent long hours doing office work and she carried out household duties as well. Prior to Peggy's taking up the job, we had Ciss Grady, Mary Connolly and Annie Greally. Christmas was the busiest time in the post office and people used to post poultry to their families in England. Sometimes the smell of dead geese and turkeys was overpowering and I dread to think of the condition they were in when they arrived at their destination.

Mick Ryan from Shanballymore was the postman was a gentle soul who cycled from the Post Office to Killuane, Kinreask, Corskeagh and Shanballard. Then he returned to the Post Office to pick up the post for Gortnalon, Tample and Clough before going home to Shanballymore. Mick never took the post bike home and we had a great time having spins on it. It had a big carrier at the front for parcels. I don't remember Mick Ryan ever being sick or absent from work.

The site of Gurteen Post Office was at the entrance to the Shanballymore lane opposite Carr's thatched house. The place is hardly recognizable now with agricultural development. Even the hill down to our house does not seem as big now as it was then. I remember taking Peggy Griffin's bike to show her how I had learned to cycle and I cycled down the hill but being inexperienced I couldn't turn the handlebars fast enough. I hit the wall and broke the front wheel.

The only phones in the parish at that time were: the post office phone in our house, James Kyne's and Burke's in Colemanstown, which was also a post office, and Gurteen 2, which was the Garda Station. The phone was operated manually and all calls had to be booked through Ballinasloe. One had to go through Woodlawn post office to get to Ballinasloe. Then one waited patiently for the telephonist in Ballinasloe to connect the call. Most people did not like speaking on the phone themselves so they asked the postmistress to pass on the message. These concerned: ordering fertiliser, booking animals into the mart or calling the AI man, vet, or doctor. Telegrams were also used for communication and were the only means of sending important messages to people who had no phone. They usually carried bad news, a death in the family sent from the hospitals or relatives in England. When a telegram was delivered, the addressee had to pay for the delivery but the post office also contributed a few pence. Sometimes people would ring the post office and ask you to give a message to a family. Occasionally people would come in the middle of the night to ring a doctor but it was often difficult to get an answer at times like these.

We were all taught to do office work, but like many small businesses there was not much money in it for the family. Mary, the oldest girl in the family, received her dowry early in life, she was the first to get her head behind the counter. When we were young we were never allowed into the office at all. There was strict secrecy about savings accounts and the like and I suppose we couldn't be trusted to keep our mouths shut.

My sister Mary took off to the Isle of Man one year and I was put charge the Post office while she was gone. I was happy because I got some money at the end of the month. One year she went to the Isle of Man and at the end of the season there, she decided to go on the Blackpool because they had a longer tourist season there. This meant that I was stuck longer in the post office. As I grew older, I didn't want to be there at all in case I became a permanent fixture there.

It used to be a nightmare watching for the postmaster from Ballinasloe, to come to check the accounts. This happened about once a year. If the money did not balance, there were letters toe-ing and froing for a long time afterwards but of course it was never too serious. There used to be great commotion in the kitchen with mother getting tea ready for the Postmaster. She would send us to the shop for delicacies and a drop of whiskey to sweeten them in case there was any error in the books. Children's allowance and pension days were also busy days. Then there was dole day, which had a different clientele collecting weekly. Occasionally, people came to collect before the due date and you had to use discretion and decide whether or not to give them money in advance. Having said that, people rarely asked for credit.

In those days neighbours shared anything they had. When a pig was killed, it was shared around with the nearest neighbours. Paddy Carr, who had the knack of killing pigs, always got a leg of the pig. Fillets of pork and homemade pudding were given to other neighbours. Paddy was also experienced in boning the pig, and when this job was complete, the meat was put into a barrel of salt to cure.

We also shared agricultural machinery and farm work was done with the loan of a horse from Markey Carr or Paddy Carr. We had only one horse and two were needed for ploughing, harrow-ing or mowing. Threshing was another day where all the neighbours helped out. When the stacks of oats were being threshed we would be watching for the rats to run away when it got near the end of the stack. We spent days on end playing on the chaff after the threshing. We loved the smell of straw, especially when it was fresh and crisp. Newly saved turf brought home from the bog had it's own distinctive smell. The little vegetable plot at the back of our house had its own beauty with different coloured vegetables such as green cabbages, carrots, parsnips and onions and rhubarb (Mother's corner). We never had an apple tree but Paddy Carr had beautiful red apples. However, they were hard, sour and plentiful because they were never robbed due to their taste. We used to get permission from Markey Carr to go to John Carr's orchard and get sweet apples. We brought home bags of them and ate our fill and next day. Our bowel movements had certainly changed colour from previous days.

Bringing home the hay was great fun. We had a float, ant it can be best described as a flat wide timber base with a rope pulley to pull the cock of hay onto it. It was horse drawn. When it was brought into the haggard we forked into the loft. Dad sat at the front of the float and we were always dangling our legs at the back.

Fishing was another past time we enjoyed. Catherine was better than the rest of us and she would go fishing to Lough Teigue or Lough na Hinch and bring home several small fish. We used to fry them in the pan on the open hearth. The fishing rods were just long thin sticks with a line and a cork for a float and a worm attached to the hook for bait. Gathering mushrooms was also done in Paddy Carr's and James Kyne's fields. They were plentiful after a shower of rain whenever it was followed by sunshine. Their pure tasted delicious. After picking mushrooms we cooked them by putting them on a red coal from the open hearth and we added a pinch of salt. Organic grown food now is in big demand. Perhaps we were ahead of the times then and didn't know it.

Playing shop was another great pastime and we had all the necessary pots and jars, tins and if you found a nest of eggs that mother could not sell in the shop you were almost as good as Supervalu is now.

We always had a bank of turf from Pakie Hynes and it was good mixture of brown and black peat so we were never short of heat in winter. We had a long rick of turf in the haggard summer and winter. I remember Jack Dilleen, Daddy's brother from America, bringing his son, John Dilleen, home on holidays with him. John fell off the top of the rick of turf and broke his arm while one year. I don't remember any serious accident on our farm, apart from the usual falls, that is. We never had any broken bones. We often hired travelling labourers. My father always hired the same man, Jack O Donnell, and he slept in the barn or in the small outhouse at the back of our house. This building was used for storing bacon(in a barrel), meal and grain and it had a fireplace where we used to boil a big pot of potatoes for the pigs and fowl.

The thatcher was Patrick Hardiman from Clough and he was much sought after because of his skills. Looking back, I believe our house was very distinctive looking, with the beautiful roses each side of the door and the white washed wall and small flower garden on one side. It had a beautifully shaped palm tree to the right of the main door. In the springtime the daffodils added colour the whitewashed wall. Of course when we were living in it we longed to have a slated house like Kyne's or Griffin's. There was a big kitchen and a parlour and another bedroom and the post office took up another room. There was a two-poster bed in the parlour with curtains hanging high over the head of the bed. We also had a folding bed. Houses like ours would be a tourist attraction nowadays. Going to the toilet meant a quick run to the back of the hen house and you could come back with more that you went with if the nettles got you.

When the electric light came to our house there was fierce excitement and the thought of being able the flick a switch and have powerful light. Electricity also meant that we could turn on the radio and our favourite programme was 'Ceili House' We liked Scottish dance music too. Later we listened to Radio Caroline. We never had a television in the thatched house but James Kyne had one. On the day of an All Ireland Football or Hurling Final he would put the television close to the window in the front room and the neighbours used to go and watch the matches.

Jim Lawless lived in the priest's lane. He had a car and we used to hire him to go to Knock. We would all buy rosary beads, scapulars, medals and little slides. Every time you clicked a button you would see holy scenes, statues and crosses. No downloading from the web in those days. Lady's Day on the 15 August in Athenry was another good outing. We used to get the train from Attymon station to Athenry. We first went to the holy well and ran around it with great speed to get back into town to the swing-boats and chairoplanes and bumping cars. We also went out to Boyhill to our Aunt Delia and she would give us a big feed. After that we'd go back to town for more fun. After the 15 August you knew that the school holidays were nearly over and it was back to the books again until Christmas.

Santa always came to us and we were at least twelve years old when we stopped believing in him. I don't know how my mother did it but we always got a stocking full of toys on Christmas morning. It might not be what you wanted but the stockings were always full to the brim. I'm beginning to wander now but penning these few lines brought me back fifty years and I realise I have only forty more years to go to live as long as mother who recently celebrated her 90th birthday.

Many people in this article are deceased and May they rest in Peace. They are part of history now for me and my family. We thank them and our neighbours and friends who still visit the post office. We hope An Post does not close it down due to decentralization because it is the centre of the social life for many of the people that live in this area.

AG CUR AN SÍOL

Sé Aibrean an mí is coitianta chun barraí a chuir . Baineadh úsáid as braillíní nó práiscíní chun é a scaipeadh ar an dtalamh. Ceanglaoidh na práiscini thart fán bholg. Bhí lámh amháin chun an práiscín a choinneáil suas agus bhí leath lamh saor chun an síol a chraobhscaoileadh ar an dtalamh. Bhí sé tábhactach an síol a dhálú go cothrom. Nuair a bhí sé scaipthe, baineadh úsáid as tor nó cliath fhuirste chun é a chuir níos doimhne sa talamh. Í dtús an chéad ní raibh spraenna ar fáil agus dá bhrí sin ní raibh le déanamh ach fanacht go bhfeicfí an coirce indias. Má bhí an aimsir feiliúnach ba ghearr go bhfeicfí iad ag fás. Bhí an cuma ceanna orthu ar dtús is a bhí ag féir. De réir mar a bhí an samhradh ag sleamhnú thart is an fómhar ag teacht, tháinig athrú ar dath na díase. Bhíodh fás árd agus dath an óir orthu ag tús an fhómhair. Cuthaire é sin go raibh an am bainte taghtha. Cúis imní é seo mar ní raibh an coirce comh docht is atá sé inniú. Tharla gur thit na diasanna go minic. Nuair a thit siad don talamh bhí sé an dheachar iad a ghearradh. Shlogfadh an coirce níos mó uisce nuair a bhí sé titithe agus ní raibh sé comh luachmhar da bhárr.

Ins na 50s ní raibh mórán innil bainte chapaill ar fáil. Dob é an spealadóir a bhain formhór na mbarraí ag an am. Théadh sé trasna na páirce ag baint sraith 3-4 ar leathadh. Lean an graineoir é ag bailiú na punnáin, ag baint úsáid as gas an phlanda chun é a cheangal. Tar éis na ceangailte cuireadh ina seasamh iad i stucainí. Tamaill gearr idiadh sin cruacadh iad. Í gceann seachtain nó dhó bhéadh an coirce sách tirim chun tabhairt abhaile. Dhéantai staicíní móra de agus fágadh san iothlann é go raibh sé in am é a bhuaileadh.

Bhí súistí acu chun é a bhuaileadh í dtús ré. Péire bata ceangailte le scloine a bhí ann. Buaileadh na gais ar an dtalamh chun an síol a bhaint de. Bhí deire leis na súistí nuair a tháinig an inneall buailte.

AN MUILEANN MÓR

Rinne an t-inneall buailte a lán torann agus bhí sé contúirteach comh maith. Bhí geataí na feirme beag agus cúng agus ní go h-annamh a bhí ar na feilmeoirí colúin a leagadh chun an measín mór seo a ligint isteach san iothlann. Bhí slua nó meitheal ag teastáil chun é a choinneáil ag obair.

Bhi fear nó dhó ag teastáil chun na stuicíní a fhorcáil go bárr an mhuilinn. Bhí beirt eile ag obair anseo, ceann ag gearrah na téadanna a bhí thart orthu, agus fear eile á gcuir isteach sa mhuilinn. Bhéadh ort a bheith go h-aireach ag obair anseo. Bhí contúirt ann go slogfadh an muilinn do chuid éadaí isteach i lár an mhuilinn agus bhéadh duine gonta go dona nó marbh dá mba rud é gur thárla seo. Bhí dainséir on scían a bhí á úsáid chun na bandaí a ghearradh freisin.

Bhí torann árd le cloisteáil on measín nuair a baineadh an síol óna diasanna. Tháinig an tuí amach ó thaobh amháin agus an síol ón dtaobh eile den mhuilinn. Bhí poill nó sleamhnain agus málaí ceangailte leo chun an siol a bhailiú. Bhí maidí stiúrtha nó luamháin chun na sleamhnáin a oscailt nó a dhunadh nuair ba gá leis Nuair a bhí mála líonta bhéadh ort an sleamhnán sin a dhúnadh go dtí go mbéadh ceann eile curtha ina áit. Dhéanadh na maidí stiúrtha an obair sin. Tógadh an síol go gtí an sciobol nó isteach sa chistin chun a thriomiú níos fearr. Is maith is cuimhin liom a bheith i mo shuí ar mála coirce in aice na tine. Bhí sé compóirdeach ar feadh achar bhig ach ní raibh taca don droim agus bhéifeá tuirseach tar eis tamall gearr.

Deanadh cocaí móra den tuí agus bhéadh sé úsáideach mar leaba nó bia dona beithigh. Thaitnigh an tuí mheilte go mór leis na cearca. Chaitheadh siad achar fada ag piocadh an ghráin ón dtalamh. Tugadh an gráin iomlán dona cearca ach meileadh é le haghaidh na h-ainmhithe. Í gcás cruineacht meilleadh, rinneadh plúr de go minic. Bhéadh sé de bua ag duine ansin nach mbéadh air an plúr a cheannach sa siopa chun arán a dhéanamh ach níor thárla seo ach fad is a bhí an Cogadh Domhanda ar siúl. Dhíoladh na feirmoiri an gráin dona ceannathoiri uaireanta freisin agus sholaithrigh sin airgead breise dóibh. Choinníodh formhór díobh a ndóthain síol í gcóir an blian dár gcionn.

ÁIT CIÚIN

Frithdhigeann é imeacht an innil bhuailte. Bhí an ciúnas ait tar éis an torann agus an clampar. (Is beag a bhí le chloisteáil ach fuamanna nádúr an tráth sin). Ní raibh aoine a ghoill an imeacht comh mór orthu ach na páistí. An torann mór a bhí as, dob é sórt cuireadh dóibh teacht abhaile go luath ón scoil, chun bheith í láthair nuair a bhí an coirce á bhualadh. Chuir sé mearbhall orthú a bheith ag féachaint air agus ag éisteacht leis an measín íontach. Bhíodh díomá orthú ag teact abhaile agus é imithe go dtí áit éigin eile. Níor thóg sé ach uair nó dhó sa chuid is mó dena hiothlainn, ach thógadh sé an lá go léir ins na feilmeacha móra. Bhí an t-ádh leo nuair a fágadh san iothlan ar feadh na h-oíche nó le haghaidh an deire seachtaine é. Aon uair a bhéadh sneacta ann ní bhéadh sé ag obair agus thárla gur fágadh san iothlann céanna é ar feadh í bhfad. Bhéadh gliondar an domhain ar pháistí muintir an tí sa chás sin mar bhéadh seans ar leith acu an t-íonadh mór seo a scrúdú go mion.

A mhalairt de thuairm ar fad is dócha a bhéadh ag bean an tí. Bhéadh uirthi béilí a chuir ar fáil don meitheal ocrach a bhí ag leanúint an measín. D'imeodh an bia blasta as radarc go mear nuair a shuí na fir chun béile. Ba dheacair an rud é freisin don fhear go raibh asma air mar bheadh deannach go tiúbh nuair a bhí an inneall buailte ag obair. Creidim nach raibh an aicíd sin comh coitianta san aimsir chaite is atá inniú mar is beag duine a chualas ag clamhsáin faoi ríamh.

Ta ré an innill buailte thart go deo. Ní fheictear in áit seachas na hiarsmalainn anois iad. Tá daonrú an tuath íseal faoi láthair agus bhéadh sé deachar go leor meitheal a fháil don obaire, dá mbéadh sé ann faoi láthair. Nil coirce, cruithneacht nó eorna á sholathair ins na feilmeacha beaga inniú. Na daoine a fhásann na barraí seo anois déanann siad ar scála mór é agus úsáideann siad inniil móra comh maith. Níl meitheal nó oibrithe ag teastáil uathu ar cor ar bith.

CASADH AN TSUGAIN

THE FORGE ON CAPPAGH HILL

By

John Corbett

'Holy smoke! No Pope elected,' we'd joke as we viewed the vast volume of black vapour issuing from the forge chimney whenever we passed by it as children. And although quite unlike the Pontiff, you could say that Larry was the High Priest of rural technology whose authority on matters of nails and horseshoes was never challenged by the devout group of followers he served at that time.

Next to our new school, stand the ruins of Walsh's forge that served the people of this area for many decades. The owner of the forge was Paddy Walsh. There was a large family of the Walshs. Most of them went overseas and spent their lives in England and America. Paddy's sons, Pat and Larry, took over the business when their father died. Pat joined the British Army and was awarded the King George V Medal for his services to the cavalry during World War 1. By all accounts he led a wild life in England and spent much of his free time in pubs in the company of strange individuals. He returned to Ireland later and used to work in the forge now and again. However, it was Larry that did most of the work there in my time.

Smiths played an important part in the lives of the local community and Larry was constantly in demand, especially at busy periods in the farming calendar. Customers from a wide area came to him to have their horses shod and the Walshs had quite a reputation for good quality work. In addition to shoeing horses, Larry made implements of various kinds. In fact blacksmiths used to boast that in addition to making the tools of their own trade, all other tradesmen depended on them to make their implements also.

The forge may have had a thatched roof originally but as far back as I can remember it was made of felt. At one stage when it was falling into disrepair, the late Eddie Bodkin and a few neighbours came together to put some new felt on it. I expect this was done on a voluntary basis because Larry's finances would be much too light to cover these kind of expenses. Anyway he much preferred to spend whatever available cash he had in the 'taproom' of the local inn.

The forge wasn't very big. There was enough room for a horse, its owner and of course the blacksmith. There was a front and back door, a small window, a chimney an anvil and a fireplace. There was a large bellows beside the fire and one had to pull hard on the overhanging handle attached to it in order to make the iron pliable enough for the blacksmith to get it into the required shape. Everyone was expected to take a turn working the bellows to keep the fire at the correct heat. Loud ringing sounds flowed out around the countryside as Larry banged and clanged on the anvil, always adding a few additional blows to blend a special kind of harmony as it were to the music of the forge. It was a warm place in cold weather and of course even warmer in the height of summer, when small rivulets of sweat rolled down Larry's face as he hammered the iron.

HAPPY AS LARRY

Larry needed a plentiful supply of iron, water, slack, hammer, sledge, files, nails and lots and lots of 'elbow grease.' The iron for the horses' shoes came in long bars. Larry used to collect these bars himself and he brought them home on his bicycle because this was the only mode of transport that he had. I don't know where he got them but I think I heard him say that he used get them in Menlough sometimes. Carrying them on a bike wasn't easy because they were long and heavy. People who knew him weren't surprised by the fact that he often bit the dust when he crashed with his load of iron. Like many blacksmiths, Larry liked to lubricate himself regularly with a liberal quantity of liquor and it was difficult to control the bike when he had a lot of drink taken.

He was fond of singing and there was nothing he liked better than to exercise his vocal chords in the local public house after, or sometimes in the middle of, a hard day's work. James Kyne, the local publican, didn't like singing on his premises at any time. He regarded such performances as a sign that the individual in question was in the early stages of intoxication and Larry was often obliged to end his renditions prematurely or risk being ejected from the pub. There were no restrictions of this kind when visiting neighbours and he didn't have to be asked twice before bursting into song whenever there were music or dancing sessions in progress. He won a prize at a talent contest organised by Jimmy Stones, a travelling showman, and this gave him a high opinion of his singing ability.

LIGHTING THE FIRE

Larry used a special kind of coal; called slack for forge work. Unlike ordinary coal which comes in lumps, slack came in small grains, very much like black grains of sand. He used to dampen the slack with water from the nearby trough. The same trough was used to cool the shoes before they were attached to the horses' hooves. How it was filled was always a mystery to me. I never saw water being put into it and it never seemed to be empty. I suppose the water was bucketed into it or perhaps a barrel was used to fill it because piped water wasn't available then. I've often heard that trough water from the forge could cure warts but I never knew of anyone with that complaint availing of it. Then again I suppose it could easily have been done without my being aware of it.

MAKING THE SHOES

Larry would shape the shoes while the iron was still very hot. He used to bend the iron by hitting it with a sledge after cutting a chunk of it from one of the long bars. This he would place in the fire and then he or one of his customers began to work the bellows to make the fire stronger. Next he would grip the iron with a pincers while it was still glowing red and beat it into a semicircle or v shape.

He used a special hammer to do this. When he was getting close to the correct shape, he had a file that he inserted into a nail hole on the outside of the shoe and he would push the shoe against the horse's hoof, checking to see what adjustments had to be made.

As the shoe sizzled into the hoof there was a lot of smoke and the smell of the burning hoof filled the forge. It's one of the odours that registers clearly in your mind and I can remember it clearly even after all those years.

When it had been shaped exactly as required, Larry would throw it into the trough to cool it down. He continued like this until all the shoes had been made. After that he would select nails, holding them in his mouth until needed, and he would hammer the shoe onto the hoof. He used seven nails for each shoe. He had a special file to smooth the hooves and he always made sure that the nails didn't protrude and that the shoes were properly secured. He had a lighter hammer for turning the points of the nails into the hooves before filing them.

SLIPPERS

Sometimes shoes that weren't well worn would get loose. In this case when the horse was brought to the forge it wasn't necessary to make new shoes. Instead the old ones could be taken off, reshaped and nailed back on again. These were called slippers. Putting on slippers took less time and cost less than new shoes. It was essential to keep horses properly shod to prevent lameness, although some farmers tried to postpone a trip to the forge until it was absolutely necessary. Larry knew when it was time to shoe and wouldn't hesitate to remind careless owners of the necessity of having their animals shod promptly.

CHANGING CART WHEELS

Although horse shoeing was the main task for Larry, he had to replace the wheels of the iron-rimmed carts that were so common at the time. This was hard work especially in hot weather. When the rims of the wheels became loose they were taken off. Then a big fire was lit and the rim was put into it and split. Unlike the fire for horseshoeing, this one was in the open air on a special piece of ground adjacent to the forge. Turf supplied by the cart owner was used instead of slack for this operation.

The rim was welded before being rejoined to make it tighter and it had to be put back over the wooden part while it was still very hot. Larry had a special wheel that he pushed around the rim in order to measure it prior to this but unfortunately the wheel used to wobble to the side a little and the measurements weren't always as accurate as they should be. Spectators, whose wheels weren't being tightened at the time, used to enjoy the process immensely but the wheel owners didn't think it funny at all. He used to mark the points with a piece of chalk when he was measuring the circumference of the wheel. Sometimes the wooden part of the wheel would catch fire while the rim was being mounted and buckets of water were spilt on it to quench it. When this occurred one had to be careful not to pour too much water on the wheel.

HOLDING THE HORSES

Most animals were quiet enough and remained calm during the shoeing process. Flighty ones could be a problem and Larry felt that the onus was on the owners to control them. He was rather short tempered on those occasions and wouldn't hesitate to tip the offending horse with a hammer. If the treatment didn't work the first time, Larry would do the same again. This of course wouldn't improve things one bit and the owner might end up outside the forge, having lost the tug of war with the jittery beast. It often happened in our own case because we had a blind pony that frightened easily.

Larry's brother, Pat, was much better in a situation of this kind. He was stronger than Larry and seldom had difficulty controlling animals.

DISTANT MEMORIES

The Walshs had a great reputation for shoeing horses and Larry was particularly proud of it. His charges were reasonable and he was never short of customers. When I was growing up the forge was a hive of activity- a kind of meeting place where like-minded individuals gathered to exchange ideas or to make mutual working arrangements, while they waited for Pat or Larry to do the needful. When there was a long interval without Larry showing up, tempers would rise and some very unparliamentary language was likely to be used but his arrival would bring an end to the cursing and the impatience of crowd would evaporate rapidly when he got back into his stride again. In a short time the horses of waiting customers were supplied with new sets of footwear that would serve them for the coming weeks.

As a youngster, I was fascinated by the ringing sounds that Larry made as he worked at the anvil. I watched in wonder at the sparks and fragments that flew off the iron as he walloped it with all his might, while beads of perspiration streamed down along his tawny face. No matter how busy he was or no matter how warm the weather was, he always took time to light his pipe. When he got paid, he couldn't relax until he quenched his thirst with alcohol. Having done so, he was ready for action and the forge fire would send clouds of dark smoke billowing into the ether all around the village of Cappalusk once more.

Eventually the demand for Larry's services grew less and less as horses, ponies and donkeys disappeared from the scene, to be replaced by tractors and the powerful modern machines of the present day. There are no queues outside the forge nowadays waiting impatiently for their horses to be shod and smoldering horses' hooves and sweating blacksmiths are just a distant memory.

Larry has joined his brother, Pat, his father, Paddy, and other members of his family and sleeps peacefully in Clonkeenkerrill Cemetery, just over a mile away from the spot where he spent his life shoeing horses, repairing wheels and making implements for local farmers.

Most of the forge still stands- a little reminder to passers-by of Larry and the skills of the hard working blacksmiths of former times who played such an important role in the life of the local community.

CHAPTER FIFTEEN

WEATHER, LAND AND SEASCAPES

DO YOU TALK ABOUT THE WEATHER OFTEN?

In Ireland, weather is one of the main topics of conversation. It has endless potential and it is a fairly safe theme to broach and even the most tactless are unlikely to offend when they comment upon it. I often wonder what would happen if we converted to the Moslem religion en masse. I'm told that devout Moslems don't discuss meteorology because they feel it would be a reflection on God to remark on the kind of weather that He has chosen to send.

Much has been said about global warming and the effects it will have on our climate. Experts tell us that pollution is causing our planet to overheat and unless we take drastic steps to change our habits the earth will become barren as the Martian landscape or as burned up as our twin in space, Venus, whose surface temperature is four times hotter than boiling water. Violent hurricanes with wind speeds in excess of 200 mile per hour are also being forecast. We rarely get hurricanes like this in Ireland and the worst storm that most can remember was 'Debbie' in 1961, which cost 14 lives. This was minor compared to 'The Big Wind' in 1839. Over 2000 boats sank, houses, churches and trees were blown down and hundreds of people died. In local lore reference is made to a severe storm that occurred in 1898. The wind blew in the door of Leonard's house in Mount Hazel. The windows were broken and the house almost caught fire as a result of the blaze being blown up the chimney.

Yet all of these are mild by comparison with the strong winds that batter America and the Caribbean. Lyall Watson has written a marvellous book (HEAVEN'S BREATH), showing how the weather can change or at least dramatically influence the course of history. A perfect example was when the Spanish Armada was blown out to sea, as the Spanish were about to attack England. The power of the wind was illustrated also when a tornado lifted a church clear off the ground and it landed at a 90-degree angle when it returned to earth. This happened in Tornado Alley in the U.S.A. Taking such things into consideration, we have a lot to be thankful for.

Modern meteorologists only claim 80 per cent accuracy in their predictions even though they use satellites and all kind of sophisticated equipment. I often wonder how their results compare with those of our parents and grandparents. Our ancestors had no scientific weather forecasts and relied on natural phenomena to predict what the weather was going to be like. The following is a list of the signs that Gurteen people depended upon:
When the sky in the east was red at sunrise, this they believed augured rain. Rain was also expected if there was a halo around the moon. A North wind and a starry sky meant frost. Low flying swallows were another sign of rain, as was a rainbow in the morning. A rainbow at night meant that the wet weather was coming to an end. They also believed that 'a wind from the east is neither good for man or beast.'

Like most of us they felt that the south wind brings heat whereas the north wind brings cold and frost. They regarded the west wind as being a harbinger of warm, wet weather.

One theory says that 'When the seagulls gathered in the land and when the cat scrapes the bags (?)', it is an indication of a storm and bad weather. 'Ragged' clouds being blown across the sky also meant a storm.

When animals gathered on the hill tops in Summer this they thought was a sign of impending good weather. Crows standing on walls and a crowing cock also meant that fine weather was on the way. When the stars were completely covered by clouds, this showed that thunder was to be expected. Rays out of the setting sun were also a sign of bad weather. In summer they believed that one could tell the kind of weather by the colour of the frog. If it was dark skinned the weather would continue to be bad but if the frog was yellow, it would be good.

MORE RAIN SIGNS
A 'half drowned moon',
Fog with the 'Old' moon,
A rough sea,
Smoke from a chimney rising perpendicularly or a blue flame in the fire,
A dog or cat eating grass,
A pony, or donkey with its back to the ditch,
When a cat or dog lies close to the fire,
Low flying owls,
When distant objects can be seen clearly or when distant sounds can be heard clearly,
When there is a black stripe across the sun or a black ring around the moon.

Judging by the number of omens dealing with rain, moisture seems to have been every bit as plentiful then as it is now. As you can see, very few of the predictions related to wind.

Check the Appendix for more data on the weather.

KYLEMORE AND ITS ABBEY

An extract from "More of my Connemara"

by

P.J. Kennelly

The imposing beauty of Kylemore Abbey in North West Connemara complement the beauty of the surrounding countryside; it is surely one of the most beautiful places in this country, if not in the whole wide world. When one dwells to sample the majestic peace and tranquility here that defies description, one is reminded of the words of Patrick Pearse "The beauty of the world has made me sad; this beauty that will pass". This is Kylemore.

Romance, drama and some sadness run through the saga of this great stone mansion, built in 1864 in the shadow of Connemara's own Twelve Pins and Maam Turk Mountains. A wealthy Mancunian merchant, Mitchell Henry, built the castle for his beautiful wife Margaret. It cost in excess of one million pounds to build and this is during the famine days in Ireland. Henry installed every luxury of the day in Kylemore; from Italian pleasure gardens to hothouses. He even harnessed the lake above the gardens to provide electricity for the mansion. For his beloved wife he duly furnished the place in stately fashion with elegantly carved wood panelling and great
mantlepieces, and a Venetian wing.

The Henry family duly came to live in the mansion. Happy with nine children, they were most hospitable and much liked in the neighbourhood.

Six years after coming to Kylemore tragedy struck. Margaret Henry caught a fever while on holiday in Egypt and sadly, died. Her husband had the body embalmed and taken back to their beloved Kylemore and it now lies within the little gothic church in the grounds of the castle. Some six years later a married daughter of Mitchell Henry was killed in a fall from a dog-cart near Kylemore.

Then financial troubles overtook the merchant from Manchester; investments in real estate failed and the Boer war wrecked his mining interests in South Africa.

KYLEMORE ABBEY

Reluctantly, Henry left Kylemore. When he died his ashes were taken back to Kylemore to rest beside the body of his wife.

Then the great house was offered for sale. It was bought by a Mr. Zimmerman from Chicago for his daughter who had married the Duke of Manchester. It was sold for a sum in the region of £65,000.

The Duchess made changes in the castle, altered the entrance hall, took out some panelling, implemented new ideas to suit her own taste.

Now, Kylemore saw a new order; but it was not for long. The poor Duchess, who loved Kylemore, had to leave it. The Duke had secretly mortgaged it - and foreclosure fell in 1913. The Manchesters left the Mansion.

So the Irish Benedictines of Ypres came to this majestic and beautiful house. This community has a long fascinating history. The sisters brought their school to Kylemore in 1920, and its eminence as a girls' boarding school is well known.

In the elegant drawing room of the old castle a silver- framed photograph stands on the mantelpiece. It appears that an Indian princess who was a pupil at Kylemore in 1929, signs the picture in affectionate remembrance of her schooldays with the Irish Benedictines.

A portrait on the wall close by is a reminder of the castle's early days. It is a full length painting of the dark haired Margaret Henry for whom Kylemore was built.

To day by courtesy of the Irish Benedictines, the traveller may visit Kylemore Abbey and walk in its lovely grounds.
Around the lakeside path, in absolute and perfect peace among the trees, is the little Gothic church built by Mitchell Henry over a century ago.

ABSENCE OF OCEAN

by

Eileen Casey

There's the story of a woman who left the West and married into the Midlands, who never saw the sea again. All those peat baked summers, bog instead of beach. No songs to gather up in singing shells. Songs that spun the dreaming spells of sights and sounds beneath the ocean swell. Ocean spells that conjured up the magic of spray and shimmering colours.

She had come to a place of dry peat. Of water solder, bulrush, gipsywort, birch. Turf brown shades. When she drew the turf with her neighbours, turf dust powdered her skin as she worked in the heat of a thirsting sun. She saw star moss and feather moss, cowberry, and crowberry. The bog blood of bog. Constant as rain pulses over Pollagh, over Clara, where rannock rushes grown. Yellow flower bog bursts flecking the landscape of bog people.

She longed for a pebbled shore with the wind rushing over the waves. White horses galloping home, racing with sea breezes that blew her hair into swirls. Where the ocean mirrored the sky, cloud swans drifting by. Whole summers spent on the white sands where her hands made her child images and where she left the imprint of her feet. Imprints that were washed away, not with sadness but with the promise of a new canvass for her to shape and shift. She yearned for the smell of seaweed drying on the rocks, the sensation of a blue world inching to the level of her bare knees. And to glimpse the sun making a lurex fabric of sea blues, sea greens that pearled the changing hues of ocean. She longed to see the glory of sunset, a red host warming cool evening waters with the last heat of the day and on rising, giving the sea its first breath of morning light.

As she watched her children play in her small backyard, she missed even the plaintive sounds of seagulls wheeling through the air. Seagulls that circled overhead with outstretched wings that embraced the vast expanse of ocean.

She often felt like a foreigner in her adopted home but over time, she adapted to the customs of her new surroundings. With her neighbours she walked the concrete paths of a place unbordered by her beloved stonewalls. Walls where stone upon stone were set in ways that could never be shaken. She grew used to the houses necklaced together with hedges the whole length of her street. Hedges that were whispered over when news would come, all battles at clotheslines patched up, forgotten in the sisterhood that united the women. She walked the road that led to the hill, crossed over the bridge where the Camcor river frothed and fizzed like lemonade. Beyond that, the Midland town. Up Main Street, past drapery shops that smelled of oilcloth and linen, shops that were canopied in bright candy striped awnings. Meeting friends, their smiles breaking upon her like sunbursts. In her garden, trees matured from saplings, brickwork weathered.
Eventually, the absence of ocean was no longer an all-pervading presence. But she never forgot her origins. The rhythms of the sea were in her blood, her heartbeat. The sea never left her voice. Across her flat, unsalted landscape, its rise and fall was like a smooth stone skimming.

CELEBRATIONS IN GURTEEN

O'BRIEN FAMILY

CONFIRMATION CLASS 2003

PEARSE'S BALLAD GROUP
BACK ROW L-R: MARY TREACY, ANNE WARD, RUTH DEMPSEY, MARY FLANNERY, JENNIFER BURKE, AGGIE BURKE   SEATED: JOAN TREACY AND SHAUNA WARD.

192

CHAPTER SIXTEEN

OUR SPORTING WORLD

OUR SPORTING WORLD

Sport has played a very important part in the life of the community
and no book on the locality would be complete without acknowledging this fact.
Not only does sport benefit the teams and the participants, it also gives
endless hours of enjoyment to spectators and fans.

We have invited the various sporting bodies in the parish to give a brief outline
of their activities and you can read these in the following pages.

1926 GURTEEN TEAM

Back row - Left to Right: Paddy Finnerty, Guard Meeany, Jim Gilligan, Sgt. MacDonagth, PakeMentane, Hubert Molloy, Mick Ryan, Pat Finn, Henry Mellody.
Middle row - Left to Right: Jack Dilleen, Simon Finn, Willie(Richie) Dillon, Tommy Coleman, Willie Dilleen (P.O.), Maher Hynes.
Front row - Left to Right: Connor Mentane, Tommy Mentant, Joe Kyne, Willie Raftery (Mascot), Lames Kyne

Galway Senior Hurling Team

New York Champions, 1964, 1965, 1966

BACK ROW (l. to r.): Mike Mahon (manager, Kinvara), Joe Burke (Abbey), Mattie Maloney (Athenry), Paddy Donoghue (Ballinakill), John Maher (Loughrea), John Joe Egan (Castlegar), Jimmy Donoghue (Ballinakill), Ken Croke (Moycullen), Mike Conway (Ballinakill), Frank Connolly (Craughwell), Mattie O'Toole (mentor, Moycullen), John Forde (trainer, Gort).

FRONT ROW: Mike Cody (mentor), Bernie Rohan (Newcastle), Mike Curtin (Kinvara), Larry Kelly (Ballinasloe), P.J. Curtin (Kinvara), Brendan Hynes (captain, Gurteen), Jimmy Kelly (Loughrea), Martin Dempsey (Turloughmore), Mick Bermingham (Dublin), Frank Connors (Ballinakill), Pat Keary (Loughrea), Jim Ryan (Ballygar).

HISTORY OF ST. KERRILL'S G.A.A. CLUB
(1990 - 2003)

By

John Mullins

For many years prior to 1990, several players from the parish of Gurteen-Ballymacward had represented various local football clubs with distinction. In fact, as far back as 1970 Stephen Cloonan played for both Galway Minor footballers and hurlers with great success.

Other players who excelled for other clubs were: Seamus Lawless, Michael Dillon, Mike O'Brien, Menlough, Seamus O' Neill, the Fahy brothers - Joe and Martin (Caltra). Both P.J. O'Connell and John Mullins played with Caltra in two North Board League finals on successive Sundays against Killererin (Junior) and Williamstown (Intermediate). They won two North Board Titles. With all these players available, it was inevitable that a football team would evolve. This happened in 1990.

It was decided to enter a Junior team in the South-East Board Football League and Championship. The name of the Club was taken from the patron Saint of Gurteen, St. Kerrill. Brendan Hardiman, Snr. was elected Chairman. Christy Connell was the first secretary of St. Kerrill's and for much of the nineties was the driving force behind the club. The Club reached the S.E. Board final at the first attempt in 1990, beating a highly fancied Loughrea team after a replay by nine points to five. They went on to contest the County Senior final against Moycullen, losing by a single point.

In 1991 they beat Kiltormer in a League final by two points. For the rest of the 90's, the Club contested four South-East Board finals without success. When things were going badly, it was the efforts of a few people that kept the club afloat. These were: Pat Clancy, Christy Connell, Eugene Murphy, Mike Carr, Seamus Lawless, P.J. Connell and Herbie Parker. The Club was in decline at this point and a new regime took over. Paraic Hillary became Secretary, Mike Carr, Chairman and Pat Clancy, Treasurer. John Mullins took over as Team Manager with Noel Moore. By the year 2000, things were changing and a more youthful team was emerging. The Club won its first trophy in 10 years by defeating St. Thomas' in the S.E. Board Final by two points. They lost the County semi-final to eventual County champions - Annaghdown. The Club was on the way up and retained the S.E. Board Championship in 2001, defeating local rivals St. Gabriel's comprehensively.

On a dull October afternoon in Annaghdown the Club made history, reaching its First County final beating a highly fancied Killanin outfit by four points in the semi-final. The County Final was played in Menlough in late November, and after an epic struggle, Kerrill's lost by one point to Milltown. It was Milltown's first title in 20 years. St. Kerrill's were now playing in the North Board and the team's football skills were improving with every game. Also in 2001, the Club had entered a minor team and they duly obliged by winning their first title, beating Eyrecourt by two points before going down to eventual County champions, Killererin-Clonberne.

All in all 2001 was a great year, with the club winning two trophies, contesting a County final and a semi-final. Noel Moore made a huge contribution as Minor manager with Pat Clancy, Mike Carr and John Mullins as his selectors. If 2001 was good, 2002 was even better. The Club retained the South Board Junior Championship, defeating Kiltormer after a replay, by two points. A three-in-a-row had been achieved and Mike Carr, a great leader, was Captain of all three.

The Minors also retained their title; defeating Kiltormer in the final. The junior team contested their second County final in a row, losing to Monivea-Abbey after a replay which went to extra time. They also got through to the North Board Junior B final losing by a single point to Claregalway. The minors were well beaten by Michael Breathnach's in the semi-final. An Under-16 team was also entered into competition with Pat Clancy as mentor and in their first year did very well in the North Board.

LAST YEAR

It was decided at the A.G.M. for 2003 to move up to Junior A and to enter a Junior C team in the North Board. Kerrills were now represented in Junior A, Junior C, Under 21, Minor, Under 16 and Under 12. Kevin Lally was now Captain in Junior A. The Junior A team did very well, winning seven out of their nine League matches but failed badly in the championship to a strong Milltown combination. They contested the North Board Junior A semi-final (League) losing to Mt. Bellew in a tough struggle. The Under 16's won five out of six of their League matches before losing out to Fr. Griffin's in the Semi-final. The highlight of the year was the success of the Under 12 Team with Noel Moore as Manager. They won their first title, defeating St. Gabriel's after a replay for the South-East Board Title.

Finally, without the help of Padraig Pearse's Club as well as several local businessmen and supporters, none of the success would have been achieved. Gurteen F.C. through Brendan Hardiman Jnr. and Woodlawn Utd. F.C., were most helpful. A great Committee is now in place with Tom Kenny as Chairman and the future for the Club is bright. There are several fine young players to call on.

This article would not be complete without a mention of the greatest Clubman St. Kerrill's has seen since its foundation back in 1990, namely Eugene Murphy. He has contributed a great deal of time and energy to the club. He has also supported us financially and his company, Murphy Plastering, is now the main sponsor of St. Kerrill's. The Club's finances are buoyant - thanks mainly to Treasurer, Pat Clancy.

Since the beginning of 2000, St. Kerrill's footballers have contested 11 finals and won 7. The Club is doing exceptionally well and we look forward to the day when a Gurteen/Ballymacward man will be wearing the maroon and white. That day is surely not far off.

S/E FOOTBALL CHAMPIONSHIP WINNERS 2000
ST. KERRILLS v ST. THOMAS'S

Back Row L-R: Kevin Lally, Shane Ruane, Niall Barrett, Martin Barry, Noel Earls, Eoin Barrett, Seamus O'Neill, Adrian Burke, Eoin Kenny, Ollie Laheen, Padraic Hillary, Paul O'Brien, John Mullins (Manager & Trainer).

Front Row L-R: Pat Burke, Tony O'Brien, Brendan Hardiman, Niall Moore, Aidan Kilkenny, David Mullins, Adrian Queeney, Sean O'Neill, Mike Carr, Kevin Moore.

2001 Team Manager and Trainer John Mullins Selectors: Pat Clancy, Noel Moore, Tom Kenny

COUNTY FOOTBALL FINAL JUNIOR B 2001
ST. KERRILLS PANEL v MILLTOWN

Back Row L-R: Eoin Barrett, Robert Parker, Sean Hardiman, Paul O'Brien, Shane Ruane, Kevin Lally, Eoin Kenny, Joe Flannery, Ollie Laheen, Martin Barry, Peter Tanian, Kevin Moore, Padraic Hillary, Anthony Kenny.

Front Row L-R: Keith Clancy, Aidan Murray, Kevin Raftery, Mike Carr, Brendan Hardiman, Aidan Kilkenny, Adrian Burke, Johnny Mullins, Sean Walsh, David Mullins, Barry Donnellan, Robbie Donnellan.

2001 Team Manager and Trainer John Mullins
Selectors: Pat Clancy, Noel Moore, Tom Kenny

STARTING TEAM 2001
COUNTY FINAL JUNIOR B v MILLTOWN

Back Row L-R: Kevin Lally, Eoin Kenny, Joe Flannery, Ollie Laheen, Martin Barry, Peter Tanian, Kevin Moore.

Front Row L-R: Mike Carr, Brendan Hardiman, Aidan Kilkenny, Adrian Burke, Johnny Mullins, Sean Walsh, David Mullins, Padraic Hillary.

2001 Team Manager and Trainer John Mullins
Selectors: Pat Clancy, Noel Moore, Tom Kenny

A BRIEF HISTORY OF PEARSE'S CAMOGIE CLUB

By

Collette Kennedy-Walsh

Formerly based in Castleblakeney, the Pearses Camogie Club as it is called today, was resituated in Ballymacward/Gurteen in 1979. The club celebrates 25 years this year and it has been a very successful 25 years.

In 1979 the club won its first County Junior title and went on to win the Connaught Junior title in the same year.

Under age success followed during the next few years. In 1980 and 1981 the club won the County under 14 title but did not compete in the Feile competition because of a mix up in registration by the County Board. In 1984 the club represented Galway for the first time in Feile in Dublin and were beaten in the semi-finals. The big break through came in 1988 in Birr when Pearses captured their first All Ireland title. They won the Division One Feile title for the first time under the captainship of Helen Geraghty helped by trainer, Michael Kennedy.

In 1989 they went back to defend their title but were beaten in the final by Freshford of Kilkenny.
.
In 1991 Pearses represented Galway in Feile yet again and captured their second All-Ireland, led by captain, Michelle Ryan, and trained by Colette Kennedy.

It was around this time that they started to make an impact on the County Senior scene. They were beaten by Mullagh in the County Senior Final. Mullagh then went on to win the Club All Ireland championship.

1992 proved to be one of our best years. Pearses defeated Davitts after a replay and won their first County Senior title, captained by the late Catherine Donnellan and trained by Michael Kennedy. After a few difficult months during which star player, Sharon Glynn, was suspended, Pearses went down to Rathnure in the All Ireland semi-final by 2 points. It was not until 1994 that they again competed at All Ireland Senior club level but were defeated by Glen Rovers in the semi-final.

In the mean-time the under 14 team under the management of Colette Kennedy, Aine Hillary and Aisling Ward won two All Ireland Feile titles back to back in Limerick.

In 1996 the breakthrough at Senior Club level finally came when Pearses captained by Ann Ryan-Forde and trained by Michael Kennedy, Pat Burke and Mike Donnellan travelled to Granagh/Ballingarry in Limerick to take home the first of 5 All Ireland Senior Club titles. In 1996 and 1997 the team was captained by Ann Ryan-Forde and the three in a row teams of 2000, 2001 and 2002 were captained by Áine Hillary. The club has won County titles every year since then. In 2003 they captured the County Junior B league and championship.

Down through the years many Pearses Camogie Clubs were awarded the Connaught Tribune Club of the Year.

During the last 25 years several people have worked with the club on a voluntary basis and we owe a great debt of gratitude to them. The club has always enjoyed tremendous support from the people of Ballymacward/Gurteen. We are grateful for this. Finally, thanks to the Padraig Pearses GAA club. They continue to support camogie by giving us the use of their facilities at all times.

At the start of 2004 we look forward to continued success for the club and another 25 years of great memories.

PEARSES — ALL-IRELAND SENIOR CLUB CHAMPIONS 1996

BACK ROW: L-R: Mike Donnellan (Sel.), Tracey Laheen, Louise Curry, Aishling Ward, Bridget Kilgannon, Michelle Glynn, Aine Hillary, Michael Kennedy (Trainer/Manager).
FRONT ROW: L-R: Collette Deely, Sharon Glynn, Ann Ryan-Forde (Capt.), Martina Harkin, Carmel Hannon, Martina Haverty, Pat Burke (Sel.), Corina Donnellan (Mascot).

PEARSES

ALL-IRELAND CLUB CHAMPIONS - 00- 01- 02

Front Row(l-r): Aoife Raftery, Nuala Burke, Aisling Ward, Martina Harkin, Aine Hillary (capt.), Patricia Burke, Orla Kilkenny, Martina Haverty, Donnellan, Lorraine Lally, Carmel Hannon, Mairead McDonagh, Mairella Power, Sandra Flannery, Caroline Curran's. Back Row (l-r): Michael Donnellan (selector) Sharon Glynn, Jennifer Hussey, Shauna Ward, Sheena Carr, Veronica Sweeney, Louise Curry, Michelle Gavin, Nickey Larkin, Ellen Finn, Anne Devilly, Rebecca Lally, Tara Wynne, Amy Reidedly, Michael Greendy Manager Pat Burke Selector.

GURTEEN SOCCER
THE STORY SO FAR

By

Kevin Ryan

Gurteen Soccer Club was founded in 1997. The first Committee with Odie Cunniffe as Chairman, Pairic Connor as Secretary and Sean Bodkin as Treasurer set about setting up a Soccer Club for the people of Gurteen. They received a great response from the people of Gurteen and with Vin Connor on board as sponsor and huge crowds at training everything was set to join the Galway District League for the first time. The aim of the Club was to bring a League Title to Gurteen and with Padraic Connor as Manager and Steve Walsh as Coach we set off on our road to glory.

The first couple of seasons were a learning experience for us and even though results did not always go our way there was never a shortage of heart and determination and with a constant influx of new young players we always felt there was potential there for greater things.

At the beginning of the 2000/2001 season a new management team of Kevin Ryan as Manager and Brendan Hardiman as Trainer was put in place. We felt the team had come along way over the previous three years we aimed to be in the top three in our first season. We had some excellent runs. On the last day of the season we defeated Loughrea to finish second in the League, thus achieving our first goal. Our next target was a League Title. With five games left to play, we had to win all of them to force a play off.

We eventually won our five games and went to Tuam Celtic grounds to the play off final for the 2C Championship. With excellent support and despite going one nil down early on we won by 2 goals to 1. We finally reached our goal of bringing silver ware home to Gurteen.

We are now in our second season in Division 2B and are already pushing for promotion.

This success is due to the hard work of the players and the support of the public. The Club has gone from strength to strength over the years from the first Committee to the present Committee with Tomás Ryan as Chairman, Tony Walsh as Secretary and Joe Flannery as Treasurer. As with any Club, it could not function without the generosity and support of the people of the parish. We greatly appreciate this and we look forward to your continuing support over the coming years.

BALLYMACWARD SOCCER 1975 -1989

By

John Mullins

Back in 1975 Soccer was regarded as a foreign game by followers of The G.A.A. However, a group of determined young men formed a soccer club in Ballymacward. They called it St. Paul's United in honour of the local church. They entered the First Division (which is called The Premier League nowadays). There were only two rural teams involved then, the other being St. Bernards.

They performed well and several fine young players soon joined. The highlights of the year were the games that they played against Dubarry and Shiven Rovers. One match was played on St. Stephen's Day and the other on New Year's Day.

Local people helped the club enormously; among them Ted Finnegan and the Late, great John Nolan from Catleblakeney. John had more success with The C.B. Trotters later on. Players from Colemanstown and Gurteen featured prominently. They included Ossie O' Grady, The Coppingers, Gerry Moran, Liam Burke and Paddy Hynes. The club entered the Roscommon league in the early nineties and the name was changed to B.M.W. Albion. This was its most successful period. The team won five trophies in three seasons and moved from the Second Division into the Premier League. They won against Ballinasloe in 1988 and were awarded The First Division Cup, despite the fact that they were missing six regular players.

Sadly the club no longer exists but perhaps it will be revived some time in the future.
Looking back, it's strange to see so many clubs in existence. Thankfully the 'Ban' mentality is no longer with us and young people can play whatever games they like without interference from any of the sporting bodies.

Finally, a special word of thanks to Frank O'Dowd and family who provided a pitch free of charge from the beginning of the club's existence.

The founder members of St. Paul's were: Willie Parker, Mike Mullins, John Mullins, Dickie Lally, Joe Raftery, John Dooley, Sean Glynn, Gerry Bracken and Herbie Parker.

26th December 1982
B.M.W. Albion

Back Row L-R: Jimmy Hartnett, P.J. Connell, W. Parker, Jim McCullagh, Adrian Mooney, Justin Lawless, Brendan Barrett, Eamon Finnegan.
Front Row L-R: Michael Mullins, Noel Hynes, Dick Lally, John Mullins, Owen Dwyer, Hugh Burke, Robbie Harrison.

GURTEEN SOCCER TEAM
BACK ROW L-R: KEVIN RYAN. TONY WALSH, BARRY DONNELLAN, KERRILL ROHAN, JOSEPH FLANNERY, TOMAS RYAN, CYRIL DONNELLAN, ADRIAN BURKE.
FRONT ROW: JASON O'GRADY, BRENDAN HARDIMAN, SHANE CONNAUGHTON, KERRILL HARDIMAN, ALAN WALSH, SEAN HARDIMAN, ALAN CORBETT.

GURTEEN SCHOOL INDOOR SOCCER
BACK ROW L-R: SHANE FINNERTY, DONAL HYNES, JOHN CORBETT, RONAN CORBETT, ADRIAN BURKE.
FRONT ROW: JOSEPH FLANNERY, TOMAS RYAN, KEVIN FINN, DAMIEN CONCANNON, SEAN WALSH.

GURTEEN GIRLS INDOOR SOCCER CHAMPIONS
BACK L-R SHAUNA WARD, CATHERINE BURKE, CAROLINE DUANE, ANN-MARIE KILKENNY
FRONT L-R AISLING DOYLE, MARY FLANNERY, MICHELLE RYAN, DEIRDRE FINN, ANN-MARIE MOLLOY.

HURLING IN TAMPLE

By

Paul Ryan

In 1968 Michael J.Kilgannon sponsored a cup known as the Kilgannon Cup for the promotion of hurling in all of the schools in Gurteen and Ballymacward. Michael asked me to organise the Gurteen end, as there was not enough boys in Tample (my old school). I was permitted to amalgamate Shanballard and Tample schools for the purpose of the competition. It was a seven a side contest played on a knockout basis.

In 1969 the Tample and Shanballard team reached the final which was played in Ballymacward pitch on the 13th. of June. This was the feast of St. Kerrill and we were hoping to bring back the cup to be displayed that night at the annual dance in honour of our local saint. It was not to be. We drew with Esker and the replay took place one week later. Esker won the replay and that ended our dream of capturing a hurling cup for Gurteen.

My panel on that day was Michael King, Tom Ruane, Tony McDonagh, Tom O'Grady, Pat Burke, Noel Burke, Gerry Dooley, Miles Dooley (R.I.P.) and Noel Finnerty (Clough).

It was an enjoyable experience but it was not to be repeated. For some reason unknown to me this competition ceased to be played after that.

PAUL & TOMAS RYAN

1969 EAST BOARD CHAMPIONS
BACK ROW L-R: K. RAFTERY J. MOLLOY, T. CLOONAN, J. CLOONAN, M. FINNERTY, J. MOLLOY, T. ROCK, FR. N. MURRAY (CAPTAIN), P. HILLARY,
FRONT ROW: S. LALLY, G. O'BRIEN, B. KILKENNY, T. BYRNES, P. RYAN, M. KILKENNY, T. MOLLOY, S. MCDONAGH

Colemanstown United F.C. 1982 - 2004

By

Martin Finnerty

In the 80's soccer became very popular in Ireland. In rural areas, however, there were little or no facilities available for players. When faced with this challenge in Colemanstown, members of the local community held a meeting and the first committee of Colemanstown United FC. was formed. The dedication and commitment of that group resulted in the club's affiliation with the Galway District League and the formation of the first junior team in 1982.

Committee 2004	Committee 1982
President - Frank Burke	President- Frank Burke
Chairman - Liam Burke	Chairman- Paddy Hynes
Secretary - Gerry Moran	Secretary- Gerry Moran
Treasurer - Martin Finnerty	Treasurer- Liam Burke
Devolvement Officer- TJ Carr	Manager- Ozzie O'Grady
Facilities Manager- PJ Finnerty	

First Team
PJ Finnerty, Liam Burke, Noel Kelly, Paddy Hynes, Joe Coppinger, Noel Finnerty, Thomas Hynes, Gerry Moran, Pa Ruane, PJ Molloy, Martin Finnerty, Gerry Rohan and Sean Moran.
Their first official league match against Kilcornan Utd (now Colga F.C.) resulted in a 9-1 win for Colemanstown. It was the first of many victories to come.

There was a variety of training venues in those early days but finally Frank Burke donated a playing pitch and this became the home of Colemanstown United. Since there were no facilities in those days, local hedgerows served as dressing rooms and the river provided much needed water for post -match showers. However, this did not deter Colemanstown's dedicated players. We had wonderful talent and this laid the foundation for the club's success. It also gained the support and respect of the local community. As time went by membership grew and as a result players came from surrounding parishes, i.e. Ballymacward, Newcastle, Menlough, Skehana, Monivea, and Abbyknockmoy.

In the mid-nineties, due to local demand, the club decided to set up an under-age structure. The aim was to train young boys and girls in the skills of football. The result of this effort can be seen both in the number of teams and the range of ages catered for today.

Currently the club has:
2 Under-age boys teams
2 Under-age girls teams
1 Junior ladies team
1 Reserve men's team
1 Junior men's team.

Each year Colemanstown hosts the F.A.I. summer camp and this encourages young people to participate in the games. The seventy students who attend this camp find the professional coaching they receive both educational and enjoyable. It is a tribute to the club that the F.A.I have chosen. to organise this event in Colemanstown.

FUNDRAISING

Fundraising is an integral part of club activity. In the past the club was involved in the Galway Utd Lotto. Current development at the pitch could not have taken place without the assistance of The Department of Tourism and Sport in conjunction with the F.Á.S. training programme. This was supplemented by various fundraising events organised by the club itself. Colemanstown United has enjoyed steadfast support from the local community for its many dances, card-games, raffles, competitions, race nights and its annual sponsored cycle. The recent 'You're a Star' competition, as well as raising substantial amount of money, was a big hit locally. Colemanstown Utd. depends on this generous, local support and loyal sponsors to fund its continued expansion and development.

CLUB ACHIEVEMENTS

85/86 Season. Division 2 Winners.
87/88 Season Athenry 5- a - side Shield Winners.
95/96 Season 2B North Cup runners- up.
96/97 Season 2B North Cup Winners.
97/98 Season Under 18 League Cup Winners.
        Under 18 League runners-up.
        Division 2B League Winners.
        League Cup Winners.
        Division 1 League Winners (Ladies)
98/99 Season Division Cup Winners.

At present Colemanstown Utd are in the First Division and for the last few seasons have come very close to gaining promotion to the Premier Division. Two seasons ago they were involved in a play off against Killtulla only to lose out on penalties.

DEVELOPMENT

The club was fortunate secure a F.Á.S. scheme under the supervision of Micheál Barrett. This has been in operation for the past four years and FÁS workers have helped to effect the changes that were required to upgrade the club's grounds. The boundaries have been beautifully enhanced by the erection of stonewalls around its perimeter. The soil in the old pitch was deemed unsuitable and consequently had to be removed. It was replaced by a mix of 80% sand and 20% soil. Much needed work was done on the drainage and levelling of the new pitch. A training area and a second pitch are currently being developed. The construction of a clubhouse, including showering and changing facilities is nearing completion. Adjoining the clubhouse, a roofed stand with seating accommodation for two hundred is also under construction at present. The Committee is hopeful that all of this work will be finished by the end of 2004.

COLEMANSTOWN CUP WINNERS 1997-98

BACK ROW (L-R): T.J. CARR, JOSEPH COPPINGER, COLIN O'GADY, P.J. FINNERY, LIAM MULLINS, DERWIN COSTELLO, GARY O'GRADY, STEPHEN CONCANNON, FRANCIS MONAGHAN, DECLN O'DEA.

FRONT ROW: RAY FINNERTY, BRIAN COSTELLO, ANDY CONCANNON, LIAM BURKE(CAPTAIN), GERRY MORAN, OLLIE CROWE, MIKE CONNOR.

COLEMANSTOWN SOCCER

FRONT ROW L-R: DAMIAM CONCANNON, DAVID MULLINS, COLIN O'GRADY, JARLATH FAHY, KENNETH DUANE, STEPHEN FARRELL.

BACK ROW; L-R GERRY MORAN (MANAGER0 KEVIN MOORE, MIKE O'GRADY, PAUL HANLON(CAPTAIN), CIARAN CANNON, DECLAN O'DEA, OWEN KENNY, ROBERT PARKER.

MISSING FROM PHOTO: OLIVER LAWLOR, NIALL ROHAN, DAMIAN DOYLE, KERRILL ROHAN, PADRAIGH FLANNERY, ROBERT BURKE.

PEARSE'S HURLING

By

Tom O'Grady

Our club was formed on the 23rd of February, 1976. Since then it has played a major role in the affairs of our parish. During the previous 8 decades the historic and economic difficulties prevailing in Ireland at the time, had a negative effect on our parish. Consequently, the success enjoyed by the respective Junior teams in both Gurteen and Ballymacward over the years was confined to one County Final Victory each.

Since the formation of Pearse's G.A.A. club some 28 years ago, a new opportunity has been created for all young people to participate in healthy outdoor pursuits on a regular basis. The club has created an opportunity for players, in all grades, to play together for the honour and glory of club and parish.

Every weekend trainers and players assemble at the pitch to prepare for the Championship and the League. The games and training are organised on a voluntary basis and have provided parishioners with entertainment and excitement for many years.
Pearses were among the first groups to generate finance for themselves by organising a local lotto. This is going well and makes the task of providing insurance and running costs easier.

Since we began in the seventies we have received wholehearted support from the people of the parish and I would like to take this opportunity to thank them for their generosity.
We have survived in difficult times and now with the advent of better times there is every reason to assume that the club will grow even stronger with the passage of time.

I think that our ancestors in Gurteen-Ballymacward would be delighted with the facilities that we have now and with the progress that we have made since 1976.

In the coming years we hope to equal our past performances which saw a number of our players feature in the county panels.

NATIONAL SCHOOL CHAMPIONS HURLING 2003
BACK ROW L-R THOMAS MCDONAGH, RORY TREACY, DERMOT SKEHILL, EDMUND FLANNERY, SHANE MCDONAGH, EMMET WARD (CAPT), BRENDAN FINNERTY
FRONT ROW: EANNA CARR, ALAN SKEHILL, SHANE DUFFY, NIALL SKEHILL, CONOR O'GRADY, FERGAL FLANNERY, ROBERT FINN, DARA SKEHILL.
MENTORS: GERRY FLANNERY, DERMOT MALONEY, MARTIN MCDONAGH.

Gurteen School Champion Footballers 2003

Pearses County Intermediate Champions 1979

LEAGUE FINALISTS IN THE 80's

BACK ROW (L-R): TOMAS O'NEILL, FR. JOE CLARKE, SEAMUS O'NEILL, TOM O'GRADY, PAT BELLEW, MICHAEL KING, MARTIN BELLEW, FRANK FINN, GERRY MURPHY, BRENDAN HARDIMAN, KEVIN DONNELLAN.

FRONT ROW: JOHN DOOLEY, FRANCIS BELLEW, MARTIN CANNON, FRANK MCDONAGH, JOHN O'GRADY, TOM O'BRIEN, GERRY MCDONAGH, AIDAN BELLEW, MARTIN RAFTERY, EAMON BELLEW.

CHAPTER SEVENTEEN

LINES AND LYRICS

THATCHER

By

Seamus Heaney

Bespoke for weeks, he turned up some morning
Unexpectedly, his bicycle slung
With a light ladder and a bag of knives.
He eyed the old rigging, poked at the eaves,

Opened and handled sheaves of lashed wheat-straw
Next, the bundled rods: hazel and willow,
Were flicked for weight, twisted in case they'd snap.
It seemed he spent the morning warming up:

Then fixed the ladder, laid out well honed blades
And snipped at straw and sharpened ends of rods
That, bent in two, made a white-pronged staple
For pinning down his world, handful by handful.

Couchant for days on sods above the rafters
He shaved and flushed the butts, stitched all together
Into a sloped honeycomb, a stubble patch,
And left them gaping at his Midas touch

THE DIVINER

By

Seamus Heaney

Cut from the green hedge a forked hazel stick
That he held tight by the arms of the V:
Circling the terrain, hunting the pluck
Of water, nervous, but professionally
Unfussed. The pluck came sharp as a sting.
The rod jerked down with precise convulsions,
Spring water suddenly broadcasting
Through a green aerial its secret stations.

The bystanders would ask to have a try.
He handed them the rod without a word
It lay dead in their grasp' till nonchalantly
He gripped expectant wrists. The hazel stirred.

THE BACHELOR

by

Margot McMahon

He owns a 'tidy' farm in sense of stonewalled fields,
the tidiness ends there, as binder twine makes do
for hinges, gate locks, trouser clips,
and straying dogs at lambing time.
Bordered by bog, he knows of cutting with a sleán,
of wheeling in bare feet,
and clamping turf against the Winter chill.

A solitary gable retains a window on his past.
Old ploughs and harrows punctuate his fields.
A pony trap lies rusting in his shed,
its wheels still iron-rimmed,
echoes of Sundays past when rattling down the road
to clopping hooves it held a cargo of believing souls.

He eats loaf bread still wistful for his mother's crusty cake
dripping with butter that smacked of buttercups,
churned deep in wooden tubs with splashing sounds.
until gathering leaned upon the dash
in readiness for rinsing,
the salting, and the laying on of hands,
butter spades in benediction.

Three nights a week he cycles to the pub,
recalling times long past
when priests poked brambles with their blackthorn sticks
in search of sinners.
He hangs wet clothes to dry beside the range-
fire hidden deep behind its shuttered doors
like his reluctant life.

When I was ten he buried my first dog
and in an act of giant gentleness belied his rugged looks,
my heart was breaking, and he understood.
I followed in the furrow of his plough,
my sadness trodden in the earthy dust,
without a word he handed me the reins,
I trusted him, and he returned my trust.

LOUGHNAHINCH

by

Ned Nevin

(Words supplied by Mrs.Kilkenny)

Long may run its waters clear and serene;
its ripples they are beautiful in silvery sheen.
Recreation on its bosom is health on a summer's day
and enhancing is the music while rousing steady and gay.
The swan in her majesty with her plumage all in white,
like Lir's only daughter when waiting for the light.

When all nature it will sing
with the music of the spring
When the woods are decked in green
And the daisy clad meadows they are seen
Tis then the little warblers, the linnet and the finch
Will be pouring forth a melody
On our route to Loughnahinch

Tis then old patrons hale and hearty
Will be crossing the brown heather
And mates so dear
Accompanying one another.
The boys will turn out with many a pretty colleen
They'll come down the hill of Coolock or the old boreen

But ochone we miss our exiled comrades
Whose home love is intense
May they be seen once more among us
In famed Loughnahinch.

Fish they abound there; the roach, the pike, the perch and eel
See yonder the anglers watching to catch them
With rod, line hook and reel. They'll hope and they'll strive
With God's blessing to make the catch immense
And the supply will be abundant
From famed Old Loughnahinch.

Try, Try again

We may not be responsible for many of the things that happen to us, but we are responsible for the way we react when they do happen.

"Tis a lesson you should heed,
Try, try again;
If at first you don't succeed,
Try, try again;
Then your courage should appear,
For, if you will persevere
You will conquer never fear;
Try, try again.

Once or twice though you should fail,
Try, try again;
If you would at last prevail,
Try, try again.
If we strive, its no disgrace
Though we do not win the race;
What should you do in that case?
Try, try again.

Time will bring you your reward,
Try, try again.
All that other folks can do,
Why, with patience, should not you?
Only keep this rule in view;
Try, try again!

A CHILD'S WORRY

Sometimes í get discouraged
Bcos í am so small,
And always leave my fingerprints
On furniture and walls.
But everyday í'm growing up,
And soon í'll be so tall,
That all those little fingerprints
Will be difficult to recall.
So here's a current handprint,
That u can put away,
So u'll always remember,
How my fingers looked,
This year on Mother's day.

AN GLEANN INAR TÓGADH MÉ

le

An Craobhín Aoibhinn
(Dubhghlas de hÍde)

Ó áit go h-áit ba bhreá mo shiúl
'S dob árd mo léim ar bhárr an tsléibh,
San uisce fíor ba mhór mo dhúil,
'S ba bheo mo chroí í lár mo chléibh;
Mar chois an ghiorria do bhí mo chos,
Mar iarann gach alt is gach feith,
Bhí an sonas romham, thall 's abhus,
Sa ghleann inar tógadh mé.

Ba chuma liomsa fear ar bith,
Ba chuma liom an domhan iomlán,
Mar rith an fhia do bhí mo rith,
Mar shruth an tsléibh ag dul le fán;
Is ní raibh rud ar bith sa domhan
Nach ndearnas (dá mba mhaith liom é;
Sa ghleann inar tógadh mé.

Gach ni a bhfhachas le mo shúil
Bhí sé dar liom. ar dhath an óir;
Is annamh a dheracainn ar mo chúl
Ach ag dul ar aghaidh le misneach mór;
Do leannainse gan stad gan scíth
Mo rún (dá gcuirfinn romhamsa é);
Do bhéarfainn, dar liom, ar an ngaoith
Sa ghleann inar tógadh mé.

Ní h-amhlaidh tá sé liom anois!
Do bhí mé luath, is tá mé mall;
Is é mo léan, an aois do bhris
Sean neart mo chroí is lúth mo bhall;
Do chaill mé mórán 's fuair mé fios
Ar mhórán   ---och ní sású é -
Mo léan, mo léan gan mise arís
Óg sa ghleann inar tógadh mé.

An Fear Gorm   (The Blue Man)
By Eileen Casey

A black rink covers the schoolroom wall,
scratchy from chalk skated over it. One slip
brings the smell of leather, stripes hands
the way liquorice blackens the tongue.
Black is heard too. In boots lurching up the street
towards blackintheface from waiting women,
in whispers of night time rosaries, fingers weaving
prayer through black beads.

In this world of black, An Fear Gorm
is the blue flame over Kitty Seery's sealshiny hair,
river blue veins in atlases, the faint ridge
around grandmother's wedding china.
His skin is the cool breeze of blue ice cream
pictured in magazines, cut out and pasted
into scrapbooks beside blue high heels
the exact shade of blueberry pie.
An Fear Gorm fills dusty inkwells,
dry as African plains
with enough blue to spill across white pages.

In this world of black,
our native language colours the Blackman blue
as if our forebears couldn't believe he ever exited,
as if a blue man is rare as a blue moon
in a pitch black sky.

HOMEWORK OH HOMEWORK!

By

Jack Prelutsky

This offering will strike a chord in all who found life at school unpleasant.

*Homework oh homework!
I hate you! You stink!
I wish I could wash you
away in the sink,
if only a bomb
would explode you to bits.
Homework! Oh, homework!
You're giving me fits.*

*I'd rather take baths
with a man eating shark
or wrestle a lion
alone in the dark,
eat spinach and liver
pet ten porcupines,
than tackle the homework
my teacher assigns.*

*Homework! Oh Homework!
You're last on my list
I simply can't see
why you even exist
if you just disappeared
it would tickle me pink.
Homework! Oh Homework!
I hate you! You stink!*

WHY GO TO CHURCH?

Submitted by Fr.Slattery

Some go to Church just for a walk
Some to stare some to talk
Some go to meet a friend
Some their idle time to spend
Some for general observation
Some for private speculation
Some to seek or find a lover
Some a courtship to discover
Some go there to use their eyes
And newest fashions criticise
Some to show their smart new dress
Some their neighbours to assess
Some to scan a hat or bonnet
Some to price the trimming on it
Some to learn the latest news
That friends at home they may amuse
Some to gossip false and true
Safe hid within a sheltering pew
Some go there to please the squire
Some his daughters to admire
Some the parson go to fawn
Some to lounge and some to yawn
Some because it's thought genteel
Some to vaunt their pious zeal
Some to show how sweet they sing
Some how loud their voices ring
Some the preacher go to hear
His style & voice to praise or jeer
Some forgiveness to implore
Some their sins to varnish o'er
Some to sit and doze and nod
But some to kneel and worship God.

PITY THE POOR STARLING

By

Geraldine Mills

The starling doesn't like Mondays
God knows she knows to keep to her roost;
hide her spangled plumage
shot through with blues and greens
muffle her raucous chacker.

She whispers to her chicks their bedtime story
(a mother has to make them skywise after all)
and they shiver in their nest when they hear
the names of Kerrill and Connell,
the brothers with their monkish ways;

how they built two chapels to the heavens,
sharing as they did and godly people do
their only sledge, their trowel,
until one bad hair day a row erupted
over who could have the tools or not
and curses flew like trowels across the airwaves,

landing with a thud on some poor old starling's head,
whose only thought was a juicy leatherjacket;
instead dropped dead on Clonkeenkerrill
and every Monday since.

Now as she tucks them under her wing
she makes them say their prayers
No corners on my bed
Feathered angels round my head
Don't let us stick our beaks out;
Don't let us dice with death.

THE LONG WAY HOME

by

Mai Dwyer

Along the cold dark roads of winter, to school
Hands blue clutching the sod of turf for the fire
Each child brought one
The dread of the day loomed before us
The drone of arithmetic Tables
White knuckles, penny catechsism, and the fear of the stick.
Fear and biting cold abides in the memory of those hard days
Sprinkled with relief of
Wet Mondays, too wet for school
In our black stockings and hobnail boots
Drawing in the fog of windows from chairs
Holding hot scones swimming in butter.

Spring cheered us with longer evenings, crocuses
Newborn lambs and Easter.
Breaking from school with a dash through the fields
Of east Galway, leaving Clonkeen behind us,
On the long way home.

Summer was forever
Long hot days stretching way out into the future
As if we would never go back to school.
Rabbits in the new mown hay
Haycocks and reeks in the haggard
Cut knees from running falls
And before we knew it

September, dragging our heels home in the amber evening
Picking fraughans and blackberries, delaying the moment
Squeezing the last out of summer
Those sultry evenings, held back after school,
Sweeping the floor, while the voices of the
other children fade into the distance.
Wishing we could fly out the window
Wishing we were grown up
Wishing it was next summer

Wishing our lives away.

MY NEW SPELLING CHECKER

Eye halve a spelling chequer
It came with my pea sea
It plainly marques four my revue
Miss steaks eye kin knot sea

Eye strike a key and type a word
And weight four it two say
Weather eye am wrong oar write
It shows me strait a weigh

As soon as a mist ache is maid
It nose bee fore two long
And eye can put the error rite
Its rare lea ever wrong.

Eye have run this poem threw it
I am shore your pleased two no
Its letter perfect awl the weigh
My chequer tolled me sew

Sauce unknown

STILL LIFE

by

Jim O'Donnell

In the sanctuary of the kitchen haggard long gone by

A donkey cart painted in a crimson red
Shafted in blue against a sugáned rick of hay
A goat and a kid munch and gorge in silence
The cidered fruit bruised beneath a rainbow of apple trees
Blackthorn sloes in hues of black and blue
Cloistering plums a ruby red, pears amber and apple green
Blackberries blobbing inkwells of brambled juice
Drip drying a tapestry in a weft of silver purls,
Spattering crystals in the dappled sun of the noon day heat
A pheasant cock walks stilted in plumage delight
Claw printing the zig zagged beaten track
Through fern and gorse yellow whins
And stools and stools of rhubarb fleshy leafed
Headlanding drills of new potato stalks
Blossoming pinks, queens, edger blues
Balls of flower in bloom
Bia, bia human word
Reechoing the famine years' decay
With food for thought in silence
Lamenting the landscaped haggard
Long gone by.

THE OLD RUGGED CROSS

by

Marian Treacy

It was a life filled with pain and desperation,
Without hope or the remedy of any man,
When a hand with the nail prints stretched downwards
Just one touch and a new life began

The Old Rugged Cross made the difference
To a life bound for heartache and defeat
I will remember His goodness forever
The Lord Jesus made the difference for me.

I am so glad that He was willing to drink the Bitter Cup
Although he prayed 'Father, let this cup pass from me.'
I am so glad He never called Heaven's Angels (saying)
'From my hands draw these nails that torment me.'

Had it not been for a place called Mount Calvary,
Had it not been for the Old Rugged Cross,
Had it not been for a Man called Jesus,
Then, forever my soul would be lost.

I believe that the Christ Who was slain on the Cross
Has the power to change lives today
For He changed me completely,
A new life is mine!
That is why by His side I will stay!

I believe in a hill called Mount Calvary,
I believe whatever the cost!
When time has surrendered and earth is no more
I'll cling to the King of that Cross.

EAMON AN CHNUIC

*Cé hé sin amuigh
A bhfuil faobhar ar a ghuth
Ag réabadh mo dhoras dúnta
Mise Eamon an Chnuic
Atá báite fuar fliuch
Ó shíor shiúl na sléibhte is gleannta
A Laogh ghil 's a chuid,
Ceard dheanfhainn-se dhuit,
Muna gcuirfinn ort beinn dom' ghúna,
'S go bhfuil púdar go tiúbh
D'A shior-shéideadh leat,
'S go mbeimís araon múchta.*

*Is fada mise amuigh
Faoi shneachta 'gus faoi shioc
Gan dánacht agam ar aoine
Mo sheisreach gan scur
Mo bhranar gan cur
Agus gan iad agam ar aon chor
Níl cara agam
Is dána liom sin
A ghlachfadh mé moch ná dhéanach
Is go gcaitfidh mé dul
Tar farraige soir
O's ann nach bhfuil aon dem ghaolta.*

NED OF THE HILL

Who is that out there still
With voice sharp and shrill
Beating my door and calling
I am Ned of the Hill
Wet weary and chill
The mountains and glen long walking

O my dear love and true
What could I do for you
But under my mantle draw you
For the bullets like hail
Fall thick on your trail
And together we both may be slaughtered.
Long lonely I go under frost under snow
Hunted through hill and through hollow
No comrade I know
No furrow I sow
My team stands unyoked in the fallow:
No friend will give ear
Or harbour me here
Tis that makes the weight of my sorrow
So my journey must be
To the east o'er the seas
Where no kindred will find me or follow.

This beautiful song is supposed to have been written by an 18th Century outlaw called Edmund O'Ryan from Tipperary. Originally it was a love song but eventually the outlaw came to be regarded as a symbol for Ireland. It was translated into English by Thomas McDonagh, one of the 1916 leaders.

THE FORGE

by

Seamus Heaney

All I know is a door into the dark.
Outside, old axles and iron hoops rusting;
Inside, the hammered anvil's short pitched ring,
The unpredictable fantail of sparks
Or hiss when the new shoe toughens in water.
The anvil must be somewhere in the centre,
Horned as a unicorn, at one end square,
Set there immovable: an altar
Where he expends himself in shape and music,
Sometimes, leather-aproned, hairs in his nose,
He leans out on the jamb, recalls a clatter
of hoofs where traffic is flashing in rows;
Then grunts and goes in, with a slam and flick
To beat real iron out, to work the bellows.

SHANBALLARD

By

Padraic Fallon

It's feeling now and dangerous
To touch, when I
Was the crown prince of birds early
With the first cock crowing;
And that was a morning,
My head pillowed and abroad
In the true blue;
Meaning I felt the world awake
And I was a county.

Meaning up heartwise the house awoke
To the call of a country
Turfsmoke curled from below
And day creaked open;
Dangling on my rafter I
Survey my kingdom,
Open fire and hanging kettle,
The doorway wide,
The feathered collie in the morning beam.

Meaning the big unsteady dawn was waiting
And the world still making,
Meaning the smoking cows halfmade
Wavered on the dews;
And there was a snail humped on a bridge
And there was the blackbird pecked him up
And there was the mare I was to ride
Butting a silly foal.
The day was starting to report.

Meaning it was zigzagged of the arrow
Head of woodcock, meaning it caught crows
Bungling a turnip field, meaning it sat
On the old crowman in the oats,
His crossbows more askew;
Green hung the crabapple's claws;
Rabbits announced me here
Comes Twolegs and his totem dog.
The thumped morse went on before me.

Meaning it went up into the breath
Of morning, meaning I bowed before
The bowlegged blackthorn in the gap

Where the sunburst met me.
And I was the bogvoice going up,
I was the beginning bees,
I was the dialogue in the curlew's mouth
And simple as a two-holed pipe;
The ripe fern turning south.

Meaning the sun was sailing me, and all
The call of crows on Lynch's knoll was mine;
And lying down I was
The newest butterfly white and green
Drying its wayward compass on a stone,
And the all around and the all to be
Turning over
To catch the three small chimneys on the hill
Treadling the morning smoke.

Meaning the cat loped after the milker
And swallows chuckled
On the byre beams above the cans, meaning
Pigs sang at the sty gate
And two old men,
Two lovely raggedly old men gossiped
By the upheeled cart, and morning
Was over, done, gone, and never
To be followed after;
Meaning I
Catching the sun upon a breakfast knife,
No longer beamed;
Housed I was and never homed again,
A swindled fellow.
Folded the buzzing miles outside the pane
Where the drunken gatepost leaned
And a single foxglove rolled its bells around
A stick tall as an umbrella.

GURTEEN SCHOOL RHYMES

The following is a selection of verses that were well known here almost a century ago:

Boxty on the griddle
Boxty on the pan
If you don't eat boxty,
You'll never get a man.

Rye bread will kill you dead
Barley bread will do you no harm
Oaten bread would redden your blood
Wholemeal bread will strengthen your arm.

This is a variation of the Lúrabog Rhyme:

Lúrabog, Larabog
Neill a priabán
Priabáin suileach
Súile a seicín
Seicín meileach
Súistín búistín
Bill a bhog a béicín
Crap isteach do mhéirín
Cos.

OTHER RHYMES

Daddy and Mammy went fighting for flies
Daddy gave Mammy a pair of black eyes.
Now says Daddy will you fight any more?
No says Mammy, my eyes are too sore

Twelve little tailors sitting in a row
One caught a fly and the other let him go.
Stick him with the needle, hang him with the thread
Hang him to the tail of a coat and leave him down dead.

A wee wee woman and a wee wee man
A wee wee kettle and a wee wee pan,
A wee wee house thatched with straw
Three blind mice and an old jackdaw.

RUDE RHYMES

Some of you may find it hard to believe that our ancestors had a vast repertoire of naughty rhymes. The first one was probably recited at Corskeagh Road when the pupils from Carhoon were parting from the other Gurteen students. Such partings were often accompanied by tough snowball or scraw battles as well as a variety of verbal assaults.

The other pieces were probably known 'off by heart' by the pupils from the other three schools.

The Carhoon Scrub
Outside the wall
A bottle of piss
Would drown them all
A greasy candle to show them light
And bury their faces in cowshite.

The cuckoo is a pretty bird she flies away to Spain
And when the weather it gets fine she flies back home again
But on the way home she met the whoring hawk
She plucked the feathers of his arse and said, 'Get down and walk.'

I see Paris,
I see France
I see up
The leg of your pants.

SIONNACH

Le

Nuala Ní Dhomhnaill

A Mhaidrín rua
Rua rua rua rua
Nach breá nach bhfuil fhios agat,
Dá mhéid a ritheann leat,
Sa deireadh
Gurbh é siopa an fhionnadóra
A bheidh mar chríoch ort.

Nílmidne filí
Pioc difriúil.
Deir John Berryman
Go ndeir Gottfried Benn
Go bhfuilimid ag úsáid ár gcraiceann
Mar pháipéar falla
Is go mbuafar orainn.

Ach fógra dona fionnadóirí;
Bígí cúramach.
Ní haon ghiorria
Í seo agaibh
Ach sionnach rua
Anuas ón gcnoc.
Bainim snap
As láimh mo chothaite.

A MEMORY

By

Fr. Seán Slattery

There is a memory of home I ne'r will forget
Its peace and tranquillity dwell with me yet,
Where oft in the Summer at eve I would dream
As I wandered the banks of the old Kerrill's stream

Neath the walls of the school it silently crept,
And on by Cloonkeen where everyone slept,
The loved ones we knew in the days that are gone
Their journey is o'er but the waters roll on.

The years have been many, I've wandered along,
Far away from the stream with its kind rippling song,
Still peacefully flowing by the old Abbey walls,
My heart is still there and my memory recalls.

And I pray that my God in His mercy will bring
An era of peace to this world again,
As calm and as peaceful a day I have seen,
When I walked the banks of Gurteen's old stream.

LIFE'S MIRROR

There are loyal hearts, there are spirits brave,
There are souls that are pure and true,
Then give the world the best you have
And the best will come back to you.

Give love, and love to your life will flow,
A strength in your utmost need,
Have faith, and a score of hearts will show
Their faith in your word and deed.

Give truth, and your gift will be paid in kind;
And honour will honour meet
And a smile that is sweet will surely find
A smile that is just as sweet.
Give pity and sorrow to those who mourn
You will gather in flowers again
The scattered seeds from your thoughts outborne
Though the sowing seemed but vain.

For life is the mirror of king and slave
'Tis just what we are and do;
Then give the world the best you have
And the best will come back to you.

Madeline Bridges

MALLACHT NAOIMH

Le

Margot McMahon

I reilig ársa Cluain Chaoin Chearbhaill
mar a bhfuil mo mhuinntir sínte
gach maidin Luain í measc na n-uaigh
tá scéal is ádhbhar iontais.
Í gcúinne dubh faoi chrainnte úir
Bíonn druidín bhallach bídeach
fad ina tost gan glór gan guth
a beatha eiteach ídithe.

Deirtear gur amllacht mánaigh é
sin bun go bárr an scéil
chuir Conall cuireadh chun bainise
chuig Cearbhaill - d'freagair seisean
'tá socraid agam Maidin Luain
níl ar mo chumas teacht',
bíodh socraid agat chuile Luain
dúirt Conall giorraisc beacht.

Thuig Cearbhaill mallacht fíor mhallaithe
is dheifrigh sé a ghuí
gur corpán éan a bhéadh dá cur
in ionad duine Dhiaga,
in ainneoin a ghliceas bhí sé
tá seanchas a luann
nach gcuirfear cónra síos fen bfód
í gCluain Caoin ar an Luain.

RAFTERY

No poetry collection would be complete without referring to Anthony Raftery, the blind poet and violinist. He spent a great deal of his time travelling in the west of Ireland and the majority of you would gave learned his poems or songs at some stage. It is impossible to do him justice in a collection of this kind so we are only including a few short extracts from his poems. The first is one of his well-known songs and poems.

TEACHT AN EARRAIGH

Le

Antaine O'Reachtaire

Anois teacht an Earraigh, beidh an la dul chun sineadh,
Is tar eis an Feile Bhride, ardoidh me mo sheol;
O chuir me i mo cheann me ni stopfaidh me choiche,
go seasfaidh me sios i lar Chondae Mhuigheo.
I Gclar Chlaoinn Mhuiris a bheas me an chead oiche,
Is an baile taobh thios de thosnois ag ol,
Go Coillte Mach rachaid go ndeanas cuairt mhi ann
I bhfoghus da mhile go Beal an Ath Mor.

EANACH DHUIN

Le

Antaine O' Reachtaire

Ma fhaighimse slainte beidh caint is trachtadh
Ar an meid a bathadh as Eanach Dhuin
Is mo thrua amarach gach athair is mathair
Bean is paiste ta ag sileadh sul.
A Ri na nGrasa cheap Neamh is Parrthas,
Nar bheag an tabhacht dhuinn beirt no triur!
Ach la comh brea leis gan gaoith na baisteach
Lan an bhaid a scuabadh ar siul. ….

Tolladh cleibe 'gus loscadh sleibhe
Ar an ait ar eagadar is millean crua
Is a liachtai creatur a dfhag se faonlag
Ag sileadh 's ag eagaoin gach maidin Luain.
Ni diobhail eolais a chuir da dtreoir iad
Ach mi-adh mor ag an gCaislean Nua
Is e criochnu an chomhra gor bathadh moran
Dfhag abhar dolais ag Enach Dhuin

THE SAINT'S CURSE

By

Margot McMahon

In Clonkeenkerrill graveyard
where my ancestors lie
tradition decrees that permission to die
is refused at the weekend lest St. Conall's curse
be fulfilled on the Monday
to make matters worse

Each Monday a starling with feathers all bright
lies cold and forlorn with no voice and no flight
in answer to prayer from Kerrill 'tis said
a person is spared while a poor bird lies dead.

St. Conall invited St. Kerrill on Sunday
to come to a wedding the very next Monday
'On Monday a funeral I must attend',
said Kerrill in answer to his holy friend.
Well Conall was raging, and feeling quite miffed
he sent back a message which caused a great rift.
'May you have a funeral each Monday morn',
he said in a voice filled with passion and scorn.
But Kerrill was quick off the mark with his prayers
and begged the good Lord as he knelt on the stairs
'Please God let a bird be the one we will bury
And that will teach Conall to be less contrary.'

QUEST FOR KNOWLEDGE

by

John Corbett

Making shapes with slates and Marla,
To unravel hidden codes,
Wearing worn out shoes or barefoot,
We went to school on potholed roads.
Deep down we feared the teachers,
And their blackboards broad and bare,
We wondered why our parents said
That our lives were free from care.

We struggled to find knowledge,
Using chalk and ink and pen.
But the classroom was a college,
That was far beyond our ken.
Our lunchtime fights, some fearsome,
Hidden by the schoolyard wall,
Likewise the games we played there,
With twine and paper ball.

We laughed, we teased, we taunted,
Testing ears and lungs and throats,
We fancied we were 'Dashers'
While those we teased were 'Goats.'
All too soon the lessons ended;
No more marla slates or rules,
No more playing with the 'scholars'
That we knew in Gurteen's schools.

APPENDIX

At the blackboard
The following are some of the people who taught in our parish schools.

at Cloonkeenkerrill N.S.

Eoin Donnelly,
Mr. and Mrs. Walsh
Mrs. Hurley
Mrs. Cogavin
Sheila Cloonan-Bellew
David McGann
Aidan Nicholson
P.J. Kennelly
Pat Burke
Mrs. Lyng
Michael J. Kilgannon

at Shanballard:

Julia Dilleen-Duffy
Mr. Clery
Tom and Mrs. Murphy
Margaret Mahon-Kitt
Mary Nally-Kyne
Maureen Blehein- Thornhill
Catherine Dilleen
Anne Ward
Dermot Maloney

Tample teachers:

Mrs. Kate duffy
Daisy Duffy
Maureen Keane- Clancy
Mrs. Lyng
Sheila Cloonan-Bellew

PARISH PRIESTS AND CURATES IN BALLYMACWARD AND CLOONKEENKERRILL PARISHES (GURTEEN)

Rev. James Dunn P.P 1716/1756
Rev. Denis Kearhy P.P
Rev. Patrick Duffy P.P.
Rev. Michael Moran C.C.
Rev. Ginnings C.C. ''
Rev. Michael Callegy ''
Rev. Patrick Connallen ''
Rev John Derry P.P.
Rev. Andrew Griffin C.C.
Rev. John Raftery C.C.
Rev. Patrick Conallen P.P.
Rev. Thomas Hoad C.C.
Rev. Gerald Dillon C.C.
Rev. John Deely C.C.
Rev. James Cahalan C.C.
Rev. Joe Cahalan C.C.
Rev. Patrick Cannon C.C.
Rev. Patrick Mullins C.C.
Rev. Dennis Coughlan C.C.
Most Rev. Dr. Healy Lord Bishop And P.P.
Rev. John Fahy C.C
Rev. Daniel Coughlan C.C.
Rev. Joseph Coughlan C.C.
Rev. James Carey C.C.
Rev. John Fahey C.C.
Rev. Joseph Pelly C.C.
Rev. Thomas O' Malley C.C.
Rev. Martin? Larkin Adm.
Rev. John Dermody C.C.
Rev. Matthew Fulham (O.P.) C.C.
Rev. Joseph Coughlan Adm.
Rev. Thomas Madden C.C.
Rev. John Keegan Adm.
Rev. Joseph M. Pelly C.C.
Rev. Tom Dunne C.C.
Rev. Patrick O' Loughlan C.C.
Rev. T.J. Joyce C.C.
Rev. Joseph Pelly. P.P.
Rev. Wm Naughton
Rev. William Naughten C.C.
Rev. J.K O' Neill C.C.
Rev. William Naughten C.C.
Rev. Michael O' Reilly C.C.
Rev. Michael Callanan P.P.
An-At S.E.S. Saidail S.E.
Rev. Declan Gordon C.C.
Rev. John Campbell P.P.
Rev J. Egan Appointed P.P.
Rev. Peter Dunne P.P.
Most Rev. Dr. John Kirby
Rev. Joseph Clarke C.C.
Rev. Martin Hough C.C.
Rev. Vincent Lawless C.C.
Rev. Gerry Sweeney C.C.
Rev. Seán Slattery P.P.

COUNTY OF GALWAY.

BARONY OF TIAQUIN.

UNION OF LOUGHREA, 1855

PARISH OF BALLYMACWARD.

No. and Letters of Reference to Map.	Names. Townlands and Occupiers.	Immediate Lessors.	Description of Tenement.	Area. A. R. P.	Rateable Annual Valuation. Land. £ s. d.	Rateable Annual Valuation. Buildings. £ s. d.	Total Annual Valuation of Rateable Property. £ s. d.
	BALLYGRANY. (Ord. S. 72.)						
a, k	Michael Nevin,		Ho., offices, land, & cottier's house,		7 5 0	2 0 0	9 5 0
b,l,q,r	James Bolton,		Ho., offs., ld., & three cottiers' houses,		7 5 0	3 5 0	10 10 0
c, n	John Barrett,		Ho., offices, land, & cottier's house,		4 5 0	0 15 0	5 0 0
d,m,o	Patrick Mullin,		House, offices, land, & two cottiers' hos.,	151 0 8	8 10 0	1 5 0	9 15 0
1 e	Martin Tuohy,	Lord Dunsandle,	House and land,		1 5 0	0 10 0	1 15 0
f	Denis Greany, jun.,		House and land,		2 10 0	0 5 0	2 15 0
g	Patrick Connolly,		House, office, & land,		2 10 0	1 0 0	3 10 0
h	John Fahy,		House, office, & land,		1 5 0	0 10 0	1 15 0
i, p	Patrick Greany,		House, office, land, & cottier's house,		2 10 0	1 0 0	3 10 0
j	Denis Greany,		House, office, & land,		2 10 0	0 15 0	3 5 0
			Total,	151 0 8	39 15 0	11 5 0	51 0 0
	CORSKEAGH (DALY). (Ord. S. 72.)						
1 a	Lord Dunsandle,	In fee,	Herd's ho., offs., & land,	726 3 33	220 0 0	0 15 0	} 221 0 0
b			Labourer's house,			0 5 0	
2	Malachy Naughton,	Lord Dunsandle,	House, office, and land,	9 3 5	5 0 0	0 10 0	5 10 0
			Total,	736 2 38	225 0 0	1 10 0	226 10 0
	CREERAUN. (Ord. S. 72.)						
1	Anthony O'Kelly,	Margaret O'Kelly,	House, office, and land,	50 3 14	5 0 0	6 0 0	11 0 0
2	James Browne,	Same,	Land,	193 3 6	118 0 0	—	118 0 0
			Total,	244 2 20	123 0 0	6 0 0	129 0 0
	GLENNAMUCKA. (Ord. S. 72.)						
1 A a	Patrick Raftery,	Lord Dunsandle,	Bog,	33 1 5	0 5 0	—	} 134 10 0
– B b			House, office, and land,	274 3 8	130 0 0	4 0 0	
			Cottier's house,			0 5 0	
2	Michael Daly,	Patrick Raftery,	House, office, and land,	15 1 13	2 5 0	0 10 0	2 15 0
3	Patrick Nevin,	Same,	House and bog,	1 3 33	0 5 0	0 5 0	0 10 0
4	John Power,	Same,	House, office, and land,	9 3 23	4 5 0	0 15 0	5 0 0
5	Patrick Hynes,	Same,	House, office, and land,	7 3 27	4 5 0	0 15 0	5 0 0
6	James Naughton,	Same,	Land,	0 3 20	0 10 0	—	} 1 0 0
1 B C		Same,	House and garden,	0 0 10	0 1 0	0 9 0	
7	James Walsh,	Same,	House, office, and land,	3 0 10	1 15 0	0 10 0	2 5 0
			Total,	347 0 19	143 11 0	7 9 0	151 0 0

VALUATION OF TENEMENTS.

PARISH OF BALLYMACWARD.

No. and Letters of Reference to Map.	Names. Townlands and Occupiers.	Immediate Lessors.	Description of Tenement.	Area. A. R. P.	Rateable Annual Valuation. Land. £ s. d.	Buildings. £ s. d.	Total Annual Valuation of Rateable Property. £ s. d.
	GORTBRACK. (Ord. S. 72.)						
1	Michael Mannion,	Robert M. Eyre,	House, office, and land,	56 3 27	5 10 0	0 15 0	6 5
2	John Kelly,	Same,	House, offices, and land,	43 2 5	8 0 0	1 5 0	9 5
3 A			Land,	6 0 12	2 5 0	—	
— B a	Patrick Molloy,	Same,	House, office, and land,	25 2 23	7 0 0	0 10 0	} 10 15
— b, c, d			Three cottiers' houses,	—	—	1 0 0	
			Land,	0 3 0	0 5 0	—	
4 A	Patrick Smyth,	Same,	House and land,	4 3 30	1 15 0	0 10 0	} 2 10
— B							
5	Michael Moran, jun.,	Same,	House and land,	4 1 20	1 5 0	0 10 0	1 15
6	Michael Moran,	Same,	House and land,	1 1 20	0 15 0	0 5 0	1 0
7 a	William Burns,	Same,	House, office, and land,	41 1 23	6 10 0	0 10 0	} 7 5
— b			Cottier's house,	—	—	0 5 0	
			Land,	0 0 4	2 10 0	—	
8 A	Patrick Finn,	Same,	House and land,	1 1 0	0 3 0	0 17 0	} 3 10
— B							
9	Anthony O'Kelly,	Same,	Land,	3 3 20	1 0 0	—	1 0
			Total,	199 0 22	36 18 0	6 7 0	43 5
	GORTEEN. (Ord. S. 72.)						
1	Lord Dunsandle,	In fee.	Herd's ho., off., & land,	223 0 10	70 0 0	0 10 0	70 10
2 a	John Naughton,	Lord Dunsandle,	House and land,	2 1 10	1 5 0	0 10 0	1 15
3	Laurence Griffin,	Same,	Land,	4 2 0	2 10 0	—	} 2 15
2 b			Cottier's ho. & garden,	0 0 10	0 1 0	0 4 0	
a	Michael Kenny,		Ho. off.ld.&cottiersho.		10 10 0	1 0 0	11 10
b	Martin Hynes,		House and land,		3 3 0	0 7 0	3 10
c	Peter Flannery,		House, offices, & land,		16 0 0	1 0 0	17 0
d	Thomas M'Gee,		House, offices, & land,		6 6 0	0 9 0	6 15
4 e	James Keane,	Same,	House, office, & land,	198 3 34	6 6 0	0 9 0	6 15
f	James Dooly,		House, office, & land,		16 16 0	0 19 0	17 15
g	John Coghlan,		House, office, & land,		6 6 0	0 9 0	6 15
h	Thomas Seery,		House and land,		7 0 0	0 10 0	7 10
i	Margaret Mullen,		House and land,		1 1 0	0 4 0	1 5
j	Thomas Tarp,		House, office, & land,		2 2 0	0 13 0	2 15
			Total,	428 3 24	149 6 0	7 4 0	156 10
	GORTNAHULTRA. (Ord. S. 72.)						
1	Lord Dunsandle,	In fee,	House and land,	370 0 18	140 0 0	0 10 0	140 10
			Total,	370 0 18	140 0 0	0 10 0	140 10

PARISH OF CLONKEEN.

	ATTIMANY. (Ord. S. 72.)						
1 a	Oliver Cunniffe,	} Lord Dunsandle,	{ House, offices, & land,	86 1 11	{ 6 0 0	0 10 0	6 10
b	Michael Kenny,		House, offices, & land,		{ 2 0 0	0 10 0	2 10
			Total,	86 1 11	8 0 0	1 0 0	9 0
	BALLYGLASS. (Ord. S. 72.)						
1 a	John Finn,	Lord Dunsandle,	{ House, offices, and land,	81 3 13	30 0 0	2 0 0	} 35 15
— c, d			House, office, & garden,	0 1 25	0 5 0	3 10 0	
— b	R. C. Chapel (no rent),	(See exemptions.)					
— e	Police-barrack,	(See exemptions.)					
—	John Finn,		Half annual rent of police-barrack.	—	—	—	7 10
2	Matthias Giblin,	Lord Dunsandle,	House, offices, and land,	71 3 39	13 10 0	0 15 0	14 5
a	Patrick Silk,		House and land,		2 7 0	0 7 0	2 14
—	Thomas Kirrane,		Land,		2 5 0	—	2 5
3 b	John Silk,	Same,	House, office, & land,	76 0 17	5 3 0	0 12 0	5 15
c	Peter Connor,		House, office, & land,		2 0 0	0 10 0	2 10
d	John Hoban,		Cottier's house & land,		0 10 0	0 4 0	0 14

VALUATION OF TENEMENTS.

PARISH OF CLONKEEN.

No. and Letters of Reference to Map	Townlands and Occupiers	Immediate Lessors	Description of Tenement	Area A. R. P.	Rateable Annual Valuation Land £ s. d.	Buildings £ s. d.	Total Annual Valuation of Rateable Property £ s. d.
	BALLYGLASS—continued.						
4 a	Patrick Kirrane,	Lord Dunsandle,	House, offices, & land,	53 0 6	4 18 0	0 17 0	5 15 0
bd	Thomas Kirrane,		House, offices, land, and cottier's house,		6 15 0	1 0 0	7 15 0
c	Patrick M'Donagh,		House, office, & land,		6 0 0	0 10 0	6 10 0
5 a	Thos. Kirrane, jun., Thomas Kirrane,	Same,	Land, Office and land,	52 1 9	18 5 0	0 5 0	18 15 0
b	John Kirrane,		Land & cottier's ho.,			0 5 0	
6 a	John Kirrane,	Same,	House, offices, & land,	38 2 15	12 0 0	0 10 0	12 10 0
b	James Ryan,		House, offices, & land,		6 0 0	0 15 0	6 15 0
7 A				51 1 28	27 0 0		
A a	Thomas Kirrane,		House, offices, & land,			1 10 0	10 13 0
b	Thos. Kirrane, jun.,	Same,	House, offices, land, and cottier's house,	—	—	1 10 0	10 13 0
c	Mark Kirrane,		House, offices, & land,	—	—	1 5 0	10 8 0
B			Bog,	36 0 0	0 9 0	—	
8	Michael Kilkenny,	Same,	House and land,	7 3 1	1 5 0	0 5 0	1 10 0
9 a	James Duffy,	Same,	House, offices, and land,	176 3 28	72 0 0	3 5 0	76 10 0
b, c, d			Three cottiers' houses, and garden,	0 2 0	0 6 0	0 19 0	
10 a	Mark Kirrane,	Same,	Land, Cottier's house & office,	10 1 0	4 15 0	0 15 0	5 10 0
11	Michael White,	Same,	Land,	10 0 16	4 15 0	—	4 15 0
12	Mark Monahan,	Same,	Herd's ho., offs., & land,	55 0 26	11 10 0	0 15 0	12 5 0
			Total of rateable property,	722 1 20	231 18 0	22 4 0	261 12 0
	EXEMPTIONS:						
1 b		Lord Dunsandle,	R. C. Chapel and yard,	0 1 0	—	8 0 0	8 0 0
c	Constabulary Force,	John Finn,	Police-barrack, office, and small garden,	—	—	3 0 0	3 0 0
			Total of Exemptions,	0 1 0	—	11 0 0	11 0 0
			Total, including Exemptions,	722 2 20	231 18 0	33 4 0	272 12 0
	CALTRAGH. (Ord. S. 72.)						
1	Patrick Mitchell,	Lord Dunsandle,	Herd's house and land,	140 0 30	90 0 0	0 10 0	90 10 0
			Total,	140 0 30	90 0 0	0 10 0	90 10 0
	CLOGH. (Ord. S. 72 & 85.)						
1 a, b	Patrick Mitchell,	Lord Dunsandle,	Herd's ho., offs., & land, Cottier's house,	174 1 38	77 0 0	0 10 0 0 10 0	78 0 0
c							
2 a	Patrick Hardiman,		Office and land,		0 15 0	0 5 0	1 0 0
b	Bartholomew Tracy,	Same,	House, office, & land,	11 1 30	0 15 0	0 5 0	1 0 0
c	Thaddeus Hardiman,		House and land,		0 15 0	0 5 0	1 0 0
3 A			House, offices, and land,	40 0 36	4 5 0	0 15 0	7 0 0
B	James Molloy,	Same,	Land,	7 0 8	1 10 0	—	
C			Land,	1 0 32	0 10 0	—	
4 A			House, offices, and land,	25 2 16	5 15 0	0 10 0	8 10 0
B	John Kilkelly,	Same,	Land,	3 3 17	1 15 0	—	
C			Land,	1 1 15	0 10 0	—	
5 A	Peter Feenaghty,	Same,	House, offices, and land,	28 3 18	14 0 0	1 15 0	21 5 0
B			Offices and land,	36 1 4	5 0 0	0 10 0	
6	Jeremiah Feenaghty,	Same,	House, offices, and land,	65 3 28	10 0 0	0 15 0	10 15 0
7	John Clonan,	Same,	House, offices, and land,	68 2 35	13 0 0	1 0 0	14 0 0
8	John Bermingham,	Same,	House, office, and land,	20 1 5	5 0 0	0 10 0	5 10 0
9	Martin Tracy, John Ward,	Same,	Land,	21 1 25	7 0 0	—	7 0 0
10 A				14 3 8	5 0 0		
B a	Bartholomew Tracy,	Same,	House, offices, & land,	—	—	0 12 0	3 10 0
b	John Ward,		House, office, & land,	—	—	0 12 0	3 10 0
B				0 0 20	0 16 0	—	

VALUATION OF TENEMENTS.

PARISH OF CLONKEEN.

No. and Letters of Reference to Map.	Townlands and Occupiers.	Immediate Lessors.	Description of Tenement.	Area. A. R. P.	Rateable Annual Valuation. Land. £ s. d.	Buildings. £ s. d.	Total Annual Valuation of Rateable Property. £ s. d.
	CLOGH—continued.						
11 A - B - C - - b	Michael Coen,	Lord Dunsandle,	Ho., offs., corn mill & ld. Land, Land, Cottier's house,	20 0 16 6 0 24 6 2 27 —	20 0 0 4 0 0 3 5 0 —	3 0 0 — — 0 5 0	} 30 10 0
12	Michael Coen, William Molloy,	Same,	Land,	4 3 5	0 10 0 0 10 0	—	0 10 0 0 10 0
13	William Molloy,	Same,	House, office, and land,	16 2 20	11 0 0	0 15 0	11 15 0
14 {a {b	Thomas Hinahan, Martin Gilligan,	Same,	House and land, House and land,	26 2 37	2 0 0 4 0 0	0 10 0 0 10 0	2 10 0 4 10 0
15 A - B	Michael M'Dermott,	Same,	House, offices, and land, Land,	8 3 0 6 0 36	5 15 0 3 15 0	1 10 0 —	} 11 0 0
16 A - B - C	John Fahy,	Same,	Land,	12 3 20 3 2 38 6 3 30	3 0 0 2 0 0 3 0 0	— — —	} 8 0 0
17 {a {b	John Fahy, Thomas M'Gann,	Same,	House, offices, & land, House, offices, & land,	88 3 23	18 10 0 18 10 0	1 10 0 1 5 0	20 0 0 19 15 0
18 A - B	Patrick Hardiman,	Same,	House, office, and land, Office and land,	3 3 34 10 1 12	2 0 0 1 15 0	1 0 0 0 5 0	} 5 0 0
19 A - B	John Kavanagh,	Same,	House, offices, and land, Land,	16 0 25 4 0 12	3 5 0 2 5 0	1 0 0 —	} 6 10 0
20	Michael Hardiman,	Same,	House, offices, and land,	14 2 10	7 0 0	0 10 0	7 10 0
21 {a {b	Denis Hardiman, John Hardiman,	Same,	House, office, & land, House and land,	25 1 4	5 0 0 5 0 0	0 10 0 0 10 0	5 10 0 5 10 0
22 a - b, c	Martin Tracey,	Same,	House, offices, and land, Two cottiers' houses,	18 3 2 —	9 10 0 —	1 5 0 1 0 0	} 11 15 0
23 A - B	Lord Dunsandle,	In fee,	Bog, House and land,	551 1 8 251 1 38	2 10 0 100 0 0	— 0 5 0	2 10 0 100 5 0
			Total,	1638 3 36	391 6 0	24 4 0	415 10 0
	CLOONBORNIA. (Ord. S. 72.)						
1 A - B - C - A a, b, c & 3 c	Lawrence Griffin,	Richard Graves,	Land, Land, Land, Four cottiers' houses and garden,	40 2 38 33 0 15 11 2 14 0 1 25	14 10 0 6 10 0 1 0 0 0 3 0	— — — 1 12 0	} 23 15 0
1 A d, e, f ba	Richard Graves,	In fee,	Four cottiers' hos. & gars.	1 0 20	0 15 0	2 0 0	2 15 0
2	Thomas Carroll, Lawrence Griffin,	Richard Graves,	House, offices, & land, House and land,	66 2 0	10 0 0 10 0 0	0 10 0 0 15 0	10 10 0 10 15 0
3 a b	Lawrence Kirrane, John Kirrane,	Same,	House, offices, and land, Cottier's house & land,	46 1 10 1 1 0	7 0 0 7 0 0 0 10 0	0 16 0 0 5 0	7 8 0 8 3 0
4 A - B a	Michael White,	Same,	House and land, Offices and land,	21 3 22 4 0 0	5 5 0 2 10 0	0 10 0 0 15 0	} 9 0 0
5 a b	Timothy Cogavan,	Same,	House, offices, and land, Cottier's house,	41 2 9 —	15 0 0 —	1 0 0 0 5 0	} 16 5 0
6	Daniel King, Malachy Kelly,	Same,	Bog,	3 0 2	0 5 0 0 5 0	— —	0 5 0 0 5 0
7 - a	Malachy Kelly,	Same,	Land, Cottier's house,	8 2 34 —	4 15 0 —	— 0 5 0	} 5 0 0
8	Daniel King,	Same,	Land,	0 2 5	4 15 0	—	4 15 0
9	Michael Cogavan,	Same,	Land,	25 0 25	7 10 0	—	7 10 0
			Total,	314 3 25	97 13 0	8 13 0	106 6 0
	FAHY. (Ord. S. 72.)						
1 A - B	Simon Curly,	Lord Dunsandle,	House, offices, and land, Land,	24 1 36 1 3 36	5 10 0 0 15 0	0 10 0 —	} 6 15 0
2	William Cogavan,	Same,	House, offices, and land,	24 2 0	6 0 0	0 10 0	6 10 0
3	Thomas Noone,	Same,	House, office, and land,	28 3 32	5 10 0	0 10 0	6 0 0
4 {a {b	Thomas Quigley, John Hoban,	Same,	House, office, & land, House, offices, & land,	58 1 14	7 10 0 7 10 0	0 10 0 0 10 0	8 0 0 8 0 0
5	Lord Dunsandle,	In fee,	Land,	70 2 3	0 10 0	—	0 10 0
			Total,	208 3 1	33 5 0	2 10 0	35 15 0

VALUATION OF TENEMENTS.
PARISH OF CLONKEEN.

No. and Letters of Reference to Map.	Townlands and Occupiers.	Immediate Lessors.	Description of Tenement.	Area. A. R. P.	Rateable Annual Valuation. Land. £ s. d.	Rateable Annual Valuation. Buildings. £ s. d.	Total Annual Valuation of Rateable Property. £ s. d.
	GORTNALONE, NORTH. (Ord. S. 72 & 85.)						
1			Land,	7 0 32	4 5 0	—	
2	Lawrence Walsh,	John E. Trench,	Land,	52 3 32	32 0 0	—	55 5 0
3			House, offices, and land,	50 1 35	15 0 0	3 10 0	
5 B b			Land,	0 3 10	0 10 0	—	
4 a	Mahony Noone,		House, office, & land,		2 15 0	0 10 0	3 5 0
b	Michael Crowe,	Same,	House and land,	42 3 9	2 15 0	0 10 0	3 5 0
c	William Coleman,		House, office, & land,		2 15 0	0 10 0	3 5 0
d	John Hynes,		House and land,		2 15 0	0 10 0	3 5 0
5 A			Land,	7 0 10	2 10 0	—	
- B a	Thaddeus Cunnane,	Same,	House, offices, and land,	23 1 8	13 10 0	2 0 0	19 5 0
- c			Land,	0 2 10	0 8 0	—	
6 b, c			Two cottiers' hos. & gars-	0 0 25	0 2 0	0 15 0	
6 a	Michael Carroll,	Lawrence Walsh,	House and land,	6 3 31	3 0 0	0 10 0	3 10 0
7 a	Michael Morrissy,	Same,	House, office, & land,	28 0 17	5 0 0	0 10 0	5 10 0
-	Lawrence Walsh,	John E. Trench,	Land,		5 0 0	—	5 0 0
8 a	John M'Qualter,		House, offices, & land,		3 6 0	0 14 0	4 0 0
b	Patrick Carroll,	Same,	House and land,	81 0 8	1 10 0	0 5 0	1 15 0
c	Thomas Molloy,		House, office, & land,		2 2 0	0 8 0	2 10 0
9 A	John E. Trench,	In fee,	Herd's house and land,	21 1 5	10 0 0	0 8 0	10 10 0
- B			Bog,	14 2 36	0 2 0	—	
			Total,	337 1 28	109 5 0	11 0 0	120 5 0
	GORTNACROSS. (Ord. S. 72.)						
1 a	Lawrence Griffin,	Richard Graves,	House, offices, and land,	17 3 20	4 15 0	2 0 0	6 15 0
- b	Nat. school-house (no rent)	(See exemptions.)					
2	Michael Cogavan,	Richard Graves,	House, offices, and land,	18 3 0	6 0 0	2 0 0	8 0 0
			Total of rateable property,	36 2 20	10 15 0	4 0 0	14 15 0
			EXEMPTIONS:				
1 b		Laurence Griffin,	National school-house,	—	—	0 15 0	0 15 0
			Total, including Exemptions,	36 2 20	10 15 0	4 15 0	15 10 0
	GORTRONNAGH. (Ord. S. 72.)						
1 a	Michael Hoban,		House, offices, & land,		11 11 0	0 14 0	12 5 0
b	John Hoban,		House and land,		4 11 0	0 14 0	5 5 0
c	John Keane,	Lord Dunsandle,	House, office, & land,	98 2 11	8 0 0	0 10 0	8 10 0
d, e	Michael Hillery,		House, offices, & land, and cottier's house,		8 0 0	1 0 0	9 0 0
2	Lord Dunsandle,	In fee,	Bog,	85 3 14	0 10 0	—	0 10 0
			Total,	184 1 25	32 12 0	2 18 0	35 10 0
	KNOCKABOY. (Ord. S. 72.)						
1	Thomas Walsh,	Lord Dunsandle.	House and land,	5 2 26	3 5 0	0 10 0	3 15 0
2	James Wade,	Same,	House, offices, and land,	6 1 7	3 15 0	0 10 0	4 5 0
3	Michael White,	Same,	Land,	0 3 10	0 10 0	—	0 10 0
4 a	John Clancy,	Same,	House, offices, and land,	64 1 31	35 10 0	0 15 0	36 5 0
- b	Lord Dunsandle,	In fee,	Cottier's house,	—	—	0 10 0	0 10 0
			Total,	77 1 4	43 0 0	2 5 0	45 5 0
	SHANBALLARD. (Ord. S. 72.)						
1	Thomas Higgins,	Lord Dunsandle,	House and land,	16 1 18	8 0 0	0 10 0	8 10 0
2 a	Edward Rochford,	Same,	House, offices, and land,	64 3 0	30 0 0	1 5 0	31 10 0
- b			Cottier's house,	—	—	0 5 0	
3 A				20 2 3	7 10 0	—	
A a	William Thorpe,	Same,	House, office, & land,		—	0 10 0	5 0 0
- b	Patrick Fallon,		House, office, & land,		—	0 15 0	5 5 0
- B				10 3 25	1 10 0	—	

VALUATION OF TENEMENTS.
PARISH OF CLONKEEN.

No. and Letters of Reference to Map.	Names. Townlands and Occupiers.	Immediate Lessors.	Description of Tenement.	Area. A. R. P.	Rateable Annual Valuation. Land. £ s. d.	Buildings. £ s. d.	Total Annual Valuation of Rateable Property. £ s. d.
	SHANBALLARD— *continued.*						
4 a	Martin Cormickan,	Lord Dunsandle,	House, office, and land,	31 3 20	9 0 0	0 10 0	9 10 0
— b	Thomas Cormickan,	Same,	Office,	—	—	0 5 0	} 17 0 0
5			House, offices, and land,	100 2 12	15 15 0	1 0 0	
6	John Connor,	Thomas Cormickan,	House and land,	9 1 37	2 0 0	0 10 0	2 10 0
			Total,	254 1 35	73 15 0	5 10 0	79 5 0
	SHANBALLYMORE. *(Ord. S. 72.)*						
1 a	Patrick Gilligan,	Richard Graves,	House, offices, & land,	263 0 15	19 10 0	1 10 0	21 0 0
b	Edmund Duane,		House, offices, & land,		9 15 0	1 0 0	10 15 0
			Total,	263 0 15	29 5 0	2 10 0	31 15 0
	SHANBALLYEE-SHAL. *(Ord. S. 72.)*						
1	Bridget Ryan,	Lord Dunsandle,	House, offices, and land,	12 0 15	2 5 0	0 15 0	3 0 0
2 A			House, offices, and land,	56 0 12	11 5 0	0 10 0	
— B	Richard Dillon,	Same,	Land,	6 0 8	1 15 0	—	13 15 0
— C			Land,	4 1 32	0 5 0	—	
3 A			Land,	5 1 0	1 5 0	—	
— B			Land,	3 3 28	0 5 0	—	6 10 0
— C	Luke Dwyer,	Same,	House, office, and land,	11 1 16	4 5 0	0 10 0	
— D			Land,	4 1 32	0 5 0	—	
4	Eleanor Mullen,	Same,	House and land,	2 0 5	0 7 0	0 8 0	0 15 0
5 A a	Malachy Daly,	Same,	House, offices, and land,	17 2 38	6 0 0	0 10 0	
— B			Land,	7 1 8	0 10 0	—	7 5 0
b			Cottier's house,	—	—	0 5 0	
6 A			House, offices, and land,	40 0 31	13 15 0	0 10 0	
— B	Patrick Donagh,	Same,	Land,	5 0 16	0 10 0	—	15 0 0
— C			Land,	6 1 14	0 5 0	—	
7	Michael M'Donagh,	Same,	House, offices, and land,	23 0 6	5 0 0	0 10 0	5 10 0
8 A			Land,	9 2 9	1 0 0	—	
— B	John Hoban,	Same,	Land,	12 0 30	3 15 0	—	5 0 0
B a			Cottier's house,	—	—	0 5 0	
9	Lord Dunsandle,	In fee,	Bog,	34 0 29	0 10 0	—	0 10 0
			Total,	261 1 9	53 2 0	4 3 0	57 5 0
	SHEEAUN. *(Ord. S. 72 & 85.)*						
1 A	Mary Gilmore,	Richard Graves,	Land,	2 2 6	0 10 0	—	2 5 0
— B			House, office, and land,	1 3 14	1 5 0	0 10 0	
2 A	Honoria Keane,	Same,	Bog,	4 1 8	0 3 0	—	6 5 0
— B			House, office, and land,	10 1 24	5 10 0	0 12 0	
3 A	Daniel King,	Same,	House, offices, and land,	68 3 3	27 0 0	1 0 0	30 0 0
— B			Land,	3 3 2	2 0 0	—	
4	Malachy Kelly,	Same,	House, offices, and land,	20 3 23	11 5 0	0 15 0	12 0 0
5	William H. Poole,	Same,	Land,	51 2 29	31 0 0	—	31 0 0
6	William Conaghton,	Same,	House, offices, and land,	14 1 10	8 0 0	1 0 0	9 0 0
			Total,	178 1 39	86 13 0	3 17 0	90 10 0
	TEMPLE. *(Ord. S. 72.)*						
1 a	William Bourke,	Richard Graves,	House, offices, and land,	56 3 7	19 0 0	2 0 0	22 0 0
b			Cottier's ho., off., & gar.	0 3 0	0 7 0	0 13 0	
2 a	William H. Poole,	Same,	House, offices, and land,	141 2 9	69 0 0	10 0 0	79 5 0
b			Cottier's house & gar.	0 1 20	0 2 0	0 3 0	
3	Patrick Morrissey,	William H. Poole,	House and land,	4 0 20	0 12 0	0 3 0	0 15 0
			Total,	203 2 16	89 1 0	12 19 0	102 0 0
	GORTNALONE, SOUTH. *(Ord. S. 85.)*						
1	Patrick Ryan, John Ryan,	John Daly,	Herd's house, off. & land,	277 0 1	70 0 0	0 10 0	35 5 0 / 35 5 0
			Total,	277 0 1	70 0 0	0 10 0	70 10 0

VALUATION OF TENEMENTS.
PARISH OF CLONKEEN.

No. and Letters of Reference to Map.	Names. Townlands and Occupiers.	Immediate Lessors.	Description of Tenement.	Area. A. R. P.	Rateable Annual Valuation. Land. £ s. d.	Buildings. £ s. d.	Total Annual Valuation of Rateable Property. £ s. d.
1 A	**LENAREAGH.** *(Ord. S. 72 & 85.)* John E. Trench,	In fee,	House and land,	14 0 25	7 0 0	0 10 0	} 11 0 0
- B			Bog,	65 2 10	3 5 0	—	
-	a		Cottier's house,	—	—	0 5 0	
	a	Patrick Finn,		House, offices, & land,		7 10 0	0 15 0	8 5 0
2	b	Matthias Finn,	John E. Trench,	House, offices, & land,	68 2 32	7 10 0	0 10 0	8 0 0
	c	Francis Finn,		House and land,		7 10 0	0 10 0	8 0 0
	d	Michael Finnane,		House and land,		7 10 0	0 10 0	8 0 0
3	Margaret Kelly,	Same,	House, offices, and land,	49 2 2	4 15 0	1 0 0	5 15 0
4	Bryan Mannion,	Same,	House, office, and land,	44 2 16	1 5 0	0 10 0	1 15 0
5 A a	Malachy Dooley,	Same,	House, office, & land,	43 0 34	8 0 0	0 10 0	8 10 0
A b	John Quinn,		House, offices, & land,	—	—	0 10 0	8 10 0
- B			Land,	17 1 30	8 0 0	—	
6 A	Michael Kirrane,	Same,	Land,	2 1 28	1 0 0	—	4 10 0
- B			House and land,	25 3 5	3 0 0	0 10 0	
7 A	Laurence Walsh,	Same,	Land,	4 0 23	2 0 0	—	3 10 0
- B			Land,	9 2 30	1 10 0	—	
8	Thomas Walsh,	Same,	House, office, and land,	19 0 8	8 0 0	0 15 0	8 15 0
			Total,	364 1 3	77 15 0	6 15 0	84 10 0
1	**CLONKEEN-KERRILL.** *(Ord. S. 59 & 72.)* Edward Barrington and partners,	Myles W. O. Reilly,	Land,	57 3 30	13 5 0	—	13 5 0
2	Bernard Flannery,	Same,	House, offices, and land,	68 1 38	11 0 0	0 10 0	11 10 0
3	John Moore,	Same,	Land,	12 3 37	6 0 0	—	6 0 0
4 a	John Golden,	Same,	House, offices, and land,	68 1 23	5 0 0	0 15 0	6 0 0
- b			Cottier's house,	—	—	0 5 0	
5 a	Robert Faire,	Same,	House, offices, and land,	342 0 26	140 0 0	0 10 0	141 5 0
- b, c			Two cottiers' hos. & gar.	0 2 0	0 5 0	0 10 0	
	Ml. Connellan, jun.,				0 6 0	—	0 6 0
6	Ml. Connellan, sen.,	Same,	Land,	8 2 39	0 3 0	—	0 3 0
	Martin Connellan,				0 3 0	—	0 3 0
7	Martin Connellan,	Same,	Land,	30 0 11	2 5 0	—	2 5 0
	Ml. Connellan, jun.,				2 5 0	—	2 5 0
	a Ml. Connellan, jun.,		House, offices, & land,		2 0 0	0 10 0	2 10 0
8	b Martin Connellan,	Same,	House, offices, & land,	5 0 12	1 0 0	0 10 0	1 10 0
	c Ml. Connellan, sen.,		House, and land,		1 0 0	0 10 0	1 10 0
-	d *Grave yard,*	*(No rent, see Exemptions.)*					
9 a	Daniel Fogarty,	Myles W. O'Reilly,	House, offices, and land,	24 2 36	13 0 0	3 10 0	16 10 0
- b	*National school-house,*	*(No rent, see Exemptions.)*					
10	Edward Barrington and partners,	Myles W. O'Reilly,	Land,	0 2 10	0 2 0	—	0 2 0
11				16 3 10	9 0 0	—	
11 a	Michael Barry,	Same,	House, offices, & land,	—	—	0 15 0	11 5 0
- b	Martin Barry,		House, office, & land,	—	—	1 0 0	8 10 0
12				30 2 27	9 0 0	—	
13	John Barry,	Same,	House, offices, and land,	18 3 38	10 0 0	0 15 0	10 15 0
	Daniel Fogarty,				6 0 0	—	6 5 0
14	Michael Barry,	Same,	Land,	104 0 0	6 0 0	—	6 5 0
	Martin Barry,				6 0 0	—	6 5 0
	John Barry,				6 0 0	—	6 5 0
- a, b	. . . . .		Two cottiers' houses,	—	—	1 0 0	—
15	Myles W. O'Reilly,	In fee,	Bog,	114 1 28	0 10 0	—	0 10 0
			Total of rateable property,	904 2 5	250 4 0	11 0 0	261 4 0
			EXEMPTIONS:				
8 d	. . . . .	Myles W. O'Reilly,	Grave-yard,	0 2 25	0 5 0	—	0 5 0
9 b	. . . . .	Same,	National school-house,	—	—	2 0 0	2 0 0
			Total of Exemptions,	0 2 25	0 5 0	2 0 0	2 5 0
			Total, including Exemptions,	905 0 30	250 9 0	13 0 0	263 9 0

PARISH OF CLONKEEN.

No. and Letters of Reference to Map.	Names. Townlands and Occupiers.	Names. Immediate Lessors.	Description of Tenement.	Area. A. R. P.	Rateable Annual Valuation. Land. £ s. d.	Rateable Annual Valuation. Buildings. £ s. d.	Total Annual Valuation of Rateable Property. £ s. d.
	COLMANSTOWN. (*Ord. S.* 59 & 72.)						
1	Edward Barrington and partners, .	Myles W. O'Reilly,	Herd's and steward's houses, offs., & land,	965 1 4	290 0 0	30 0 0	320 0 0
2	Daniel Fogarty, .	Same,	Land,	0 2 20	0 2 0	—	0 2 0
3	Thomas Kenny,	Same,	Land,	6 0 8	2 5 0	—	2 5 0
4	John Lyons,	Same,	House, office, and land,	7 1 13	1 10 0	0 10 0	
5			Land,	12 1 7	1 10 0	—	4 0 0
– a, b			Two cottiers' houses, .	—	—	0 10 0	
6 a	Patrick Kelly,	Same,	House, offices, and land,	8 2 24	2 0 0	0 10 0	
– b			Cottier's house, .	—	—	0 5 0	2 15 0
7	Martin Laffan,	Same,	House, offices, and land,	28 2 11	8 10 0	1 5 0	9 15 0
8	Patrick Reynolds,	Same,	House, offices, and land,	40 0 18	6 5 0	0 15 0	7 0 0
9	John Moore,	Same,	House, offices, and land,	41 1 11	11 0 0	0 15 0	
13 b			Office,	—	—	0 5 0	12 0 0
10	Michael Moore, .	Same,	House, offices, and land,	31 2 26	8 15 0	1 5 0	10 0 0
11 a	Patrick Lally,	Same,	House, office, and land,	49 3 33	11 15 0	1 5 0	
– b			Cottier's house, .	—	—	0 10 0	13 10 0
12	John Ruane,	Same,	Land,	5 3 32	1 10 0	—	1 10 0
13 a	Catherine Ruane,	Same,	House, offices, and land,	17 3 8	10 0 0	1 0 0	11 0 0
14	Martin Devany, .	Same,	House, office, and land,	16 2 24	7 10 0	0 15 0	8 5 0
15	Sarah Jordan,	Same,	House and land,	5 1 29	1 0 0	0 10 0	1 10 0
16	Peter Flannery, .	Same,	House, offices, and land,	75 1 6	17 0 0	1 0 0	18 0 0
17	Myles W. O'Reilly,	In fee,	Bog, .	143 2 31	1 0 0	—	1 0 0
			Total, .	1456 2 25	381 12 0	41 0 0	422 12 0

PARISH OF CLONKEEN.

No.	Townlands and Occupiers.	Immediate Lessors.	Description of Tenement.	Area. A. R. P.	Land. £ s. d.	Buildings. £ s. d.	Total. £ s. d.
	KILLOOAUN. (*Ord. S.* 72.)						
1	John F. Browne,	In fee,	Land,	153 2 21	15 10 0	—	15 10 0
2	Thomas Mannion,	John F. Browne,	House, offices, and land,	28 0 11	8 5 0	0 15 0	9 0 0
3 a	Patrick Dooley, .	Same,	House, office, and land,	21 2 20	4 5 0	0 10 0	4 15 0
b	Mary Loughnan, .	Patrick Dooley, .	House,	—	—	0 5 0	0 5 0
	Peter M'Cann, .	John F. Browne,	House and land,	2 3 37	0 15 0	0 2 0	0 17 0
	Luke Roche,	Same,	House and land,	2 0 25	0 12 0	0 3 0	0 15 0
	John Cooge,	Same,	House and land,	3 1 21	1 5 0	0 5 0	1 10 0
	John Geoghegan,	Same,	House and land,	4 1 33	2 0 0	0 5 0	2 5 0
	Patrick Ward, .	Same,	House and land,	7 2 21	2 10 0	0 5 0	2 15 0
	Catherine Murray,	Same,	House, office, and land,	5 0 0	3 0 0	0 12 0	3 12 0
	Bartholomew Mannion,	Same,	House and land,	1 0 5	0 14 0	0 6 0	1 0 0
a	Patrick Connor, .	Same,	House, office, & land,	72 0 38	10 5 0	0 15 0	11 0 0
b	William Connor,		House and land,		10 5 0	0 10 0	10 15 0
c	Patrick Gavin, .	Patrick Connor,	House,	—	—	0 5 0	0 5 0
d	Mary Cuilkeen, .	Same,	House,	—	—	0 4 0	0 4 0
e	John Daly,	Same,	House,	—	—	0 5 0	0 5 0
f	Vacant,	Same,	House,	—	—	0 5 0	0 5 0
			Total, .	302 0 32	59 6 0	5 12 0	64 18 0

PARISH OF KILLOSCOBE.

No.	Townlands and Occupiers.	Immediate Lessors.	Description of Tenement.	Area. A. R. P.	Land. £ s. d.	Buildings. £ s. d.	Total. £ s. d.
	AGHANAHIL. (*Ord. S.* 59 & 60.)						
1, b	Edmund J. Concannon	In fee,	House, offices, herd's house, offices, & land,	220 2 35	125 0 0	20 15 0	145 15 0
	Bryan Neill,	Edmund J. Concannon	House and land,	2 2 28	1 15 0	0 10 0	2 5 0
			Total, .	223 1 23	126 15 0	21 5 0	148 0 0

WORDS WHICH WERE ONCE PART OF EVERYDAY SPEECH

Back load of Hay	– Hay gathered onto ropes for carrying on the back.
Banbh	– A young pig.
Barge	– A crabbit woman.
Barge	– The cement along the corner of the galvanised roof, to stop the wind lifting the iron.
Beestings	– Milk from a newly calved cow.
Belly-band	– Part of the harness going under the belly of horse.
Big Supper Night	– Christmas Eve night.
Binder	– Strip of cloth, wrapped around the navel of the new born baby, also worn at one time by women around their breasts after childbirth.
Bit	– Piece for the mouth of horse/donkey.
Bláther	– Nonsense or silly talk.
Bócan	– A dry fungus.
Bodice	– An upper undergarment, once worn by female children.
Booley	– Summer pasture for cows/cattle
Booreen	– Small road or laneway.
Brag	– To show off.
Britch	– Part of the harness going under the tail of horse or donkey.
Bróg	– A boot.
Broom	– Brush.
Buchallan	– Poisonous week (ragworth).
Butter Prints	– Small Rolled pieces of butter.
Butter Spades	– Small grooved timber spades with a short handle, used to shape the freshly churned butter.
Cant	– Stall at fair selling second hand clothes.
Cár	– A sarcastic grin.
Carabuncle	– Large boil.
Ceileing	– To go to a ceile house, or go visiting other homes.
Ceili-house	– House where people gather for story telling and crack.
Ceisóg	– Sow pregnant with first litter.
Channel	– Drainage space in the byre for manure.
Chaser	– A fine comb for head lice.
Christmas Box	– A token from a shop at Christmas.
Churched	– Cleansing prayers by the priest, for women after childbirth.
Churn	– Vessel for making butter.
Ciotóg	– A left-handed person.
Cipins	– Small twigs for kindling the fire.
Ciseán	– A basket.
Clab	– A person who tells everything i.e. a big mouth.
Clábar	– Wet and runny mud.
Clamps	– Larger piles of turf built when the turf was dried.
Clocker	– Broody hen.
Clods	– Small pieces of turf.
Clot	– Sloppy or dirty woman.
Clout	– To strike or hit a blow.
Cnócan	– Small hill.
Cob	– A small horse.
Cogar	– A whisper or to speak quietly.
Collar	– Neck piece for donkey/horse.
Consumption	– T.B. (Tuberculosis).
Corr	– A grin or ugly face.
Crate	– Detachable wooden sides for cart, used on cart when carrying hay or turf.
Creel	– Wicker-work basket used for carrying turf, and fitted on the straddle of the donkey.
Cricket	– An insect that lived in the chimney of old houses. It came out at night around the heart and made a clicking sound. It was pale brown in colour.
Crock	– A vessel made from crockery, kept in the dairy, used to collect milk or the churning.
Crubeens	– Pigs feet.
Dallóg	– Cover for the eyes.

Dash	– Long handled wooden instrument, used for churning.	Hasp	– Larch or gate/window.
Daub	– Sticky sub soil.	Hob	– Stone seats on either side of open-fire.
Deor	– A drop.	Hock	– Back of the knee (animal).
Doirín	– Handle on the end of a scythe.	Hussie	– Bad girl.
Donnie	– Sickly person.	Kesh/Ceis	– A small bridge over a drain or shruch, made with plants, branches and scraws.
Drauci	– Warm, wet, misty weather.		
Dudeen	– Clay pipe.		
Duds	– Something of no value (old clothes).	Lachico	– A playboy or "devil may care" fellow.
Dúl	– A loop on a twine rope or wire.	Laps	– Handfuls of hay loosely folded, to help dry it.
Dunkil	– Dunghill.		
Elder	– Udder.	Lee	– Freshly turned ground.
Endboard	– Part of a cart.	Leipreacháin	– A fairy-man.
Fabóg	– A big lie or exaggeration.	Links	– Large piles of turf or small ricks, left on the bog over the winter.
Farl	– Triangle of soda bread or boxty.		
Fibber	– A liar.		
Flaithúl	– Very generous.	Loc	– A small amount.
Fly-boy	– Cute or wise.	Long acre	– Grass along the roadside.
Fodder	– Winter feeding for cattle.	Loy	– Implement with long handle and a long blade, used for cutting out sods or turning soil.
Fornist	– Opposite or in front of.		
Fort	– Fairy place usually left undisturbed.		
		Mar-dhea	– By the way, pretending (mauryah).
Futtin'	– Arranging turf sods on their ends to dry.		
		Méarann fence	– Fence or ditch between farms/ditch.
Futty	– Careless or slipshod.		
Galavanting	– Running a bit wild.	Meitheal	– A crowd, gathered together to work on farm i.e. gathering in the hay/harvest.
Gallon	– A tin can of various sizes, with a handle on the top, used to carry water or for milking cows.		
		Mí-ádh	– Misfortune or bad luck.
Galore	– Lots of everything.	Moithered	– Troubled.
Gap	– Opening in a field through a ditch or fence.	Mote	– Something in the eye.
		Naump	– A big piece take off or cut out of something.
Geansey	– Jumper.		
Glam	– A handful.	Oinseach	– Fool (female).
Glár	– Muck or dirt.	Pioc	– A bag cough.
Gob	– Mouth.	Pip	– A disease n the throat of chickens.
Goody	– Bread soaked with hot milk and sugar.		
		Pistróg/Pisóg	– Superstition.
Grape	– Four pronged fork for manure.	Plamás	– Flattery or false praise for a person.
Griddle	– An iron frame, placed in front of the hearth fire, to bake an oaten cake.		
		Po	– Chamber pot.
		Poitín	– Home made brew.
Gripe	– Ditch, with water, draining two fields.	Ponger	– Tin vessel holding about a quart, with a handle on the side.
Guggaring Bag	– Bag of cloth, used to carry the potato splits. Worn on the front of the body for easy access.	Pooka	– Ghost.
		Poteens	– Small potatoes used for pigs and hens.
Haggard	– Enclosed area where hay/oats were kept.	Press-bed	– A fold away bed, concealed by two doors.
Hait	– Little or nothing.		

Purdóg	– Used for spreading manure, like a creel, and made of wood with loose bottom.	Stripper	– A cow bought for winter milk, (not in calf).
Quick	– Small hedge.	Stubble	– That which is left in the field after cutting oats/barley/wheat.
Rack	– A large toothed comb.	Sweep	– Married woman, going around with other men.
Raiméis	– Foolish talk.		
Raked fire	– Ashes put over fire at night to keep it alive till morning.	Tacklings	– Harness for horse / donkey.
		Tatties	– Potatoes.
Ranai	– A thin person.	Thaillaght	– Pain in the wrist, one wore a black silk band or a leather band to cure it.
Rift	– Burp.		
Rigado	– Fuss.		
Ruala-Buala	– Confusion or chaos.	Thránins	– Wisps of hay or blades of grass. Used also to describe a very light person.
Sally	– Willow tree.		
Scaldí	– A young wild bird in the nest.		
Scallops	– Sally rods shaped like hairpins used to keep the thatch in place.	Tint	– Small drop.
		Topcoat	– Overcoat.
Scheme	– To mitch from school.	Trap	– Horse drawn vehicle for conveying people.
Scraw/Scraí	– Top layer of turf. Used under the thatch. Name given to top sod of earth.		
		Trimaddens	– Belongings, bits and pieces.
		Twig	– Large bottom made of heathers or broom, used to sweep the kitchen floor.
Scythe	– Used for cutting hay by hand.		
Settle bed	– Folded type seat that opened out as a bed.		
		Visits	– A religious practice, to make as many visits to the Church for the Holy Souls on November 2nd.
Shanking	– Trimming along the bottom of a cock of hay.		
Sheaf	– Approximately 30 stands of oats tied with a piece of itself.		
		Will-Ó-The-Wisp	– Flighty person.
Sheebeen/Shíbín	– A house where liquor was sold without a licence.	Winkers	– Used for the sides of the eyes of the horse / donkey, a part of the bridle.
Shift	– Woman's vest.		
Shillelagh	– Blackthorn stick.		
Shindy	– A row or commotion.		
Shruch	– Large drain or small stream dividing fields.	Pounds, Shillings and Pence	
		£	S D
Sideboard	– Board along the side of the cart.	Bob	= 1/-
Skeilp	– A slap.	Florin	= 2/-
Skillet	– Small iron pot.	Half Crown	= 2/6
Skitter	– Diarrhoea.	Crown	= 5/-
Sláin	– Used for cutting turf.	Guinea	= £1-1-0
Sláumy	– Wet or messy.	Farthing	= 1/4d
Splits	– Potatoes cut, with an eye in each part, and then planted.	Halfpenny	= 1/2d
		Truppence	= 3d
Stake	– Tying for cow.	Kids Eye	= 3d
Stirabout	– Porridge.	Tanner	= 6d
Stook	– Four sheaves each side, with two on top.	Penny	= 1d
Strap	– Four sheaves each side, with two on top.		
Strap	– Troublesome person (usually female).		

Values of Rainfall amount (mm) as recorded at Birr.

	Jan	Feb	Mar	Apr	May	June	July	Aug	Sept	Oct	Nov	Dec	Year
1872					52.2	83.9	55.7	121.6	85.1	113.8	93.7	135.5	-
1873	136.1	20.8	107.6	47.0	53.3	36.3	106.3	124.5	96.7	106.1	52.3	29.5	916.5
1874	69.7	41.4	44.5	45.4	58.0	44.4	73.8	131.5	103.0	100.8	91.6	106.4	910.5
1875	123.3	29.9	26.7	20.1	49.2	81.4	65.9	78.0	166.4	77.5	66.5	49.9	834.8
1876	30.6	105.7	112.8	52.4	19.0	40.0	43.2	87.2	112.5	81.3	63.4	125.1	873.2
1877	120.4	58.9	67.3	76.4	52.7	94.8	58.8	111.0	65.5	88.9	138.1	85.2	1018.0
1878	72.6	41.8	30.7	36.3	86.9	131.2	65.0	96.3	79.4	73.2	44.7	31.1	789.2
1879	42.8	83.6	40.5	56.9	64.8	124.5	76.3	115.3	116.9	31.4	21.8	47.2	822.0
1880	25.0	68.3	90.2	103.2	35.3	64.5	186.4	43.1	53.0	64.3	91.1	77.6	902.0
1881	9.8	86.2	60.7	35.4	63.4	106.2	48.7	120.3	101.2	64.5	105.8	110.0	912.2
1882	58.6	61.3	64.1	79.5	69.9	77.7	112.0	85.9	40.6	85.8	135.1	86.5	957.0
1883	126.3	91.0	16.1	44.5	66.1	43.7	100.1	103.4	84.8	92.2	111.8	47.7	927.7
1884	100.8	79.2	76.5	40.5	55.8	19.7	82.0	34.6	48.0	72.5	69.8	107.4	786.8
1885	61.2	71.0	56.4	76.2	48.5	30.7	55.6	77.9	138.2	91.1	49.0	24.3	780.1
1886	103.1	49.4	69.9	49.2	80.9	42.8	66.3	58.8	78.1	112.8	77.4	126.5	915.2
1887	71.4	31.9	33.3	48.0	35.0	8.6	74.1	63.2	42.4	67.0	55.3	66.0	596.2
1888	54.3	15.6	78.8	41.3	52.9	122.9	113.6	61.2	17.9	34.8	62.5	98.1	753.9
1889	60.2	49.3	69.9	51.1	84.2	31.5	49.1	127.5	25.2	91.5	40.3	93.2	743.0
1890	148.5	20.6	79.2	17.6	38.3	63.5	56.6	84.0	82.4	60.0	135.5	49.2	835.4
1891	48.1	4.3	36.5	47.8	79.0	77.1	54.5	177.5	51.6	86.9	68.1	152.0	883.4
1892	44.5	74.0	14.8	25.7	120.0	48.5	93.6	199.0	111.4	58.4	98.8	32.8	921.5
1893	73.5	75.5	19.7	20.8	68.9	66.7	55.6	95.6	58.3	79.9	47.9	101.0	763.4
1894	99.7	82.8	53.1	124.0	63.6	48.4	102.9	77.7	7.8	83.7	88.6	73.4	905.7
1895	56.1	21.7	75.7	49.0	17.4	20.8	90.9	123.4	11.3	72.8	111.6	94.1	744.8
1896	25.3	36.9	117.3	23.0	8.6	54.1	135.9	65.6	141.2	63.2	26.7	108.5	806.3
1897	46.2	41.6	117.3	110.2	33.8	96.2	59.3	107.1	56.5	67.2	130.9	99.2	965.5
1898	47.3	40.9	20.4	90.8	67.6	83.4	28.1	161.1	76.6	53.2	131.5	62.3	863.2
1899	87.8	58.0	32.3	75.3	85.3	47.0	87.0	111.7	59.7	40.4	71.6	99.0	855.1
1900	104.4	59.7	18.8	54.9	58.4	98.3	45.7	190.4	35.5	111.3	104.6	102.9	984.9
1901	69.7	33.3	73.7	51.0	46.0	71.9	31.0	70.3	98.7	66.8	104.5	75.9	792.8

METEOROLOGICAL SERVICE
Values of Rainfall amount (mm) as recorded at Birr.

	Jan.	Feb.	Mar.	Apr.	May	June	July	Aug.	Sept.	Oct.	Nov.	Dec.	Year
1902	77.1	50.9	58.7	50.7	50.5	38.7	49.9	62.2	39.8	42.8	118.4	74.0	713.7
1903	120.6	82.2	139.4	35.3	42.4	30.1	129.0	132.1	81.0	113.3	63.8	66.4	1035.6
1904	89.7	112.5	70.9	51.0	82.7	41.3	94.3	83.0	59.7	63.0	60.2	48.6	856.9
1905	58.5	40.1	107.7	47.2	23.1	37.3	34.2	137.3	36.1	34.0	63.0	48.2	666.7
1906	101.3	67.6	57.6	43.4	89.8	57.4	88.7	88.4	29.8	117.7	42.2	60.0	843.9
1907	29.1	43.7	69.5	63.4	73.3	75.9	124.7	83.2	26.4	122.5	71.7	89.8	873.2
1908	76.6	59.4	74.7	44.2	71.6	39.8	64.9	95.5	137.8	39.9	62.7	80.9	848.0
1909	70.6	24.6	77.4	107.6	66.0	43.7	50.1	29.9	53.3	109.5	50.1	94.0	776.8
1910	90.9	106.9	50.0	69.0	54.0	95.0	76.4	112.7	17.6	42.9	73.2	78.6	867.2
1911	42.6	68.2	33.5	41.4	32.0	56.1	72.9	60.4	42.4	103.6	103.9	129.8	786.8
1912	68.5	81.0	90.9	25.3	33.8	125.9	121.3	117.5	9.7	55.1	43.2	104.2	876.4
1913	121.2	32.0	100.1	99.2	88.1	83.2	26.0	32.9	81.3	92.2	78.2	64.3	898.7
1914	31.3	114.3	86.9	53.0	40.2	23.1	60.7	104.7	42.9	46.5	89.4	135.2	828.2
1915	102.7	105.3	20.3	43.8	12.4	50.0	117.2	100.5	37.0	74.2	76.8	108.0	848.2
1916	64.4	105.3	51.2	76.0	126.3	72.8	70.3	80.4	61.7	151.1	95.1	75.6	1030.2
1917	24.8	46.3	62.4	29.2	83.6	39.2	65.9	229.2	44.3	99.1	63.2	36.8	824.0
1918	55.6	95.2	54.2	26.2	51.9	30.3	88.3	60.2	133.9	92.0	77.7	120.5	886.0
1919	(70.4)	(34.7)	47.2	38.3	64.1	95.5	45.0	(59.7)	65.1	23.3	52.6	132.5	(728.4)
1920	113.1	93.3	71.8	75.5	66.1	30.5	110.4	54.0	42.9	146.9	76.0	67.2	947.7
1921	94.1	23.4	71.9	20.1	51.1	19.3	101.9	85.4	55.8	67.1	71.5	106.8	768.4
1922	71.9	100.2	41.8	57.5	46.9	34.8	66.9	80.6	97.1	29.3	21.3	101.8	750.1
1923	74.4	121.4	59.8	73.7	33.8	23.7	71.8	136.5	85.0	114.1	75.0	81.1	950.3
1924	100.3	31.1	19.7	84.1	107.5	73.2	74.8	95.8	171.5	87.4	103.9	136.2	1085.5
1925	83.8	133.7	11.9	96.5	120.8	13.9	100.9	46.4	46.8	55.1	54.4	43.8	808.0
1926	115.5	55.2	26.3	47.4	65.3	66.2	127.0	74.4	52.5	55.7	84.8	25.0	795.3
1927	85.9	61.7	87.5	39.1	20.1	70.6	75.3	109.1	124.0	48.5	63.1	54.9	839.8
1928	98.7	98.9	82.3	46.8	55.0	110.6	53.5	104.1	39.3	137.9	99.4	89.4	1015.9
1929	37.4	83.5	13.4	23.0	65.3	42.9	88.2	126.0	21.0	103.2	101.0	165.0	869.9
1930	125.0	14.1	95.0	46.5	41.8	45.8	79.8	145.0	98.1	117.8	74.8	87.6	971.3

Values of Rainfall amount (mm) as recorded at Biri,

	Jan.	Feb.	Mar.	Apr.	May	June	July	Aug.	Sept.	Oct.	Nov	Dec	Year
1931	47.0	64.2	53.7	77.0	71.5	101.8	99.5	64.8	63.5	50.1	156.5	55.1	904.7
1932	100.1	5.9	32.1	56.4	69.8	14.4	93.8	37.2	94.3	83.8	32.6	110.6	731.0
1933	72.6	59.0	84.3	25.1	51.3	63.7	79.2	59.2	35.6	53.6	29.2	49.0	661.8
1934	112.7	4.2	73.9	48.1	50.7	49.0	45.8	116.2	127.6	88.1	34.7	130.5	881.5
1935	31.4	76.6	34.6	44.9	26.5	121.4	23.9	82.1	143.9	98.4	102.3	37.5	823.5
1936	100.5	45.3	39.0	58.0	25.0	75.2	156.0	48.8	118.5	49.5	77.9	79.6	873.3
1937	113.7	105.5	52.3	67.5	69.7	52.0	97.8	84.6	101.7	48.9	37.3	49.3	880.3
1938	111.6	36.7	34.4	3.9	92.2	87.5	170.3	103.9	51.7	184.9	118.8	84.0	1079.9
1939	127.7	69.6	68.5	27.4	33.8	57.9	91.3	36.8	57.1	22.0	187.8	56.4	836.3
1940	62.9	98.1	53.8	63.9	23.0	27.3	85.9	12.8	53.6	157.9	106.3	89.1	834.6
1941	56.1	93.0	58.4	42.4	66.7	19.1	70.8	78.6	24.7	67.9	123.3	58.7	759.7
1942	105.8	24.0	71.0	47.1	88.8	7.7	98.2	138.2	111.6	63.6	16.7	95.1	867.8
1943	127.6	44.7	21.4	38.3	81.9	76.4	50.8	112.9	63.5	95.7	69.1	56.1	838.4
1944	101.4	35.1	14.0	39.7	81.2	44.7	77.5	96.7	110.9	113.0	128.7	98.2	941.1
1945	51.1	79.4	43.1	33.4	82.4	92.6	106.8	59.5	91.8	73.9	17.0	105.6	836.6
1946	125.3	132.0	36.7	26.6	51.4	90.2	117.4	171.4	133.5	33.4	91.7	122.9	1132.5
1947	89.7	48.0	115.6	98.2	117.0	113.8	73.5	21.2	95.0	96.4	110.2	73.2	1051.8
1948	178.0	55.2	71.8	51.8	60.6	97.8	51.2	72.8	83.7	95.9	74.1	144.9	1037.8
1949	50.6	66.0	57.6	58.1	44.5	18.2	74.4	98.3	25.7	161.7	82.2	103.0	840.3
1950	32.4	100.5	42.9	66.3	31.0	47.2	136.6	112.3	138.1	79.9	70.6	57.2	915.0
1951	95.1	64.9	97.9	45.6	44.8	35.2	41.3	103.5	115.6	49.3	78.8	144.6	916.6
1952	112.9	21.9	28.4	49.2	96.6	56.3	40.7	73.9	53.8	131.4	51.5	74.8	791.4
1953	40.2	39.4	10.9	73.2	43.8	25.1	83.5	121.2	68.6	78.7	69.1	71.0	724.7
1954	54.8	103.7	59.7	30.4	101.5	62.1	90.5	104.4	124.3	125.9	99.7	97.3	1054.3
1955	67.6	60.2	37.3	69.7	82.6	105.0	13.5	33.2	88.0	39.3	64.7	108.9	770.0
1956	74.6	21.7	50.2	22.3	33.8	59.6	116.3	128.6	119.4	61.4	48.0	107.0	842.9
1957	105.7	77.7	93.0	40.2	52.1	21.0	115.4	43.9	86.8	107.4	17.9	69.5	830.6
1958	95.6	86.9	39.5	37.5	101.2	85.1	100.2	153.3	101.0	46.1	51.6	88.7	986.7
1959	53.3	28.5	55.7	87.9	45.6	58.2	65.5	18.4	36.1	142.7	81.4	179.9	853.2
1960	84.7	44.6	42.0	59.3	68.9	78.7	145.4	112.5	130.1	67.1	151.7	127.6	1112.6

METEOROLOGICAL SERVICE

Mean Daily Air Temperature (°C.) at Birr.

	Jan.	Feb.	Mar.	Apr.	May	June	July	Aug.	Sept.	Oct.	Nov.	Dec.	Year
1872					9.3	12.8	16.0	15.2	12.7	7.4	6.0	4.9	
1873	4.7	2.6	5.1	8.1	10.6	13.9	15.3	14.6	11.5	7.9	6.5	6.8	9.0
1874	5.8	5.4	7.8	10.0	10.8	14.0	15.8	14.7	12.5	9.2	7.6	2.3	9.7
1875	7.4	4.3	6.2	9.0	12.0	13.1	14.6	16.0	14.9	9.7	5.7	4.2	9.8
1876	5.0	5.3	4.6	8.5	10.2	13.5	16.6	15.8	12.9	11.0	7.0	6.1	9.7
1877	5.4	6.9	5.7	8.1	10.0	15.2	14.4	15.0	11.3	10.8	6.7	5.2	9.6
1878	5.7	6.6	6.8	8.9	11.7	14.7	17.3	16.6	13.7	10.8	2.8	-0.9	9.5
1879	1.2	4.2	5.0	6.9	9.2	12.7	13.5	13.9	11.8	9.6	5.8	2.3	8.0
1880	3.9	6.4	8.0	7.9	11.0	13.2	15.0	17.1	14.5	6.1	6.0	4.7	9.6
1881	-1.0	4.6	6.0	7.7	12.0	12.9	15.1	13.5	11.9	8.6	9.3	3.6	8.7
1882	6.4	7.4	7.6	8.5	11.1	12.6	14.1	14.9	11.2	9.1	5.7	2.4	9.2
1883	5.7	5.7	3.6	7.7	9.7	13.2	13.6	14.2	12.5	9.1	6.2	5.0	8.8
1884	6.8	5.8	6.5	7.4	10.7	13.1	15.1	15.3	13.6	9.1	4.7	4.2	9.4
1885	4.2	5.3	4.7	7.1	8.4	12.7	15.5	13.7	11.3	6.9	6.9	4.7	8.5
1886	1.9	3.8	4.8	7.4	9.8	13.6	15.2	14.7	12.4	9.9	6.8	2.2	8.5
1887	4.4	5.2	4.4	6.0	10.1	16.3	16.3	14.8	11.1	7.4	4.4	3.1	8.6
1888	5.0	2.7	3.4	6.5	10.6	13.4	13.3	13.8	11.5	9.0	7.6	5.0	8.5
1889	4.5	4.1	5.7	7.1	11.9	14.0	14.1	13.6	12.8	7.6	7.3	5.5	9.0
1890	5.6	4.3	6.2	7.9	11.1	13.4	13.6	13.2	14.4	10.4	6.3	1.8	9.0
1891	3.0	6.3	4.2	6.8	8.5	14.7	14.2	13.4	13.1	8.1	4.6	5.2	8.5
1892	2.3	4.3	3.1	7.4	11.1	12.4	13.6	14.3	11.4	6.0	7.2	4.0	8.1
1893	3.5	4.8	8.1	10.4	13.0	15.1	15.3	16.5	12.2	8.9	4.5	4.9	9.8
1894	3.5	6.2	6.7	9.7	9.0	13.5	14.5	13.7	10.4	8.4	6.8	5.7	9.0
1895	0.7	-0.4	6.1	8.2	11.7	14.2	13.6	14.3	14.3	6.6	6.6	4.3	8.4
1896	5.8	6.3	6.9	9.2	12.4	14.9	14.6	13.6	12.1	6.0	5.0	3.3	9.2
1897	1.9	6.9	6.2	7.0	9.7	14.7	15.7	14.9	11.4	10.4	8.0	5.9	9.4
1898	7.5	5.4	4.6	8.4	9.9	13.2	15.0	15.2	14.8	10.9	6.8	7.5	9.9

Mean Air Temperature (°C.) at Birr.

	Jan.	Feb.	Mar.	Apr.	May	June	July	Aug.	Sept.	Oct.	Nov.	Dec.	Year
1899	4.6	5.8	6.0	8.1	9.9	15.1	15.8	17.2	12.2	9.4	8.9	4.1	9.8
1900	4.5	1.5	3.5	9.0	10.5	13.7	16.1	14.6	12.8	9.2	6.0	6.8	9.0
1901	4.4	2.4	4.2	8.2	11.7	12.8	16.6	14.9	13.0	8.6	5.6	3.9	8.9
1902	5.0	3.2	7.3	7.6	9.1	13.3	14.5	14.2	12.9	9.7	7.1	5.3	9.1
1903	4.3	7.1	5.9	6.9	11.0	12.7	14.4	13.3	12.7	9.4	6.3	3.3	9.0
1904	4.7	3.5	4.8	7.9	10.3	13.7	15.5	14.4	12.2	9.3	6.0	5.4	9.0
1905	5.5	5.1	6.0	7.4	11.0	14.8	16.3	13.8	11.5	6.9	3.9	7.2	9.1
1906	5.5	3.5	5.6	6.6	9.8	14.5	14.6	15.8	13.2	9.1	6.9	3.9	9.1
1907	4.5	3.5	7.2	7.3	10.1	11.9	15.0	13.7	14.0	8.3	5.2	4.8	8.8
1908	4.4	6.6	4.6	6.3	11.9	13.2	15.5	14.0	12.4	12.2	8.0	5.9	9.6
1909	5.4	5.2	4.1	8.5	10.5	12.2	13.9	14.7	11.9	9.5	3.9	4.3	8.7
1910	4.1	5.0	6.2	6.7	10.7	13.8	14.3	14.5	12.0	10.1	4.2	6.1	9.0
1911	4.3	5.1	5.4	7.3	12.2	13.7	16.5	16.3	12.3	9.3	5.3	5.7	9.5
1912	5.5	5.8	7.0	8.7	11.6	12.8	13.8	11.5	10.9	8.4	6.5	6.7	9.1
1913	4.8	5.5	5.4	7.3	10.5	12.6	14.2	14.5	12.9	10.2	7.8	5.3	9.3
1914	4.5	6.4	5.7	9.7	10.7	14.2	15.2	15.6	13.1	10.1	6.2	3.6	9.6
1915	4.0	3.5	5.1	8.4	10.9	14.1	13.9	14.6	13.6	9.3	3.3	4.9	8.8
1916	7.7	3.9	3.4	7.8	10.4	11.7	15.1	16.4	13.5	10.9	7.2	2.5	9.2
1917	1.8	1.9	4.4	5.7	12.2	13.0	15.9	14.6	13.1	7.5	8.3	3.3	8.5
1918	4.6	7.4	6.1	7.6	12.5	13.4	14.7	15.1	11.0	8.3	6.2	7.5	9.6
1919	3.6*	3.6*	3.3	7.5	12.6	13.0	13.8	15.3*	11.8	9.2	2.6	5.6	8.5*
1920	5.4	6.7	5.8	7.3	10.7	13.6	13.1	13.3	12.7	10.9	8.3	4.0	9.3
1921	7.3	5.1	7.2	8.3	10.1	14.8	17.6	14.0	13.4	12.2	7.5	8.0	10.5
1922	5.4	6.2	5.5	5.5	12.2	13.0	12.9	13.3	12.1	8.7	7.3	5.6	9.0
1923	6.2	6.6	6.7	7.3	8.9	13.3	16.2	14.5	11.9	9.4	3.5	5.6	9.2
1924	6.3	4.8	5.7	6.9	10.9	14.0	14.5	13.7	12.1	9.8	7.6	7.2	9.5
1925	5.9	4.5	5.5	7.0	9.9	14.8	15.1	14.7	11.3	10.7	4.1	3.6	9.0

* denotes estimated value.

/...

METEOROLOGICAL SERVICE

Climatological data for Birr

Period 1955-1980

	Jan.	Feb.	Mar.	Apr.	May	June	July	Aug.	Sept.	Oct.	Nov.	Dec.	Year
Precipitation.													
Mean Rainfall Amount (in millimetres)	77	51	54	57	62	54	70	75	78	78	78	85	819
Greatest Rainfall Amount in a day*	27.8	23.5	18.4	30.8	17.5	24.2	31.1	36.3	31.6	33.8	30.2	44.2	44.2
Mean number of days with 0.2 mm or more	18	15	17	16	17	16	17	17	18	18	18	20	207
Mean number of days with 1.0 mm or more	14	11	12	11	13	11	11	13	13	13	13	14	149
Wind.													
Mean Wind Speed*(in knots)	7.9	7.6	8.3	7.3	7.1	6.5	6.1	6.0	6.8	7.0	7.2	8.2	7.2
Highest Wind Speed in a gust (in knots)	85	67	62	60	56	51	44	58	81	65	66	69	85
Highest Mean Wind Speed over a period of 10 minutes (in knots)	51	42	36	36	31	30	27	35	39	40	39	43	51
Mean number of days with gales /	0.3	0.3	<0.1	<0.1	0.0	0.0	0.0	<0.1	<0.1	<0.1	0.2	0.2	1.3
Other Phenomena.													
Mean number of days with snow or sleet	4.8	4.6	2.4	0.8	0.2	0.0	0.0	0.0	0.0	<0.1	0.7	2.4	15.9
Mean number of days with snow lying at 9hGMT	3.0	2.2	0.8	0.2	0.0	0.0	0.0	0.0	0.0	0.0	<0.1	0.6	6.8
Mean number of days with hail	0.6	0.9	2.3	1.6	1.2	0.4	<0.1	0.1	0.3	0.7	0.4	0.4	8.8
Mean number of days with thunder	0.2	<0.1	0.2	0.2	0.8	0.8	1.1	1.1	0.4	0.2	0.1	<0.1	5.2
Mean number of days with fog at 9h GMT	1.2	1.0	0.8	0.4	<0.1	0.1	0.0	0.4	1.0	1.6	1.0	0.9	8.4
Mean number of days with fog (at any time)	4	2	2	3	1	2	2	4	4	5	3	3	35
Mean number of hours with fog	24	14	11	11	5	7	8	17	20	31	20	22	190
Mean number of days with air temperature less than 0.0°C	10	12	8	4	1	<0.1	0.0	0.0	<0.2	2	3	8	48

* "Day" is taken as a period of 24 hours commencing at 6h GMT.

** Based on periods of 10 minutes at each hour over the years 1955-1961 and mean hourly wind over the remainder of the period.

/ Mean wind speed 33.5 knots or more, for a period of at least 10 minutes.

METEOROLOGICAL SERVICE

Climatological data for Birr

Period 1955-1980

Lat. 53° 05'N Long. 7° 53'W HT. above MSL 70 metres

	Jan.	Feb.	Mar.	Apr.	May	June	July	Aug.	Sept.	Oct.	Nov.	Dec.	Year
Air Temperature (in degrees Celsius).													
Mean Daily Maximum	7.3	7.8	9.8	12.3	15.0	17.8	18.9	18.9	16.8	13.8	9.8	8.2	13.0
Mean Daily Minimum	1.6	1.7	2.7	3.9	6.2	9.0	10.9	10.5	8.9	6.9	3.4	2.6	5.7
Mean Daily	4.5	4.8	6.3	8.1	10.6	13.4	14.9	14.7	12.9	10.4	6.6	5.4	9.4
Mean Monthly Maximum	12.0	12.2	14.6	17.5	20.6	23.7	24.3	23.4	21.5	18.2	14.5	12.8	25.8*
Mean Monthly Minimum	-5.8	-4.4	-4.0	-2.3	0.3	3.8	5.4	4.4	2.3	-0.3	-4.5	-4.9	-7.6✓
Absolute Maximum	14.5	14.5	19.7	23.7	24.7	31.2	30.5	29.3	26.3	23.2	17.5	14.3	31.2
Absolute Minimum	-11.6	-10.5	-10.5	-4.6	-2.1	-0.3	3.1	1.2	-0.8	-4.0	-7.2	-9.4	-11.6
Relative Humidity.													
Average percentage at 0h GMT.	90	89	88	88	88	88	88	89	90	90	90	90	89
Average percentage at 6h GMT.	90	90	90	91	90	91	91	92	92	91	90	90	91
Average percentage at 12h GMT.	85	81	74	69	67	68	71	71	74	79	83	86	76
Average percentage at 18h GMT.	87	82	75	69	67	69	71	73	78	84	87	88	78
Sunshine.													
Mean Daily Duration (in hours)	1.77	2.54	3.43	4.78	5.67	5.30	4.34	4.54	3.70	2.76	2.05	1.45	3.53
Mean Duration (in hours)	55	72	106	143	176	159	134	141	111	86	62	45	1290
Greatest duration in a day	7.5	9.2	11.7	13.8	15.2	15.8	15.2	13.8	11.5	10.0	8.0	6.7	15.8
Mean number of days with no sun	12	6	5	3	2	2	3	2	4	6	9	10	64

* Mean of highest each year.   ✓ Mean of lowest each year.

Ballymacward (Clonkeen)

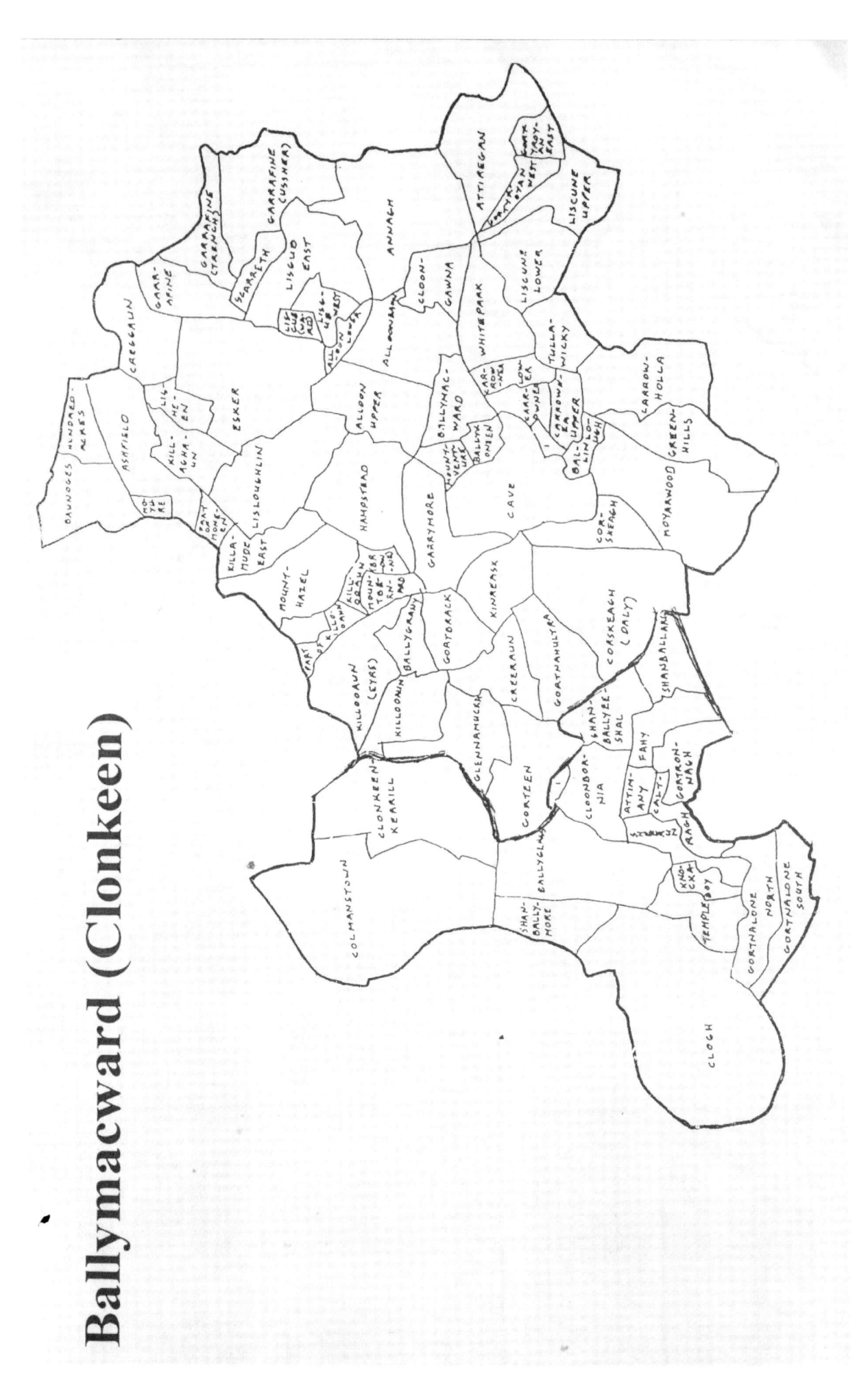

Pierce 2-Horse Victor Open Gear Mower No. 4.

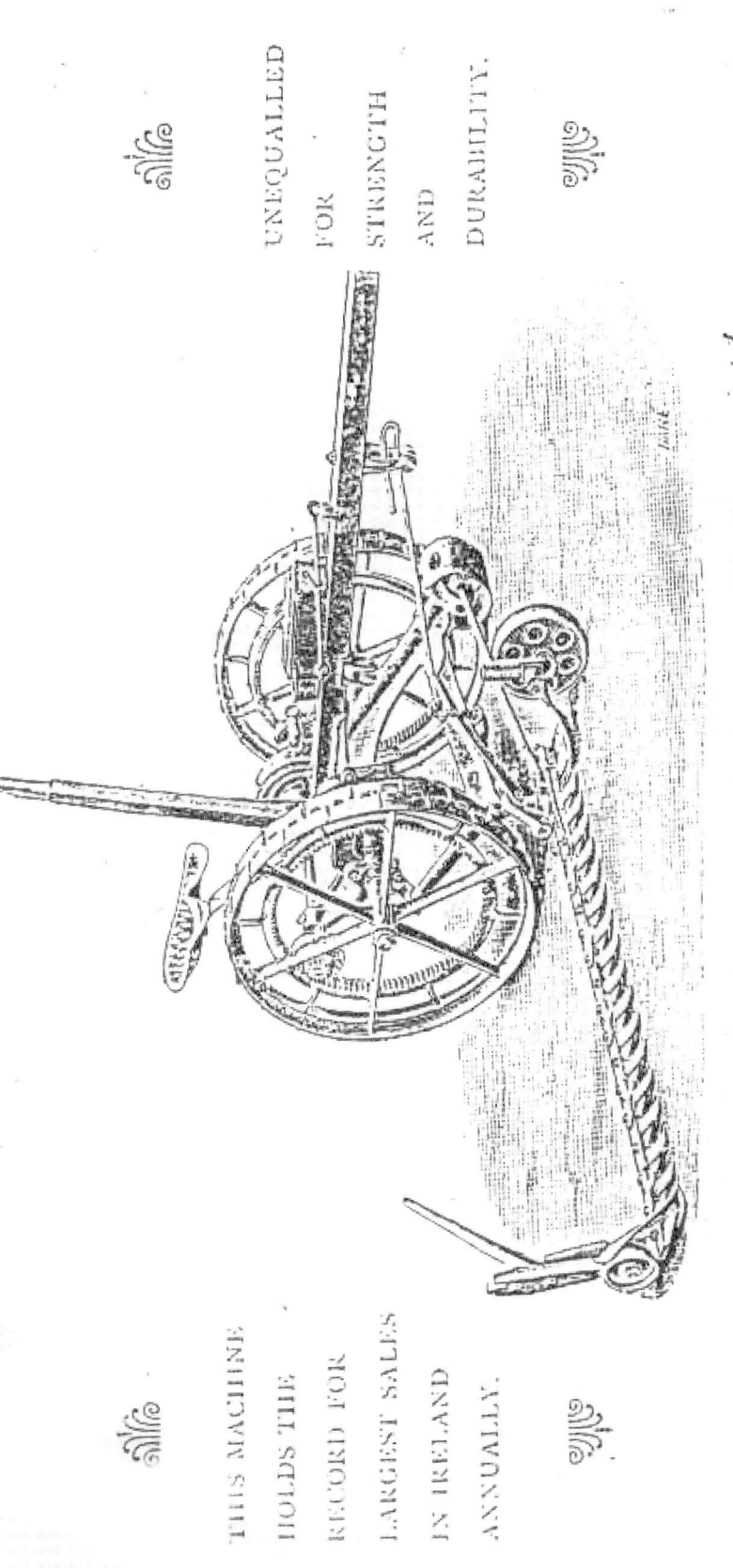

THIS MACHINE
HOLDS THE
RECORD FOR
LARGEST SALES
IN IRELAND
ANNUALLY.

UNEQUALLED
FOR
STRENGTH
AND
DURABILITY.

THE PIONEER OF HIGH WHEEL MOWERS.

Our No. 4 has an excellent reputation; its extraordinary strength makes breakage almost impossible and reduces wear to a minimum, saving expense, replacements, and loss of time, all of serious importance to present-day Agriculturists. A few shillings for Sections often represent the necessary outlay for many years, and even these parts have double the life of any other Makers. Foot and Hand Levers give easy control of Finger Bar, raising it over obstructions with the least exertion; with young or spirited horses the Foot Lever is specially convenient. Neckweight is counterbalanced by placing driver's weight at rear of main axle; pressure on horses' necks is entirely relieved thereby.

Alignment is always retained by the construction of Hinge Shoe and Main Brace; no irregularity can take place, however slight, which means freedom from breakage of knife heads, connecting rods, etc. Twenty years' continuous work will not alter the solidity and efficiency of the principal parts of this Machine. The high Wheels are invaluable, rolling smoothly over all obstructions.

Pierce Through Axle Horse Rake.

Complete with Seat and Two Levers.

Height of Wheels 4ft. 6in.;

Extreme Width 8ft.

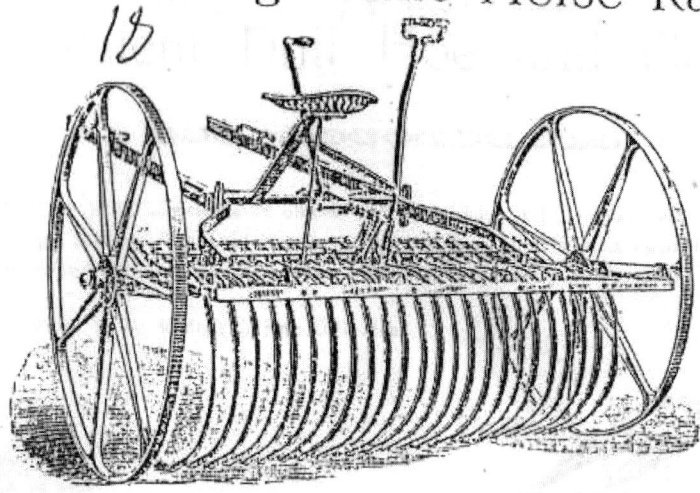

Complete with Seat and Two Levers.

Height of Wheels 4ft. 6in.;

Extreme Width 8ft.

OUR RAKE is well known owing to its Gigantic Strength, Enormous Capacity, and extra Height of Wheels—in fact, there cannot be any doubt in the mind of the practical Farmer as to its excellence. Where the Crops are heaviest, these Rakes are thickest, as the weaker and inferior class quickly collapse. For Hay Gathering and Stubble Raking, no Machine can get through its work with such ease. The Frame, Stays, etc., are of

BEST WROUGHT STEEL.

The Axle of Spring Steel, turned, tapered, and capped at each end. The teeth are of the strongest section and specially shaped to offer the least resistance in filling or discharging. A man or boy can get through many acres per day without hitch or difficulty, discharging by hand or foot with the smallest possible pressure. At any price a better Rake cannot be offered.

Pierce New Victor Wheel Rake.

Supplied Complete with Seat and Two Levers, 24 Teeth, 7ft. 8in.

Height of Wheels 4ft. 4in.

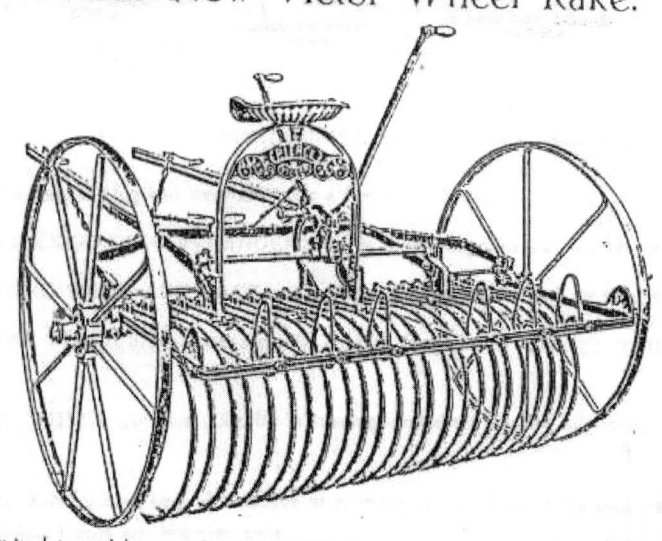

Supplied Complete with Seat and Two Levers, 24 Teeth, 8ft. 2in.

Height of Wheels 4ft. 4in.

Quite the most up-to-date and improved form of Wheel Rake, just completed on popular lines, embodying every desirable feature. Light and free moving, yet strong and durable, a distinct advance is evident even on superficial examination. Our main frame is of steel throughout, made in one piece, with stays hot rivetted for greater rigidity.

Discharge is effected by Unbreakable tooth quadrant, and levers are arranged to work with the slightest exertion.

Either foot or hand levers can operate Rake, whereas in other rakes the foot lever is practically powerless without aid of hand lever.

The Through Main Axle is Steel and of extra strength to resist strain in rough work.

Wheels possess extraordinary strength, and renewable sleeves are provided, allowing of inexpensive replacement.

Teeth are made of special section to facilitate discharge; their shape ensures clean raking without a chance of a foul. Alternate teeth are coupled, imparting increased strength.

Shaft adjustments are instantaneous and will suit any horse.

The general finish is of PIERCE quality, notably excellent in construction and fitting.

Old Farm Machinery

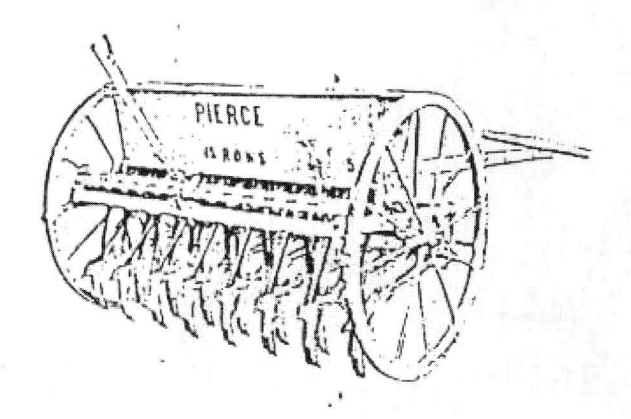

Victor Corn Drill.

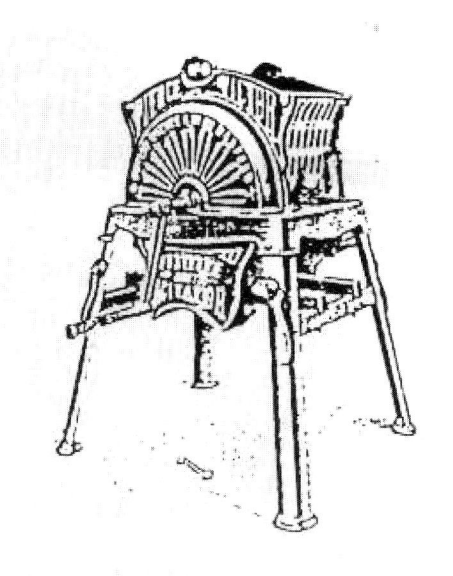

Double Root Cutter.

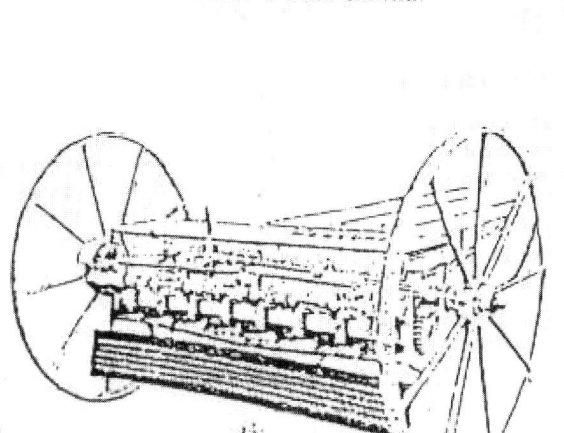

Pierce Manure Distributor.

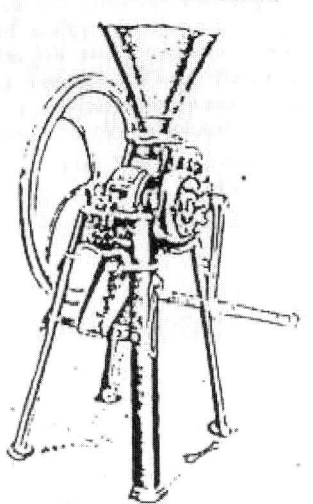

Hand Crushing Mill.

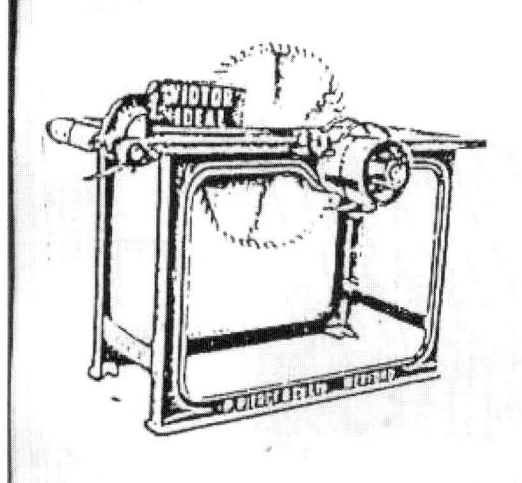

Saw Bench.

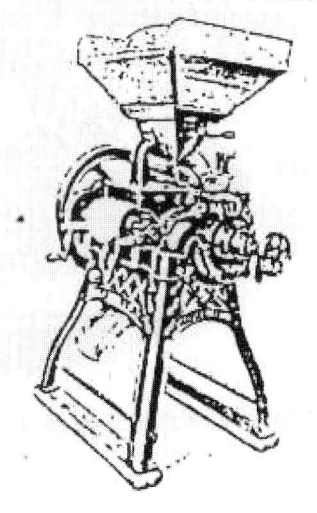

Crushing and Grinding Mill.

TURNIP & MANGOLD SEED SPACER.

NEW AND IMPROVED MACHINE.

The advantages of sowing Turnip and Mangold Seeds in bunches instead of continuous rows are undoubted, and to successfully accomplish this we have designed a New Spacer of original type. This Machine was patented by us in Season 1911, and since that time we have been experimenting and perfecting details, with the result that we now offer a Machine which sows with wonderful accuracy and is positive in its feed. Simplicity is an outstanding feature of this new Machine, and all Valves, Rods and Levers are dispensed with. Seed spacing ensures healthy plants, spares fertilisers, obviates labour of hoeing, and it uses only one-quarter usual quantity of Seed per acre.

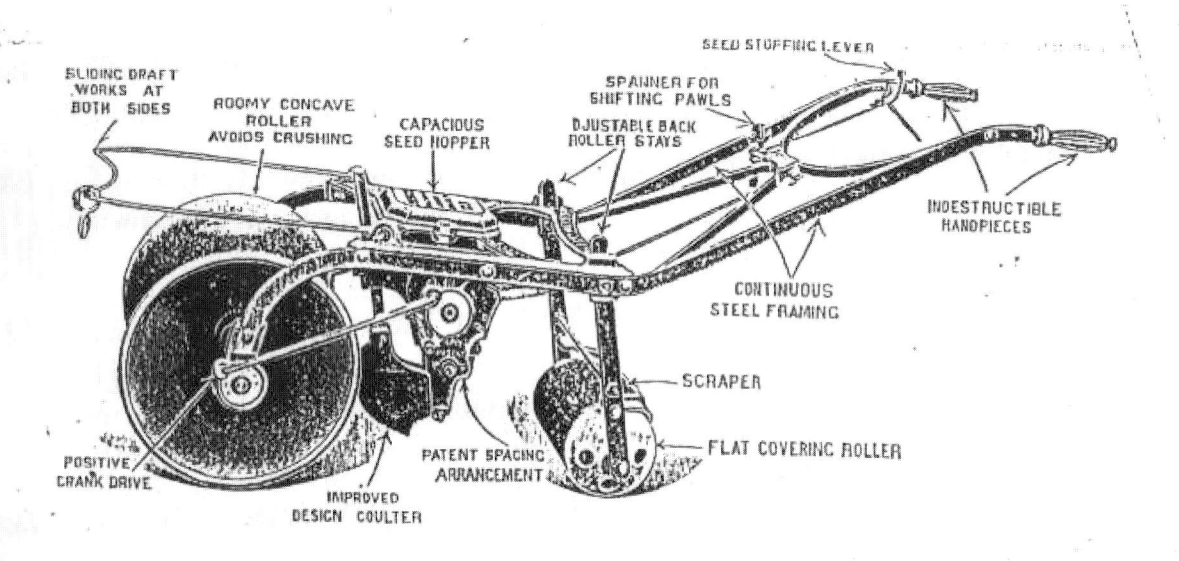

POSITIVE DELIVERY.   EXTREMELY SIMPLE.

CAN BE INSTANTLY CHANGED FOR SOWING IN ROWS.

TAKE AN EARLY OPPORTUNITY OF EXAMINING THIS LATEST CREATION.

An Roinn Oideachais

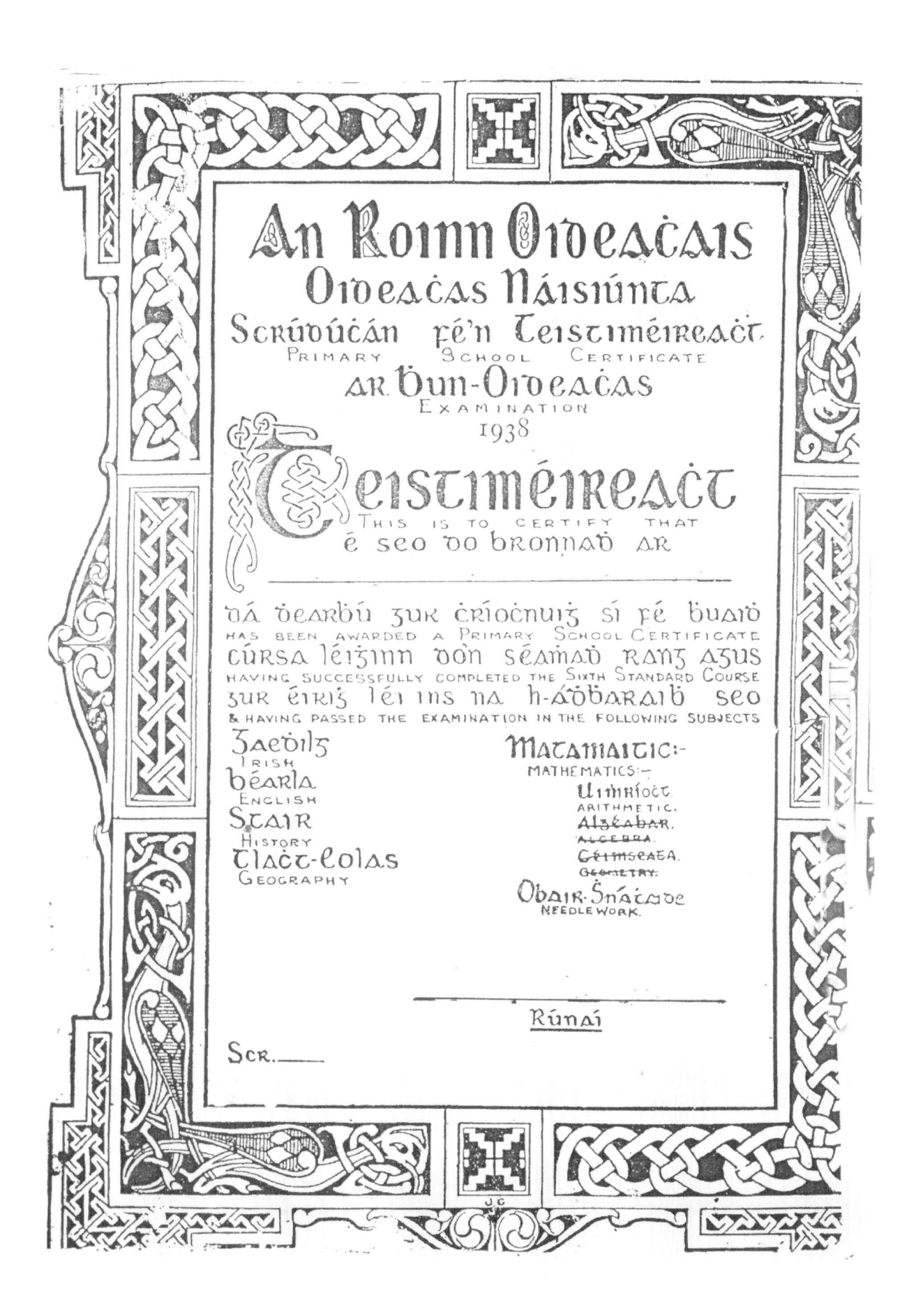

Oideachas Náisiúnta

Scrúdúcán fé'n Teistiméireacht
PRIMARY SCHOOL CERTIFICATE

ar Bun-Oideachas
EXAMINATION
1938

Teistiméireacht
THIS IS TO CERTIFY THAT

é seo do bronnadh ar

_____

dá dearbú gur críochnuig sí fé buaid
HAS BEEN AWARDED A PRIMARY SCHOOL CERTIFICATE

cúrsa léiginn don séamad rang agus
HAVING SUCCESSFULLY COMPLETED THE SIXTH STANDARD COURSE

gur éirig léi ins na h-ádbaraib seo
& HAVING PASSED THE EXAMINATION IN THE FOLLOWING SUBJECTS

Gaedilg — IRISH
Béarla — ENGLISH
Stair — HISTORY
Tlacht-eolas — GEOGRAPHY

Matamaitic:— MATHEMATICS:—
Uimhríocht — ARITHMETIC
Algéabar — ALGEBRA
Céimseaea — GEOMETRY
Obair Snáitide — NEEDLEWORK

_____
Rúnaí

Scr._____

REGISTRATION OF DOGS.

I hereby certify that the following persons have taken out Licenses in the Petty Sessions District of GURTEEN, in the County of Galway, for the number of Dogs set opposite their names, for the Year ending 31st March, 1886.

NAME AND RESIDENCE.	No. of Dogs	NAME AND RESIDENCE.	No. of Dogs	NAME AND RESIDENCE.	No. of Dogs	NAME AND RESIDENCE.	No. of Dogs
A H Blake, Esq, Attymon	1	Michael Devaney, Cross	1	Francis Leslie, Gurthmore	1	John Smith, Liscune	1
Peter Flannery do	1	Thomas Egan do	1	John Mintane, Green Hills	1	Edward Donohoe, Lisheen	1
Owen Flannery do	1	Mary Golden do	1	Michael Quinn do	1	Michl Donohoe do	2
Peter Galvin do	1	Ellen Kelly do	1	Thomas Burke, Garratine	2	John Donohoe do	1
Patrick Barrett, Alloon	1	Martin Leeaon do	1	John Burke do	1	Pat Faby do	1
Martin Commins do	1	Martin Mulowney do	1	Michael Griffin do	1	Patrick Cahill, Lishane	2
John Costello do	1	Connor O'Dowd do	1	Wm Hillier do	1	Michael Costello, Liscub	1
Pat Costello do	2	Arthur Potter do	1	Pat Higgins do	1	John Costello do	1
Patrick Fynn do	1	Bartly Scanlon do	1	John Kelly do	1	Tim Conaheeny do	1
Patrick Forde do	1	Thomas Carroll, Clunbonia	1	Wm Kenny do	1	Pat Cassidy do	1
Michael Farrell do	1	Timothy Cogavin do	1	John King do	2	Thos Keane do	2
James Green do	1	John Kirrane do	1	Martin Lally do	1	James King do	1
Thomas Kenny do	1	Thomas Clancy, Carraterrikeen	1	Denis Morrissy do	1	Wm Morrow do	1
Bartly Kenny do	1	James Gavin do	1	Thomas Neil do	1	Bridget Mullins do	1
George Kenny do	1	James Ruane do	1	Laurence Griffin, Gurteen	1	Pat McEvoy do	1
Joseph Kelly do	2	Francis Fenaghty, Corinacoo	1	James Kyne do	1	Edward Conaghton, Leanaresgh	1
Thomas Lally do	1	Peter Quinn do	1	Bryan Naughton do	1	John Carroll do	1
Martin Murry do	1	Pat Culkeen, Courskeagh	1	Patrick Raftery, Gurteen Lodge	1	James Cannon do	1
James Murry do	1	John Kenny do	2	Martin Duggin, Garbally	1	Pat Cannon do	1
James Madden do	1	James Kelly do	1	Pat Gready do	1	John Dooley do	1
Roger Coffey, Annagh	1	Patrick Mullin do	1	Michael Jordan do	1	Patrick Fynn do	1
Wm Dilleen do	1	Malachy Naughton do	1	James Laugheen do	1	William Hussion do	1
Michael Groden do	1	Pat Ruane do	1	Michael McDermott do	1	Pat Morressy do	1
John Kelly do	1	James Dooley, Coppaluch	1	Martin Nolan do	1	Michl McGann do	1
John Kelly, junr do	1	John Barry, Glenkeen	1	Michael Tanvane do	1	Thomas Murphy do	1
Laurence Lyons do	1	Martin Barry, senr do	1	James Cogavin, Gurthnacross	1	Michl Gullane, Loughtanora	1
Martin Lydon do	1	Martin Barry, junr do	1	Pat Forde, Glananmucka	1	William Cleary, Mountventur	4
Thomas Manion do	1	Martin Connallin do	1	John Tully do	1	Michl Cahill, Monaveea	1
John McDonagh do	1	Owen Donnelly do	1	Pat Cannon, Gurthnalone	1	Daniel Kelly do	2
Thomas McDonagh do	1	Martin Hession do	1	Patrick Hussion do	1	Patrick Raftery do	1
Pat Madden do	1	Ulick Burke, Cahoverteown	1	Pat Walsh do	2	John Kelly, Muneen	1
Patrick Murry do	1	Pat Crehan do	1	Pat Burns, Gurthbrack	1	John Royne do	1
Owen Neil do	1	Michael Devaney do	1	Honor Daly do	1	Pat Burns, Moyarwood	1
John Neil do	1	Michael Flannery do	1	Mark Fitzpatrick do	1	Michl Dwyer do	1
Margaret Wiley do	1	William Forde do	1	Pat Kelly do	1	James Mercer do	1
John Cahill, Beefield	1	Timothy Fahey do	1	James Lydon do	1	Edward Brophy, Mounthazle	1
Thomas Cahill do	2	Michl Higgins do	1	Pat Moran do	1	Andrew Consheeny do	1
Martin Mullin do	1	John Kelly do	1	Catherine Molloy do	1	Pat Clancey do	1
Edward Duffy, Beech-Hill	1	John Lyons do	1	John Cannon, Gurthrush	1	Michl Costello do	2
Thomas Moran do	1	Michael Lally do	1	James Cannon do	1	John Costello do	1
Thomas Moran, junr do	1	Pat Lally do	1	Bernard Falton do	1	John Dempsey do	1
John Moran do	1	Darby Laffey do	1	John Ryan do	1	The Marquis de Stackpool, do	1
E C Villiers, Esq, J P do	1	Michael Manning do	1	Patrick Scarry do	1	John Egan do	1
Mark Carr, Ballyglass	1	James Queeney do	1	Patrick Hillery, Gurthrunagh	1	Michael McDermott do	1
John Griffin do	1	John Quinn do	1	Michael Hooban do	1	Michael O'Dea do	1
Thos McDonagh do	1	Pat Ruane do	1	James McDermott, Gurthnacloogh	1	Michael Queeney do	1
Sarah Raftery do	1	Michael Tyrell do	1	Pat Donohue, Gurthlemon	1	John Raftery do	1
						John Kelly, New-Inn	1
Michl Kindrigan, Ballinlough	1	John Connier, Cluncagh	1	James Gibbons, Hampstead	2	John Kelly, New-Inn	1
Pat Ward do	1	Pat Cosgrove do	1	Miss Mahon do	1	Bryan Naughton, Pulsubrone	1
Martin Kelly, Ballymoneen	1	Michael Laffey do	1	John Fahey, Highpark	1	Mary Scanlon do	1
Thomas Kenny do	1	Thomas Laffey do	1	Thomas Baker, Keave	1	John Scanlon do	1
Stephen Donohue, Ballymacward	1	Pat Laffey do	1	Martin Broderick do	1	Pat Craven, Streamsford	1
Bridget Farrill do	1	Thomas Mitchell do	1	Patrick Kelly do	1	John Cannon do	1
Bridget Fynn do	1	Pat Mintane do	1	Michael Noone do	1	Michl Gullane do	1
Martin Kenny do	1	Thomas Mintane do	1	Francis Nevin do	1	Bridget Kelly do	1
Pat Mahon do	1	Pat Murry do	1	William Parker do	1	Francis Murry do	1
John Morgan do	1	Timothy Naughton do	1	Michael Dwyer, Kinreask	1	John Moran do	1
Thomas Woods do	2	Daniel Walsh do	1	Patrick Dwyer, do	2	Wm Neil do	1
Thomas Connelly, Ballygreany	1	Michael Walsh do	1	John Fynn do	1	Pat Reardon do	1
Patrick Naughton, Ballynulty	1	Denis Coen, Clough	1	Thomas Flanery do	1	Timothy Sheridan do	2
John Royne do	1	John Glynn do	1	Pat Kilkenny do	1	Thomas Walsh do	1
Timothy Manion, Ballyarra	1	William Molloy do	1	Timothy Kelly do	1	Owen Dwyer, Skehenane	2
Stephen Kenny, Clunbenis	2	Michael Treacy do	1	Martin Kilkenny do	1	James Murry do	1
John Manion do	1	Michael Ward do	1	Thomas Manion do	1	Julia Murry do	1
Michael Glynn, Cloonahinch	1	Pat Cannon, Cappannoole	1	James Mahon do	1	Michl Sirk do	1
Thomas Earles, Carrahulla	1	Pat Carroll do	1	John Dolly, Kilbeg	1	Martin Connor, Shanbailymore	1
James Glynn do	1	John Molloy do	1	Edward Fahey do	1	Pat Carr do	1
Josiah Holland do	1	Pat Mahon do	1	Patrick Hynes, Killoghaun	1	John Gilligan do	1
Richard Kelly do	1	Michael Cannon, Clunamorris	1	Pat Loughnane do	1	Pat Hynes do	1
Joseph Kelly do	1	Michael Mullin do	1	John Neil do	1	Thos Royne do	1
William Kelly do	2	Malachy Naughton do	1	James Tanvane do	1	Pat Sirk do	1
James Molloy do	1	Edward Cunniffe, Doonane	1	Owen O'Neil do	1	John Bodkin, Shanballyeshal	1
Michael Quinn do	1	John Connelly do	1	William Connors, Killevaun	1	Pat Cogavin do	1
John Clarke, Clungowna	1	Thos Connelly do	1	Wm Hussion do	1	Hubert Dilleen do	1
Bridget Faley do	1	Thos Glynn do	1	Pat Laffey do	1	Michl McDonagh do	1
John Madden do	1	Pat Gilligan do	1	Thomas Murry do	1	Pat Keane, Sheaun	1
John Murry do	1	Michl Gavin do	1	John Manion do	1	Michl Kelly do	1
James Quinn do	1	William Kelly do	1	Bryan Manion do	1	Pat King do	1
John Raftery do	1	Peter Kelly do	1	Michael Clarke, Killaghmore	1	Pat Connors, Tyaquin	1
Michael Raftery do	1	Pat Lally do	1	S J R Donlan, Esq, J P do	1	John Dunne do	1
J R Parker, Church Hill	3	Michl Laffy do	1	John Donohue do	1	Michl Fenaghty do	1
Thomas Madden, Carrowmore	1	Michl Touhey do	1	John Forde do	1	Pat Gilligan do	1
Patrick Quinn do	1	Edward Fahy, Dernamana	1	James Hynes do	1	James Grendy do	1
James Craughwell, Cloonaholle	1	Thos Murray do	1	Martin Lally do	1	Pat Glynn do	1
John McDonagh, Caltracreen	1	Pat Coppinger, Derrough	1	John Lally do	1	Martin Roughan do	1
Thomas Naughton do	1	Michael Brien, Esker	1	Michael Fahey, Lisloughlin	1	Peter Ward do	1
Mark Ruane do	1	John Burns do	1	Walter McDonagh do	1	Wm Burke, Tample	1
Pat Ruane do	1	Michl Coen do	1	Martin Barrett, Liscune	1	Pat Kelly do	1
Timothe Burke, Coodoo	1	Thos Dooley do	1	Thomas Barrett, do	1	Hubert Kelly, Vermount	1
Peter Glynn do	1	Pat Dempsey do	1	Laurence Barrett do	1	Martin Manion do	1
Martin Glynn do	1	Michl Guinan do	2	John Cassidy do	1	Lord Ashtown, Woodlawn	22
Edward Kelly do	1	Pat King do	1	Michael Higgins do	1	Michl Hentley do	1
John Kelly do	1	Martin Kitt do	1	Michael Kelly do	1	Stephen Grent do	1
Thomas Murphy do	1	Henry Lynch, Esq. do	2	Patrick Kelly do	1	James Hughes do	1
Thomas Murphy, junr do	1	John Murphy do	1	John Kenny do	1	John Kennedy do	1
Mark Monahan do	1	Thos Mason do	1	John Kelly do	1	Connor Kelly do	1
Mary Murphy do	1	Martin Steaken do	1	Richard Kelly do	2	Michl McDonagh do	1
Malachy Ruane do	1	Michl Tierney do	1	Thomas Lally do	1	Ellen McDonagh do	1
Denis Ruane do	1	Anne Hooban, Faha	1	Martin Lally do	1	Thomas Quin do	1
Pat Ruane do	1	Michael Burns, Garrymore	1	Pat Murry do	1	John Sweeney do	1
Hugh Touhey do	1	Patrick Hynes do	1	Pat Nulty do	2	Michl Feeney, Whitepark	1
John Breaden, Carana	1	Richard Hansberry do	1	Simon Nulty do	1	Edward Groden do	1
Peter Culkeen do	1	Patrick Murphy do	1	John Nulty do	1	Michl Lyons do	1
Thomas Griffin do	1	James Molloy do	1	Michl Nulty do	1	Matthew Lally do	1
Michael McLoughlin do	1	Michael McDonagh do	1	Michl Nulty, junr do	1	Joseph Morgan do	1
William Murry do	1	Michael Griffin, Gurthmore	1	Michl Nulty, senr do	1	Michl Naughton do	1

Ballymacward, 8th April, 1885.

J. R. PARKER,
CLERK OF PETTY SESSIONS.

Portion of Map 20
L. Nahinch
Clonkeen
Kerrill
Gurteen
Tample
Gorthnalone
3618
2931
3935
3950
2101
1436
3677
2100
3208
4099
3415
3416
1025
2495
3739
3339
3493
4005
4052
3496
2921
3876
1665
3628
2736
2734
2735
3985
3063
1661
3599
3704
3648
2419
2724
2958
3060
1565
4091
2359
2624

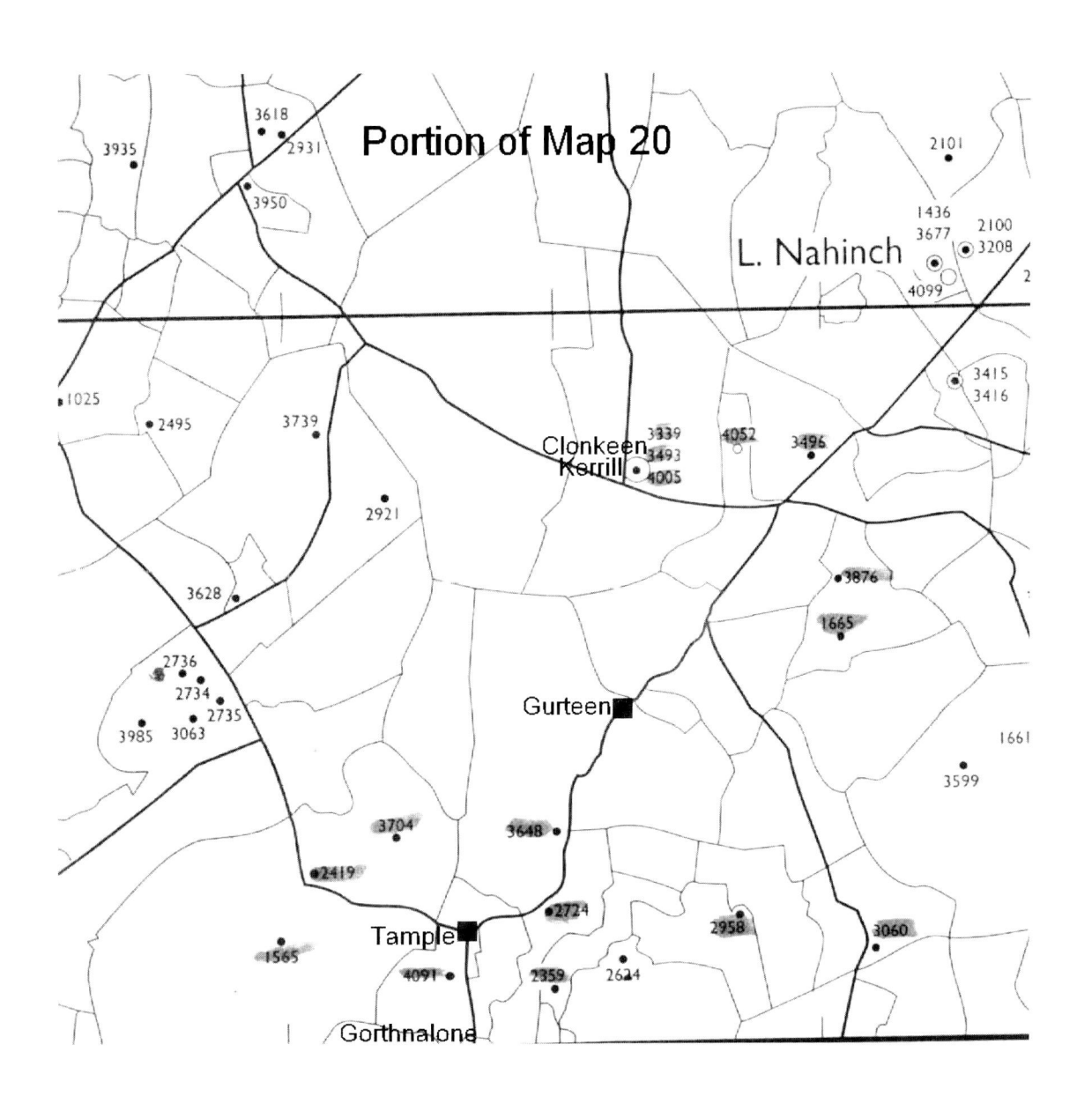

BIOGRAPHY

Burke, Jim is a native of Cuddoo. He attended Cloonkeenkerrill N.S. in the twenties but later transferred to the new school in Tiaquin.

Carr, Maura is a Social Welfare Officer. She likes Drama and is a member of Loughnahinch Players. She has been active in quizzes in Macra na Feirme and while attending secondary school.

Casey, Eileen is originally from the Midlands. She has been writing and facilitating workshops for some years. Her work, both prose and poetry, has appeared in national and international outlets. Awards include: The Scottish International Poetry Award, The Golden Pen (Galway), Citta Di Olbia (Italy), The Library of North America, and prose winner in Listowel Writer's Week, 2002, among others.

Clarke, Fr. Joe is a native of Mullagh. Fr. Joe is a keen sportsman and played with Pearse's Hurling team when he was curate here.

Cloonan-Bellew, Sheila is a native of Clough and taught in several parish schools before retiring. She is an avid reader and is au fait with current educational developments. She has a very positive outlook on life and has always taken a keen interest in the welfare of her students.

Coen-Cormican, Nancy is a member of a talented family who has been active in Galway City business circles for most of her life. She has many fond memories of her schooldays in Shanballard N.S.

Cogavin, Jimmy lives in Dublin. He travels extensively in his role as Company representative and takes every opportunity he can get to spend time in Gurteen.

Connaire, Sean is from Killimordaly and writes prose and poetry. His works can be found in the books that are published by BAFFLE.

Connaire, Sonny was an enthusiastic fair goer. He has a wealth of local lore that he shares with his friends.

Corbett, John is a former teacher who spends much of his free time writing.

de hÍde, Dubhglas was a member of the Gaelic League and was particularly interested in the writings of the old Irish poet, Raftery. He was also the first President of Ireland.

Dillon, James N., lives at Lisduff, Attymon. He taught in The Mercy Convent, Tuam for a number of years. He took early retirement and devotes his time to writing, gardening and a wide range of hobbies. He has written extensively on land ownership and his material has been published in a number of books.

Doyle, Alfie works with The Department of Agriculture. He has produced a marvellous model of The Quaker Farmyard which once existed in Colemanstown.

Dwyer-Laheen, Mai is from Kinreask. She has many relatives in the parish and has strong views in the educational system that was current when she was attending school.

Fallon, Pádraic was a writer and broadcaster. He has written many poems and plays and his family continue to promote creative writing. For more information see The Literary Connections at the beginning of the book

Finnerty, Martin is a talented tradesman. When not busy installing living room units, he likes to watch sporting events. He is a leading member of Colemanstown Football Club. He is also interested in local history and is the great grandson of the first Headmaster in Cloonkeenkerrill National School.

Flaherty, Gerard lives in Ballygreaney. He farms extensively and is involved in local affairs. He is Chairman of Ballymacward Hall Committee and has helped enormously with the development of the Social Centre.

Flannery, Eileen is a native of Kinreask but now lives in Co. Meath. She is a member of a large family. She was active in local drama before she moved to the Midlands.

Garvey, Fr. John is a former pupil of Shanballard N.S. He keeps close contact with local people. He is presently involved in pastoral duties in the town of Ballinasloe.

Gavin, John was born in England but his father was a pupil of Cloonkeenkerrill N.S. He works in the aircraft industry. He is very interested in Irish affairs and visits here regularly.

Greaney, Declan is a member of a very musical family. He teaches in Wales but likes to come back to Ireland on his holidays.

Heaney, Agnes lives in Ballyhaunis. She edits a beautiful magazine entitled 'Annagh' which is published annually. She also contributes to St. Kerrill's Journal.

Heaney, Seamus is one of Ireland's most famous poets. He has won countless awards, including the Nobel Prize for Literature.

Henry, William is an archaeologist, local historian and author. He is a native of Galway City, and has had a life-long interest in history, archaeology and folklore. He is a committee member of the Galway Archaeological & Historical Society and the Old Galway Society, and he is also a director of Galway Civic Trust. His works include, The Shimmering Waste, the Life and Times of Robert O'Hara Burke, St. Clerans, the Tale of a Manor House and a historical mini series of twelve booklets. He has also been a contributor to a number of other publications and at the moment he isi n the final stages of two other books.

Hynes, Brendan has travelled extensively and was formerly a member of the U.S. Army. He runs a number of businesses in the States and maintains regular contact with the Irish emigrants who live there.

Kennedy- Walshe, Collette teaches in St. Cuan's College, Castleblakeney. She is a member of Pearse's Camogie Club and coaches many of the school teams also.

Kennelly, P.J. N.T., lives in Connemara and has been active in politics for most of his life. His articles on his local area have been published in The Irish Independent.

Kenny, John lives on the family farm at Cappalusk. He is a great conversationalist and has taken an active part in politics over the years.

Kilgannon, Micheal J. taught in Cloonkeenkerrill National School from Nov '61 to July '66. He came as Principal; the Assistant was Mrs. Pam. Lyng. Michael J. obtained his BA. and H.D.E. in addition to being an N.T. He served on Galway Co. Council for a number of years and will be a candidate in the forthcoming local elections.

Kilkenny, Julia formerly Julia Hessian from Kinreask, has had a life long interest in music. Although ninety years of age, she still plays the accordeon and her power of recall is wonderful. The musical tradition is still strong in her family and her children and grandchildren have made many records.

King-McKiernan, Sheila is a native of Ballyglass and former student of Tample N.S. She is the sister of Oliver King, Treasurer of The Reunion Committee.

Lally-McGann, Gráinne is a granddaughter of John Joe McGann. She teaches in Ballinasloe and lives near the family home. She is active in many local organisations.

Lawless, Fr. Vincent lives in Kiltulla. He worked in Africa for many years before returning to Ireland. He was always active in parish life and is vice president of St. Kerrill's Committee.

Mannion, Joseph N.T., is a former principal of Woodford National School. He is the author of a new book on St. Kerrill and has a comprehensive knowledge of the history of this area.

McGann, John Joe is a retired farmer who lives with his family in Carhoon.

McHugh, Dr. Peter lectures at N.U.I.G. He is interested in bio technology and is currently involved in researching projects of this nature

McMahon, Margot is a daughter of Mrs.Hurley, the former principal of Cloonkeenkerrill N.S. She is a talented poet who lives in Galway City. She is also a former prizewinner in The Golden Pen Competition.

Mills, Geraldine is a prolific writer. Her work includes short stories and poetry. She won first prize in the first Golden Pen Competition in Gurteen. Since then she has had two poetry books published. She has written Pity The Poor Starling specially for the occasion.

Mitchell, Tommie is one of the most extraordinary men in our village. He was a building contractor who was always in demand due to the high standard of his work. Although in his nineties, he is still able to do a good deal of work of this kind.

Mullins, John is from Ballymacward and has been noted for his involvement with various sports. He is particularly interested in Gaelic Football and Soccer and has coached members of St. Kerrill's Football Club for a number of years.

Ní Dhomhnaill, Nuala is a well-known writer who has produced several books of poems in Irish. She is one of the adjudicators in Listowel Writer's Week.

Noone, Breda teaches at Esker School, Athenry. She is secretary of The Reunion Committee and takes an active interest in community affairs. She was one of the leading members of Macra na Feirme during her time in Gurteen.

O'Donnell, Jim is a native of Tipperary who now lives in Dublin. He is an accountant by profession. He has written extensively and was a prizewinner in the Gurteen Golden Pen Competition.

O'Flaherty, Michael spent his early years in Clough. He later moved to Dublin where he began a successful career in the Defence Forces. He likes sport and spends much of his free time refereeing hurling matches.

O'Grady, Tom is a member of Gurteen Pastoral Council and is an officer of Pearses Hurling Club. He is very interested in sport and rarely misses a hurling or football match.

O'Reachtaire, Antaine, file a mhair idir 1784 go dti 1835. Chaith se a shaol ag seinm ceoil agus ag cumadh amhran.

Parker, Noreen is a tireless worker who devotes a great deal of her spare time to youth and drama. She has had many successes with 'The Tops of The Club' and Foroige.

Roche, Tom is one of the most resourceful individuals in the parish. He has invented several machines, including his highly successful pole erector. He is a mechanical wizard who generated his own electricity while still at school. He was the first editor of St. Kerrill's Magazine.

Ruane, Mary (Sr.Vera) is a native of Colemanstown. She comes from a family of nine and has spent most of her life teaching. She is very supportive of local events and returns to Ireland regularly on vacation.

Ruane, Oliver has been involved in local drama for many years. Last year he was shortlisted for 'best comedy actor' in The Mid and North West Radio Drama Awards.

Ryan, Kevin works in Galway. A keen sportsman, he has been involved with the local soccer club for several years.

Ryan, Paul is an avid Gaelic hurling fan. He and his wife, Renie, have been involved in community affairs for decades.

Scarry, Paddy worked locally before emigrating to America. He keeps in touch with local events, even though he is separated by the Atlantic from his native Cappalusk.

Slattery, Fr. Seán is the Parish Priest in Ballymacward-Gurteen. He is a stalwart advocate of local enterprises and was actively involved in The Pioneer Association until recently.

Spellman, Marian teaches in Presentation College, Athenry. She is also interested in Speech and Drama and conducts classes in her native and in her adopted parish each week. She is a wonderful dancer and her team of 'Strawboys' is eagerly sought after.

Sullivan (nee Dilleen), Bridget worked in Dublin for a time. She is now married in Leitrim. She has done a great deal of research in family and social matters. Her help in compiling this book has been invaluable.

Sweeney, Fr. Gerry spent much of his life in the African Missions. He is actively involved in community life and has set a number of projects in motion since his arrival in Gurteen.

Treacy, Marian lives in Athenry and likes to write poetry in her spare time.

Treacy, Noel T.D. Minister of State. He was elected to the Dail in 1982 and has been active in politics since then. He is active in local affairs and is a member of The Schools' Reunion Committee.

Ward, John Joe is a painting and decorating contractor. He lives near the Abbey and has a wonderful collection of stories relating to the locality.

Ward, Anne teaches in St. Kerrill's National School. She has been in charge of the Church Choir since her arrival here and is the mainstay of the Scór talent competitions.

GURTEEN SCHOOL SEVEN-A-SIDE WINNERS 1991

WILLIAM HENRY

William Henry is a native of Galway City. He has a life-long interest in history and archaeology, and is committee member of both the Galway Archaeological and Historical Society and the Old Galway Society.

MRS. KITT N.T. AND HUSBAND JOE

273

Printed by KPW Ballinasloe. Tel: 090 9642297.
Published by Gurteen Schools' Reunion Committee April 2004.
Layout & Design: Padraic Judge.
Cover and Illustrations: Francis Kennedy

© Copyright Gurteen Schools' Reunion 2004.
All rights reserved.
No part of this publication may be reproduced or transmitted in any form or by any means, electronic or mechanical, including photography, recordings, or any information storage or retrieval system, without permission in writing from the publishers.
The book is sold subject to the condition that it shall not, by way of trade or otherwise, be lent, re-sold or otherwise circulated without the publisher's prior consent in any form of binding or cover other than that in which it is published and without a similar condition including this condition being imposed on the subsequent purchaser.